THE ART OF
STORYTELLING

Creative ideas for preparation and performance

MARSH CASSADY

MERIWETHER PUBLISHING LTD.
Colorado Springs, Colorado

Meriwether Publishing Ltd., Publisher
Box 7710
Colorado Springs, CO 80933

Editor: Theodore O. Zapel
Typesetting: Sharon E. Garlock
Cover design: Tom Myers

© Copyright MCMXCIV Meriwether Publishing Ltd.
Printed in the United States of America
First Edition

Library of Congress Cataloging-in-Publication Data

Cassady, Marsh, 1936-
 The art of storytelling : creative ideas for preparation and
performance / by Marsh Cassady.
   p.   cm.
 Includes bibliographical references.
 ISBN 1-56608-002-9
 1. Storytelling. 2. Folklore--Performance. 3. Oral
interpretation.   I. Title.
GR72.3.C37   1994
808.5'43--dc20
                                                          94-12938
                                                            CIP

 2   3   4   5   6   7   8   9   99   98   97

To
Herb Kulman
and
Rick Treat

CONTENTS

Part I:

Choosing Stories to Tell

CHAPTER ONE

WHAT IS STORYTELLING?

I'll never forget the time when I was in ninth grade general science, and one of my classmates was acting up. Dropping books on the floor, scooting his desk around, making a general nuisance of himself. His name was Billy Findlay, and ever since first grade, he'd fancied himself class clown.

The teacher was an old guy, near retirement. His name was Mr. Thomas, and I guess he just got fed up with the whole thing — the noise, the lack of discipline, the disrespect. All at once he slammed his book down on his desk and stormed back to Billy's seat.

The rest of us watched spellbound as Mr. Thomas picked up the kid, desk and all, and carried him to a storage closet in the back of the room. Holding the desk in one hand, he opened the door and tossed the kid and the desk into the closet and slammed the door.

Well, I'll tell you, it was so quiet that nobody even dared breathe. Mr. Thomas, blue eyes shooting fire, strode to the front of the room, picked up his book and took up the lesson right where he'd left off.

Funny thing was old Billy Findlay never made a sound, and, of course, neither did anyone else. At the end of the period we all filed out two by two just like we'd had to do in first grade, for heaven's sake.

What's weird about all this is that nobody ever heard from Billy again. Some of the kids said he really must have been scared, petrified like those trees in the Petrified Forest and so became kind of mummified. But even if that's true, why did nobody ever see him in that condition?

Other kids said that he probably was so embarrassed he sank right through the floor. We looked in the basement, of course, but never found a trace.

And what about Mr. Thomas? Well, you can bet your boots that from then on nobody ever made a sound in his class, except, of course, to stutter out answers to the questions he asked.

I heard a week or so back that Mr. Thomas celebrated his hundredth birthday. And so far as I know, he never once brought up the incident involving Billy and the desk and the closet. It was like it never happened.

Storytelling is a common form of communication that people engage in nearly every day. For instance, a parent asks how things went at school, and you tell about something silly a friend did.

"You should have seen what happened," you say.

"What was it?" someone around the dinner table asks.

"Well, Mr. Franklin asked Joe Reynolds if he'd done his homework. You know how Joe is. He never does anything he doesn't want to do."

"Yes?"

You start to laugh. "So he gets up and walks to the front of the room. And in this deep voice, trying to imitate Mr. Franklin, he says (and here you imitate the voice), 'Well now, class, it seems as if some people think they can get away without doing their homework.' "

"You're kidding," someone else at the table says, which encourages you to go on and tell what happened, adding things here and there to make the story funny.

Or maybe you go to visit your grandparents Sunday afternoon, and your grandpa starts to talk about when he was a young man:

"Well, you see, we lived on the farm back then. There wasn't much money, none at all for extras. And wouldn't you know one day the teacher at school asked us all to bring in newspaper because she wanted us to make papier-mâché animals as gifts for our folks for Christmas. Well, my family didn't get a newspaper. We couldn't afford it. But did you think I was going to admit that in front of the class? No siree!"

"So what did you do, Grandpa?" you ask.

"I didn't want to tell Mom and Dad 'cause it would only make them feel bad. I thought about it for a long time, what I was going to do, I mean. We didn't need to bring the papers in till the following week. One day on the way to school I noticed that sometimes people had stacks of newspapers sitting out on their back porch, not knowing what to do with them. So I got this idea. I'd go around town. It was a little place, maybe a couple hundred people. A grocery store, a bank, a clothing store and post office combined. Anyhow, I decided to tell folks that for a nickel a month — starting right away — I'd come around each week and collect their papers.

"Now let me tell you," Grandpa continues, "a nickel was worth a heck of a lot more in those days than it is now. So I had stacks of papers people didn't want and a lot of us kids needed, and I was making money besides.

"I think maybe it taught the teacher a lesson, too, when she saw how eagerly some of the other kids took those papers."

"And that's what started you on the road to being an entrepreneur," your dad jokes.

"You better believe it," Grandpa says, and goes on to tell how in junior high school he parlayed this newspaper collection into a whole distribution center for all sorts of things other people wanted and which he got for free or nearly so. All afternoon the stories continue.

Or at lunchtime you rush up to your best friend. "Hey, Lynn," you say, "I heard the funniest joke this morning."

"What is it?" Lynn says.

"Well, there was this man . . ."

All of the foregoing are forms of *storytelling, which is nothing more than sharing a narrative tale of experiences, either real or imaginary, with someone else.* The examples so far could be based, at least in part, on actual experiences. The tale about Mr. Thomas and Billy Findlay, of course, continues on into fantasy. The only "true" part of the following is some of the background information about Mexico.

5

THE FLIGHT OF THE NIÑOS

Manuel Ortega was twelve years old before he knew he could fly. One night he stood at his bedroom window and simply spread his arms. They sky was filled with *niñas y niños.* Manuel glided toward Eduardo Rodriguez.

"You too?" Eduardo said. "You are flying. I myself have never flown before. I find it a little bit frightening."

Manuel saw a man in white robes flying beside him.

"Buenas noches," el hombre said. "My name is David Martinez, and it is time to gather at the top of the mountain." He swooped to the rocky earth. Manuel and Eduardo landed beside him.

On the highest rock stood *un hombre* in robes so white they seemed to glow. *"Buenas noches,"* he said. "My name is Señor Viejo. I will explain how it is that you can fly."

Eduardo nudged Manuel. "He is *muy viejo* all right, older even than my great-grandfather."

"A long time ago," the old man said, "we visited this *planeta* because our own world was dying. You see, we had searched for a place to rebuild our civilization. We could find no world that was empty of people."

"Could this be the truth?" Manuel asked Eduardo.

Señor Martinez leaned toward the two boys. "You must listen; then you will understand."

"We failed in our search," Señor Viejo said. "Yet we found another world we thought we could tame. Our scientists have struggled for generations, but still the task is unfinished."

A girl hesitantly raised her hand.

"What is your name, *niñita?*" Señor Viejo asked.

"Maria Eléna."

"Do not be afraid, Maria Eléna."

"You said that only scientists stayed on that *planeta?*"

"That is correct."

"What happened . . . to the others?"

He smoothed the ends of the white moustache that hung past the corners of his mouth. "You are the descendants of those *hombres y mujeres.*"

Suddenly, everyone was speaking.

"I cannot believe this," Manuel said. "It is a dream."

"*Mi madre y padre* are not . . . space people," said a boy of fourteen or fifteen. "*Mi apellido* is Calderón, an ancient and honorable name. Umberto Calderón."

"*Si,*" Señor Viejo answered. "Your *padres* took that name to fit in; they knew they would never see their new home. They were content to be wayfarers, understanding that their descendants would reach the stars once more."

"What do you mean, Señor?" Eduardo asked.

"You, *amigo,* you and all these others, will travel to the home that has been chosen for you. Not your *padres.*"

"I will not leave *mis padres!*" Manuel shouted. "You cannot make us leave."

"You are telling us tales," Eduardo said.

"How is it then that you can fly?" Señor Viejo asked. "You are not human, though very close. Earth was meant only as a stopping place."

All around *los niños* were talking among themselves.

"Children! You do not understand. This is the purpose for which your great-grandparents were left on this world."

"If this is true," Umberto said, "why have not our *padres* told us?"

"*Si,*" a boy shouted, "why have we not been told?"

"The settlers were forbidden to communicate our origins. Your own *padres* did not know who they were nor that they could fly."

Everyone tried to speak at once.

7

"*Silencio!* We have worked hard for this, for our dream of a planet to support us."

"I will not leave," Eduardo shouted.

"I see the uselessness of this," Señor Viejo said. "We will disband, but you will be summoned again."

The next morning Manuel thought what had happened had surely been a dream and decided to see if he could fly. He rose toward the ceiling. "No!" he shouted and dropped back down.

"Manuel," his *madre* called, "it is breakfast time."

Downstairs his *padre* sat at the table eating *machaca*, scrambled eggs with bits of beef, and a corn tortilla. A cup of steaming coffee sat by his elbow. "*Buenos dias*, Manuel," he said.

"*Papá*, a strange thing happened last night." His *padres* would think he was *loco* if he told them.

"It is about the flying, is it not?" his *madre* said, scrambling more *huevos* in the skillet.

His *padre* pointed to the newspaper. "Look, Manuel, it is here." There were pictures of children high above the earth.

"*Si!* Last night, many *niños*, I among them, flew to the top of the mountain outside Tijuana."

"Aiiiee!" His *madre* sat at the table, as if she could no longer stand. "Is it true then?"

"*Si, mamá, es* true."

When your *papá* and I were children, our *padres* told us a story. We thought it only a fairy tale to amuse us."

That our ancestors could fly," his *padre* said.

"And one day," his *madre* continued, "great ships would come to take our children to a promised land." Tears ran down her cheeks.

Manuel could not stand to see his *madre* cry. He leaped from his chair and raced outside. On the street, other *niños* looked as sad and upset as he was.

Carlos Espinoza, Manuel's best friend, ran up to him. "Did you hear," he said, "about the flying *niños?*"

"I heard," Manuel answered.

"*Mi madre* thinks it is only a hoax to sell more copies of the newspaper."

Manuel's first class was mathematics, followed by his foreign language, English, where they were reading a novel called *Great Expectations* by *un hombre* named Charles Dickens. Manuel found it hard to concentrate.

At noon, school was dismissed for two hours for lunch and a *siesta.* On the way home, the urge to fly came upon him. He saw Eduardo struggling to resist. Suddenly Eduardo shot into the air. And so did Manuel. Everywhere *niños* hovered just off the ground.

He saw Umberto Calderón outside the high school. The older boy rose up, came back down, rose up and came back to earth once more. "We can fight against this," he said.

Manuel half-floated and half-walked to the group forming around Umberto.

"We must talk to them," a *niña* said, "and tell them how we feel.

"Talk?" Eduardo answered. "Why should we?"

"We must convince them," Manuel said, "that we will not leave earth."

"I agree," Umberto answered, "but how can we do that?"

"Make them see that they are wrong to take us from all that is familiar," Manuel answered.

"But will they listen?" Maria Eléna asked.

Other students from both the lower and upper school stood watching.

"We have to talk to Señor Viejo now!" Manuel said.

"I agree," Umberto replied. "To delay only makes

9

things harder."

Like a flock of *pájaros* the group rose and flew together.

Señor Viejo and other *hombres* and *mujeres* were waiting. "So you have come back," he said.

"We found that we can oppose you. We can resist the urge to fly," Manuel said.

"*Sí,*" Señor Viejo said, sounding discouraged. "But all of our plans . . ."

"Señor Viejo," Manuel said, "Earth is all we have known. Did anyone think that maybe we would not want to leave it?"

"You are right," Señor Viejo said. "It was difficult for all of us to leave our *niños* here on earth. Even for me it was sad, and I had none to call my own. It must have been hard for those *niños* too. But the home we left was old, and *el sol* was dying." He stroked his moustache. "I am the only original scientist alive. These others you see are their descendants, born after we left their brothers and sisters on earth."

"What happened?" Manuel asked.

"La *planeta* did not choose to be tamed. She fought against us." He looked from one to the other. "We need you to take over, and someday . . ."

"Do not be so sad," Maria Eléna said.

"It is a sad situation. Everyone needs a homeland. It is not right to wander in space forever. We must —"

"Our home is here!" Manuel said.

"Is it all for nothing? Have our years been wasted, a hundred people lost to the untamed *planeta?*" Señor Viejo's voice trembled. "I am old. I cannot fight any longer, and life is passing me by. Am I but to die on a world which now I know will never be a home for my people?"

"*Abuelo mio?*" Manuel said, for the old man did remind him of his grandfather.

10

"*Sí?*"

"Maybe somehow you could learn to like this world, the one we are on."

"I do not understand," the old man said.

"There is a room that is standing empty in *mi casa*. I will talk to *mis padres*, but I am sure . . ."

"You would take me in after resisting me? After I would all but kidnap you?"

"*Sí*, I would do that," Manuel answered.

Señor Viejo looked to the other scientists. "And what do you think of this?"

"Perhaps," David Martinez said, "you should listen to this boy. He speaks with intelligence."

"But what about you?"

"We will survive." He looked to the other *hombres y mujeres*. "Perhaps one day we will tame the *planeta.*"

The other scientists nodded assent.

"Then it is done." Señor Viejo, tears flowing down his checks, went to each of the *hombres y mujeres* and embraced them. Then he placed a hand on Manuel's shoulder. "You will be so kind," he said, "as to show me the way to my home."

* * *

In the years that followed, it was nearly forgotten that Señor Viejo and the last members of a race of people had come from the distant stars. Yet if anyone happened to look up when the moon was bright, sometimes there could be seen *niñas y niños* soaring and gliding high above the hills of Tijuana.

DEFINING STORYTELLING

So far, you've read examples of several different types of stories. So you have a pretty good idea what is involved in the communication process called storytelling. A more complete definition follows:

**Storytelling *is an oral art form for preserv-
ing and transmitting ideas, images, motives and
emotions with which everyone can identify.***

This pins down what storytelling is, but still the definition
is lacking because storytelling is not so cut and dried as the
definition. It is ever changing — with the situation, the teller,
the audience, the purpose, and the mood. It is a kind of art
that involves spoken sounds and words. Yet people who tell
each other jokes or funny incidents probably are not thinking
in terms of an art, just as kids playing pretend games probably
don't think of themselves as actors in a play. But some of the
same elements are there. The only major difference is that the
presentation of a formal storytelling event or theatrical play
involves more preparation, polishing and practice.

Our definition states that storytelling preserves and
transmits. A storytelling event takes place when one person
wants to communicate with another, and the second person
wants to listen.

Why does this occur? There can be many reasons, but the
most important probably is for *entertainment or fun.* That's
why jokes are so popular and why sometimes people can hardly
wait to share something they saw happen or something that
happened to them. Rather than rushing up to your best friend
and saying, "I aced my English test," you include much more
information, much more background to build suspense and
interest. You say:

"I was really worried about my American Lit. test because, you know, I didn't have time to study. I had to cram it
all into a couple of hours yesterday. And I just skimmed that
novel we had to read. The one by Harper Lee that takes place
in the South?"

"So what happened?" your friend asks.

"Well, it's weird, but the movie based on the book was
on TV when I went over to Mike's house. And I didn't think I
was going to like the book, but I really liked the movie. So
anyhow, I came home and stayed up almost all night reading
it. Man, was I tired the next morning.

"I had to read the last couple of chapters on the way to

12

school. There weren't any seats on the bus, and this man with really bad breath like he'd been eating garlic or something . . ."

The telling is a sharing with others, a way of saying: I know you and I are very much alike. We have the same needs and wants, and so you'll be interested in what I have to say. It is *a way of being close to others,* which is the second reason for telling stories. This is the sort of story you are most likely to hear when families get together and begin reminiscing about earlier times.

STORYTELLING IS AN ANCIENT ART

In all probability storytelling is nearly as old as spoken language. Most certainly it existed for years before written language came into being, and it continued on up through the centuries when only a small percentage of the population knew how to read.

During the middle ages, troubadours and minstrels traveled from community to community to sing and tell stories. Storytelling became a folk tradition that continued up until the present.

For a time the art seemed to be dying out, but in the past few decades there has been a resurgence of interest. There is even an organization called NAPPS, the National Association for the Preservation and Perpetuation of Storytelling, with headquarters in Jonesborough, Tennessee. It was started by a man named Jimmy Neil Smith.

Many believe storytelling is making a comeback because people are tired of having their entertainment all prepackaged and slick. Storytelling is much more intimate than film or television or even plays; it provides a greater means for interaction among audience members and performer.

Many of the reasons that storytelling continued through the ages are still valid today. *One reason is to learn about the past.* That's why there are collections of stories for telling from many different ages and why storytellers often concentrate on telling this type of tale.

Many tales, both from the past and from modern times, illustrate facets of various cultures. There are Native American

13

tales, Jewish and African stories, Russian folklore and so on. Stories often make many different cultures come alive for the teller and listener.

Stories encourage good listening. Young children improve their language skills and vocabularies by hearing stories. They have an easier time inferring the meaning of unfamiliar words in a told story than in a written one. Told stories have more impact, and so children remember them better. Children who hear stories view literature in a more positive manner and are more apt to enjoy reading than children who are not exposed to storytelling.

Stories acquaint or reacquaint us with human emotions and drives, both in traditional tales based on mythology and legend, for instance, and in those based on personal experience and background. Often stories change or alter throughout the years so that they are more relevant to contemporary needs and concerns. Many cultures have the same stories, but adapted to fit the images and familiarity of that particular culture in which they are told.

Stories teach us how to live moral lives. They reinforce the idea that stealing or lying is wrong, but they do it painlessly.

No matter what the story, each teller makes it his or her own. Each adds a unique background and a unique perception to every story, whether original or already in existence. Each has had a different set of experiences and so views the world in a different way. Each has certain tastes and expectations. All these things influence the way a story is told.

Because of these differences, any story a person tells will be different from anyone else's. And each time a person presents the story a little differently. This is due to changes in the teller's mood and feelings.

Each person can relate to certain experiences, but they affect each differently. This is why some people dislike a movie or book that others think is good.

To test this idea try a little experiment. Divide into groups of five, and choose a well-known children's story. Everyone should tell the story in front of the class. Notice how one person makes the telling funny or even silly, while another builds up suspense and tension.

When we tell stories, we cannot help but add our own experiences and backgrounds, our own likes and dislikes of each character and event.

A definition of a storyteller then might be:

> *A storyteller is a person who wants or needs to share experiences and who likes communicating with others. This individual takes a story, original or already in existence, adds his or her sense of humanity to it, and makes it come alive for an audience of one or more. The storyteller interprets life, presents truth and helps an audience enter into other realities for enjoyment and to gain understanding.*

Our views of the world differ from those of our grandparents or great-great grandparents. Yet we feel the same emotions; we are concerned with the same sorts of values and morals. They are just in different settings than occurred fifty or five hundred or five thousand years ago. So when we tell a story about the value of honesty, we might want to set it in modern times, in a contemporary city, rather than in the marketplace of ancient Athens.

We often choose stories to tell that illustrate how we feel. We are saying, in effect, that because a character in a story feels a certain way, we know this feeling exists; it's common and natural to feel that way. This reassures both the teller and the audience and proves we are similar to others.

Further, by the way we tell the story, we show that what the character does with a feeling is appropriate or not. Rumpelstiltskin gets angry and stamps his feet, thus making him appear childish. So we tell the audience — probably young kids for this type of story — that the character's emotion is natural, but his behavior is extreme.

The storyteller and the listener have a contract they've agreed upon just by the fact that they both are attending a storytelling event. The audience has a right to expect that the teller will present a story or stories to the best of his or her ability. The teller in turn has a right to expect that the audience will pay attention and absorb the story.

The teller has to have prepared the story as well as possible, and the audience must try its best to follow and understand.

Sometimes the teller will lose an audience for various reasons — the mental or emotional state of the listener and teller, or even a poor location with a lot of outside noise.

In the best performance it should be difficult to separate the teller from the story. They should be a part of each other. And the audience should become another part.

In effect, *a storyteller adapts a story to suit his or her personality and individual style of presentation while using language — both verbal and nonverbal — with which the audience is familiar.*

The teller must take into consideration the reactions of the audience, and the audience should be changed by what the teller says, just as a person is changed in some way by any form of communication. For instance, you meet up with a friend, and your dour mood is changed to a happy one. A teacher tells you your grades are slipping, and this creates tension.

The teller is influenced and affected by the audience and adapts to it. Much of this is an unconscious melding. We are a part of the community, state or world in which we exist, and they are a part of us. We relate to them and speak their language. It's common, for instance, for a northerner to have a southern accent after living for several years in the south.

Yet, as storytellers, we must understand that any "community" is broken into segments, and we have to understand how these segments differ from each other. In simplest terms, we might tell one set of stories to preschoolers at a library hour and another set to a group of adults at a storytelling convention.

There is a commonality of experiences in being human, and this comes across in the teller-listener relationship. Even so, sometimes the audience and the teller simply do not connect. But if there is adequate preparation on both sides, this should be rare.

16

REASONS FOR TELLING STORIES

There are many reasons for telling stories.

1. *Something we've experienced or read about affects us strongly, and we want to share the experience.*

2. *When we tell stories, we feel more alive,* just as actors and other performers do.

3. By choosing a story, preparing it and presenting it, *we learn about ourselves.* Stories help crystallize our views, our feelings and our priorities. When we look at a story with the idea of telling it, we see fairly quickly whether what it says is important to us.

4. *Telling stories helps us imagine and build worlds and characters both for ourselves and others.*

5. *When we tell stories from our lives, we assess what has happened, which brings about a catharsis or an understanding of the event.* This certainly is the case with the following excerpt from a long work, told from the viewpoint of a seven-year-old boy who becomes very upset about something that has been said to his father.

REVIVAL MEETING

We're having revival services. And these two weird people are here. I hate them. They're two sisters. They're horrible and they're ugly. They're fat and have black hair pulled into knots behind their heads. They always dress in black. They have hairy moles on their faces. I heard them in church Sunday morning, and then we went back Sunday night. The only thing I liked was when they lit a cigarette and stuck it in a rubber tube with a bulb at the end, and the tube stuck through a dummy's mouth. They squeezed the bulb, and the dummy smoked. This was just so they could say how bad cigarettes are. That was funny. But then they started to sing their stupid songs and yell at everyone to be saved.

I hate to hear their voices. They're loud and mean and keep shouting about hell. They sing together. "Jesus is calling thee tenderly home, calling today, calling

17

today . . ." If Jesus is calling me tenderly, why do the ugly sisters scream their songs? One of them went through the church and whispered to people about whether they were saved or not. She walked up to my dad and told him he was going to go to hell. She's a stupid old witch. No! I can't think that. It's bad. But I go to Sunday school and church too. I know better than this old hag. There I did it again. Aunt Helen said never to call anyone a hag. But this dumb old hag's a hag. Dad goes to church, and he's good. I hate her. My dad isn't going to hell.

6. *Telling stories helps us see that we are similar to others and so creates a bond with these others.* We often feel closer to those who hear our stories.

In the following, an excerpt from the novel *Alternate Casts,* although the character may be different from the way we are, he is experiencing similar feelings: a need to see new things and a hope for a better life.

> The railroad spur had been abandoned for years, yet Willie heard the mournful echo of a far-off train.
>
> He lay now in his sister's house, staring up at the banana-colored beams that ran under the roof and across the top of the attic, wide awake, the springs of the old brass bed poking into his back.
>
> He'd dropped in for a visit a few days earlier, and already Herman, his brother-in-law, was starting to get to him. Herman, with the $400 suits and the big gut that hung way out over the top of his belt with the solid-gold buckle, telling Willie that with his brains he could have done whatever he wanted.
>
> It was true, Willie thought. He was fifty-six years old and had never amounted to much, his life the path of a playful breeze. A loner, he made friends as easily as eating the sections of an orange, left them as easily as spitting out the

seeds. Balding, with a white Pancho Villa moustache, he was a little runt of a guy, five-and-a-half feet tall.

Throwing back the sheet, he plopped his feet on the rough wood floor, bumped his head on the sloping walls. The trouble was, Willie thought, he was born too late. A hundred years back he might have amounted to something — become rich in the Klondike gold strike or traveled the theatrical circuits.

He grabbed an old blue bathrobe from the nail by the bed and walked over to the single window, a circle of glass with spokes. In the ghostly light of the moon, the two-lane road twisted and curved through fields of ripened grain. In the yard a giant willow, the tiny leaves on its trailing branches shiny with dew, guarded the silver mailbox. "Herman von Althaus," the letters said. "Box 897, Route 1, Randolph, NJ."

Off in the distance he heard it again, saddest sound in the universe. The whistle of a steam locomotive, the kind he'd heard in his youth. If he closed his eyes, he could bring back the memory as real as ever he'd seen it. The old iron horse, coming ever closer, wheels chugging, the engineer pumping the cord, cowcatcher in front.

Maybe if he went outside he'd find the explanation. Maybe it was the wind through the trees. Except there wasn't any wind. He pulled on a pair of athletic socks, boxer shorts and dark blue work pants. The night air was cool, so he grabbed a flannel shirt from the closet and slipped it on. He tossed his bathrobe over the nail, grabbed his shoes and tiptoed down the steps.

It was a beautiful night, peaceful — the first cool spell after a mid-August heat wave. A

19

delicate scent of newly cut grass rode softly on the air. Willie tugged on his shoes, pushed open the weathered gate and crossed the narrow road. Down a bank through tall grass and this-tles he slid to the railroad track.

He heard again off in the distance the mournful whistle, like the keening sigh of a widow. It touched a chord in him, an itch to travel on.

He'd go back to the house, he decided, and pack a few belongings. The whistle blew again, now a siren of the sea, irresistible. Willie started to run, to race toward the sound that logically couldn't exist. Down the rusted tracks and rotting railroad ties over a road that hadn't been traveled in decades. Yet he knew it would be now.

He couldn't take time to do any packing or to leave a note. Sis and Herman would under-stand, would be glad to get rid of him. Maybe later he'd drop them a postcard. Maybe he wouldn't.

Off in the distance he saw the locomotive illuminated in the spill from its headlamps. The tracks began to vibrate and grumble. Puffs of steam escaped, hung, faded into wisps like cot-ton candy out in the rain. With a screech of wheels and the bucking protest of cars the train shuddered and stopped. The engineer leaned from the cab. A red-faced man with fiery hair, he wore overalls with pale blue stripes against a background of white. His cheeks puffed out like a chipmunk's filled with nuts.

"I'm glad you're coming aboard," he said.

ACTIVITIES

1. Take a story you remember from your childhood, such as "Goldilocks and the Three Bears," and tell it to the class in

your own words.

2. Choose one of the shorter stories from this chapter and tell it to the rest of the class. Remember that you don't have to use the exact words that are used in the written version.

3. Take a happening from your own life and build it into a story to tell the class. It should be about one to two minutes long.

4. The story that opens this chapter is based on an actual happening, a teacher's picking up a student, desk and all, and locking him in a closet. Take a happening or set of circumstances from your life and turn it into a story that then departs from the truth and goes into fantasy.

5. Choose one of the story excerpts from the chapter, finish the story and tell it to the class. You can make it realistic or silly.

21

CHAPTER TWO

CHOOSING A STORY TO TELL

It is important that you like the story you choose. The story should be enjoyable. It should be fun to read and fun to tell. You should be excited about it. You should become involved in it. It may have unexpected twists such as occurs at the end of "Who Are You and Why Are You Here?", or it may be funny like "A Wag's Tale," both of which appear later in the chapter.

It is important to enjoy your story because you will be spending a lot of time with it. If you don't like it at the beginning, you certainly will not want to spend hours learning and preparing it for presentation.

If you hope to keep on telling stories, you will want to build a collection on which to draw for different occasions and audiences. So you need to choose those that you think you will want to tell over and over again. Of course, all of us make mistakes. If after a time you find you don't like a story, don't feel that you have to stay with it.

The story should suit you and the type of person you are. You should feel comfortable with it. If you are an extravert, you may not want to tell a quiet story but one that allows you a lot of movement and changes in voice. If you are not so outgoing, you probably will not want to choose a story that needs a lot of exaggeration.

You should agree with the content. If the story presents ideas that go against your beliefs, you shouldn't choose it. On the other hand, a story which enforces your beliefs may be a good one to tell.

For example, if you believe hunting game is wrong, you probably wouldn't want to choose a story about a person's enjoyment in going out one morning to shoot his first deer. Yet you may choose a story that takes the position that the sport is cruel.

23

A WAG'S TALE
by Carl Catt

Graham wore bib overalls faded near to white from wear and washing. His beard was white too, except for tobacco stains around his mouth. He stretched his lanky frame, readjusting himself on his rocking chair. Then he rubbed his leg, looked at Parlez Vous and said, "I can feel a thunderstorm acomin'."

Parlez Vous twitched one of his floppy ears, whined, but didn't move. His long pink tongue, speckled with black, quivered as he panted. Saliva dribbled onto the floor.

"Oh, yes, PV, my weather predictin' bone is right here below the knee. Ephraim was splittin' wood, usin' an old steel wedge and a ten-pound hammer. He was thirteen and feelin' his oats, swingin' that sledge like he thought he was Paul Bunyan. Well, wham damn come that hammer, and a shard of that steel wedge flew into my leg, right smack into the bone." The dog lifted an eyelid momentarily, as if letting Graham know he had heard the story, but Graham pressed on. "Now let's see, hit was nineteen and thirty-three. I recollect because hit was the year that Roostervelt and his toothy hen got to be King and Queen of America."

"Talkin' to your dog again?" snapped Ephraim as he hobbled up the porch steps.

Graham nudged Parlez Vous with his foot and said, "Now don't you pay him no mind." He started rocking again, harder than before and spoke louder. "I was just a tow-headed five-year-old, born on the very day them Dem-o-crates nominated a New York City mackerel-snapper, Alfred E. Smith. Paw wanted to name me Martin Luther to get even, but maw held out for Graham, seein' as it was the same day that grandpaw died."

"Only five," he repeated as his brother slumped onto the other rocker. "Ephraim shoulda knowed better — lettin' a youngin' go chasin' around by the wood pile."

"Why do you talk to Parlez Vous? He's just a dumb

animal. And besides, he went deaf, year 'fore last, and," continued Ephraim with a deep sigh, "even if he weren't deaf, he couldn't hear ya under his big ears. And dumbbell, even if he could hear ya, dogs don't know nothin' other 'an sit, fetch, and a few things like that."

Parlez Vous growled.

"Now PV," said Graham, leaning over, patting his dog, "hits that shard of metal that makes my leg so smart. Lotsa folks what's got old, healed-over broken bones can foretell the weather too, but hit's that shard of Bessemer steel that makes my weather predictin' the best in the West, by God, Virginia."

"Don't talk to the dog, Graham, someone might hear ya, and hit would be mighty embarrassin' — a grown-up man talkin' to a dog."

"Hit wouldn't be polite."

"What wouldn't be polite? What wouldn't be polite?" said Ephraim.

"Hit wouldn't be polite not to answer PV."

Ephraim shook his head, said, "Parlez Vous don't talk. Maybe sometimes, when he whines, hit sounds like he's sayin' Graham or yes or no, but hit only sounds that way. Dogs don't talk."

"Maybe you don't listen careful-like. After all you're old and goin' deaf yourself."

"I tell ya, I wish I was deaf so I couldn't hear you sayin' things to a dumb dog that can't understand nothin' and can't hear nothin' and, sure as shootin', can't talk."

"Ephraim, you're just a stubborn old fool. You always was and always will be. Maw said, more'n once, that you was old even when you was young."

"Why hell, everybody knows," said Ephraim, "that a dumb animal can't talk. If I don't say he can, hit's not bein' stubborn, hit's bein' smart, which you ain't."

Parlez Vous rolled over on his back and whined.

25

"Yes, I suspected it would," said Graham looking at his dog.

"What did your flea-bitten dog say?"

"You don't believe in dog talk, so why should I tell ya?"

"Maybe I will believe in it if I know what Parlez Vous said."

"He said 'a storm's acomin' . . . from the northwest . . . with winds gustin' up to forty miles an hour.' "

"Oh, hell, I heard that on the radio more'n an hour back."

"I suppose PV did too," said Graham," 'cause he mostly ain't much good at predictin' the weather."

"Horsefeathers, Graham, you ain't gonna play the fool with me *no* more. I heard that dog, and he didn't say nothin'."

"Well, you see, big brother, you don't understand PV 'cause he talks French. I was over in France in nineteen and forty-four while you stayed here to run the farm."

"Oh, hell, you didn't learn no French talk. And as I recollect, you didn't even learn to speak American 'till you was four or five."

"Like hell, I didn't learn no French. I learnt it real good and learnt it to PV too."

"Then say something in French."

"Like what?" said Graham.

"Like anything," said Ephraim. "Like anything."

"How about, 'cut the grass?' "

"Yeah, say that."

"Mow de lawn," said Graham. He broke out laughing and Parlez Vous barked, "ruff, ruff."

Ephraim stomped into the cabin and slammed the screen door.

Graham laughed harder, slapped his leg. Parlez

Vous wagged his tail. Then they settled down to rocking and panting.

The air was hot and muggy. Graham shooed flies away and looked through the porch vines to the thunderclouds moving up the valley. He rocked his chair slowly, and soon he and Parlez Vous dozed off.

Later, Graham jolted awake when a crack of thunder shook the cabin. Parlez Vous ran in circles, barking. Then the wind blew over a table, and flower pots smashed onto the floor.

Graham and Parlez Vous scurried inside. Parlez Vous hid under the kitchen table. Graham and Ephraim latched the windows. A crack of thunder shook the cabin again, rattling dishes and jars.

Graham and Ephraim exchanged wide-eyed stares as they smelled smoke. "We got hit," said Ephraim, "sweet Jesus, we got ourselves a lightnin' fire."

"Where?" said Graham.

"Hell, I don't know."

"Ruff, ruff," barked Parlez Vous.

"Hit's in the roof," shouted Graham.

They looked up and saw a smoldering rafter and then looked down at Parlez Vous. He was wagging his tail.

"Well sometimes," said Graham, "when hit's real important, he speaks American too."

FURTHER CONSIDERATIONS

Even when you find a story you think you would like to tell, there are other important factors that you need to judge.

There should be only a few characters. If there are too many characters, or even if they are similar, such as twins Rodney and Roderick, an audience may lose track of them. This would be even worse if there were little differences in their personalities and looks.

In other words, *there should be contrasts among the char-*

27

acters in looks and personality.

Besides being different from each other, *the characters should be interesting.* You should care what happens to them. In the children's story that follows, you should feel empathy for Little Bit of Darkness. Just as important, you should believe in the theme.

This means, of course, that *you need to consider whether the story has meaning beyond providing entertainment.* "Into the Light and the Darkness" is a story that should capture a child's attention due to the characters and their dilemma. But more than that, it teaches a lesson in acceptance, in not fearing others just because they are different.

A story often deals with a theme that is important to the lives of the audience or that at least should be important. Often it can be stated as a common premise, something which most people believe. Examples are: War is wrong; everyone should be equal under the law, and so on.

INTO THE LIGHT
AND THE DARKNESS

Little Bit of Darkness looked out the window where children were tossing a ball back and forth. She wished she had friends. Sometimes Mama and Papa played hide-and-seek with her or read to her from a big storybook up on the shelf, but it wasn't the same.

"May I go outside?" she asked.

Mama sat on the end of the sofa watching shadows move across a dark TV screen. "The light from the sun will make you disappear."

"Mama, please." The big yellow sun shone down on grass and big houses. It didn't look scary.

Girls and boys laughed and called to one another as they threw a ball back and forth.

"You know that none of our people ever go out there," Mama said. "Grandma told me once about a little boy who went into the light, and no one ever saw him again."

28

Did Mama think the sun would chew someone up and swallow her whole?

Little Bit of Darkness leaned across the back of the sofa, her chin on her fists and watched the children.

Mama leaned over and gave her a hug. "If only your cousins lived nearby . . . I know you must be lonely."

Uncle Willie always kidded Little Bit of Darkness by telling her a goblin was going to get her nose. Then he pretended to steal it right off her face. She knew he was teasing.

"Are you teasing me, Mama?" Little Bit of Darkness asked.

Mama shook her head scattering dark shadows across the black room. "I tell you, Little Bit of Darkness," she said, "that children who live in the light and children who live in the dark were never meant to get together. Even in the darkest nights, those who live in the light have flashlights and lamps. They cannot see in the darkness."

"But I can see in the light," Little Bit of Darkness said.

"Maybe so. But the light will shine through you, and you will be nothing."

Little Bit of Darkness thought about what Mama had said and decided to see for herself.

Since it was nearly lunch time, Mama went to the kitchen to fix black bean soup and to bake a licorice cake.

Little Bit of Darkness's heart thumped hard against her ribs as she tiptoed to the front door. She looked back and saw that Mama was still in the kitchen. Little Bit of Darkness quickly opened the door and rushed outside. The light felt warm on her face.

"May I play? May I?" Little Bit of Darkness asked as she ran toward the children.

Nobody answered.

29

"I'd like to play ball," she said.

"Did you hear something?" Katy asked.

"I think I did," Gary answered.

"There's nobody here," said Rob. "It's just your imagination."

"It's not your imagination," Little Bit of Darkness said. She was getting mad.

The children looked around.

"Do you see anyone?" Shannon asked.

Little Bit of Darkness reached out and grabbed Katy's wrist.

Katy screamed. "I felt something touch me," she said.

"I did. I touched you," Little Bit of Darkness said. She ran from one to the other grabbing their hands. She saw that they all were scared. She wondered why. Then she looked at her hand, and it wasn't there.

"Oh, I've disappeared," she said.

"Who are you?" Gary asked.

"My name is Little Bit of Darkness."

"Why can't we see you?" Shannon asked.

Little Bit of Darkness started to cry. "Mama said I would disappear if I came into the light. I didn't believe her."

"I don't understand," Shannon said.

"Me either," Little Bit of Darkness said.

"I bet I know," Gary said. "When you turn on a light, the darkness disappears."

"Except for shadows sometimes," said Shannon.

"Are you a shadow?" Katy asked.

"No!" said Little Bit of Darkness. "I'm just as real as you are."

"I'll tell you what," Rob said. "If we go under the tree, maybe then we can see you."

"Because there's a shadow under the tree!" said Little Bit of Darkness as she ran underneath the thick branches.

"I see you," Katy said. "I see you."

"Now you can play with us," Rob said. He threw her the ball. Soon all the children were playing and having fun.

"Oh, Little Bit of Darkness," Katy said, "I'm glad you came out to play."

"I am too," said Little Bit of Darkness. "I never had anyone to play with before, except my cousins. But they live far away and can only travel at night. It takes a long time to get here, so I see them only on special days like Thanksgiving and the Fourth of July."

"Do you celebrate the Fourth of July?" Rob asked.

"Of course," said Little Bit of Darkness. "And Valentine's Day and Halloween and —"

"Little Bit of Darkness!" Mama called. "Where are you? Lunch is almost ready."

"I'm here, Mama," Little Bit of Darkness yelled. She ran out from under the branches and into the light.

"Oh, my goodness, I hope you aren't outside."

"It's okay; I'm with my friends."

"Your friends?" Mama asked.

"The children I saw playing. I was playing too."

"Are you feeling all right? Do you have any pains?"

Little Bit of Darkness laughed. "I'm fine, Mama. When I go into the shadows under the tree, my friends can see me."

"Oh, my, I never heard of such a thing," Mama said.

"Mama?"

"Yes?"

"May I bring my friends inside?"

"Don't you think they will disappear?"

31

"We will," Gary said. "We never can see each other in the darkness. But we know we're still there."

"It's the same thing with you, Little Bit of Darkness," Katy said. "You disappear in the light, but still you are there."

"Mama," Little Bit of Darkness called. "Can my friends eat lunch with us?"

"There is plenty of black bean soup and licorice cake," Mama said. "And I bought a whole gallon of dark chocolate milk."

"Come on," Little Bit of Darkness shouted. She grabbed Shannon's hand and started to run. Katy and Gary and Rob ran after her.

Inside, it was very dark. Katy and the other children who lived in the light kept bumping into furniture.

"Ow," Shannon said.

"Double ow," said Rob.

"I thought you might disappear forever like the boy did long ago," Mama said. "But I think maybe that was just a story to frighten us so we wouldn't go into the light."

"Oh, this is scary," said Gary. "I can't see anyone, not even myself."

Little Bit of Darkness laughed and looked at her own arms and legs. Now she could see them as plain as night. "Here," she said grabbing Katy's hand, "I'll lead you all to the chairs." One by one she helped them sit down. "It's funny that I can see you all better now than I could outside, and best of all, I didn't disappear forever."

Gary jumped up from his chair. He ran to the window and stuck his head outside. "I didn't disappear forever either," he said.

Mama dished up the bean soup and cut big pieces of cake.

"Mama?" Little Bit of Darkness said. "Now I won't

have to be lonely anymore."

Her mother smiled as she poured the dark chocolate milk.

The characters and action should be believable within the framework of the story. Little Bit of Darkness is not a human character, and logic tells us that nobody would really become invisible in the light. Yet the story creates a world in which this is possible and believable. In the story that follows the older Deborah Ann may have come entirely from Carl's imagination. Yet this is believable in the world that the storyteller has created. Carl is an inventor and writer. He is interested in quantum physics and says he has worked out the concept of time travel. So within the "universe" of the story, it is conceivable that Deborah Ann did come from the future.

WHO ARE YOU
AND WHY ARE YOU HERE?

As I walked inside the coffee shop, I saw she was there as usual, a little old woman in a red suit, gold tennis shoes and a wide-brimmed hat. Stooped, she walked with the support of a silver-headed cane and chattered incessantly to herself.

Not for the first time, I wondered what she was saying. I walked to the self-serve counter and poured myself a cup of decaf and ordered a cherry almond scone, my favorite. I paid the bill and sat at a table in the corner. The place was crowded with men and women, some hunched over business papers, others engrossed in conversation.

I set down my cup and scone and looked up to see the old woman standing on the other side of my table.

"You wonder why I talk to myself when no one's around. You wonder if anyone can make sense of what I say. You wonder who I am and why I'm here when you are."

I felt my face flush. "Uh —"

"It's all right," she said. "I understand. May I join you?"

I jumped to my feet, my chair thunking against the wall and rattling a shelf of mugs.

"No need to get up," she said, pulling out her chair, leaning heavily against the table as she sat down. "I suppose if I were in your place, I'd wonder too. A young man like you, who —"

"Not so young," I replied. I was thirty-five.

She laughed. "Anyone under the age of fifty is young."

I smiled. "Well, then I certainly qualify."

"Go ahead and ask," she said.

"All right then, why do you talk to yourself?"

"I suppose it must appear that way," she said.

"You mean you're talking to someone else?"

"My husband." She leaned close. "He's right here beside me."

I frowned. Had I been right all along? Was she out of touch with reality?

"No, I'm not a fruitcake," she said, the word somehow at odds with her appearance. "I suppose that's what you must be thinking." She turned as if to talk to someone beside her. "Don't you suppose that's what he's thinking?" she asked and paused as if listening to an answer.

I began to feel uncomfortable. How could I gracefully drink my coffee, eat my scone and then leave?

"Don't let me keep you," the woman said. "Go on and finish."

"How is it that you seem to know what I'm thinking?"

"Do you want the truth?"

I nodded.

"All right then," she said, "but eat your scone as you listen to my story.

"Once upon a time I was happily married. My

husband and I didn't have a great deal to live on, but we were young and in love. Oh, I'm being immodest, but let me tell you, I was a beauty back then, and I thought he was the handsomest man who ever lived."

"What happened?" I asked.

"He was an inventor and a self-made physicist. Particularly interested in quantum mechanics, Schröedinger's cat and that sort of thing."

"Quantum physics!" I said. I myself was a writer, interested in quantum physics. My stories were fanciful, fantastic (in the original sense or so my public seemed to think) and brought me my meager living. But you see, I truly believed what I wrote. I believed in worlds parallel to ours, worlds that had broken off when things might have gone one of two ways. I believed that all time was simultaneous and thought I knew how to travel in time, except for having money to build a device to do so.

"I know of your interests. Why do you suppose I've come here every day when you have? Every day for the past few weeks trying to work up my nerve?"

"It's true, isn't it? Every time I've come here lately, you've been here too. It seemed a strange sort of coincidence."

"I'm from the future, another world, another probability, whatever you want to call it, Carl."

"How did you know my na —"

"I want to stop you. You cannot go on with this. It causes too much disruption."

"I don't understand."

"Carl, there's only one way to say this, and that's straight out. Once you knew, will know, had known — Merciful heavens, I don't know the proper verb form."

Suddenly, she looked familiar to me, and I thought to imagine her as she had been. "Deborah Ann! Your name is Deborah Ann." Chills ran up and down my back. I frowned. "Why did I call you that? How could I possibly know your name?" I tried to make light of it. "There must

35

be something in this coffee."

She looked uncomfortable. "You wondered who I talk to all the time, as if I'm out of my mind."

"I'd never say that sort —"

"Of course you wouldn't, Carl, you were always too much the gentleman."

"Who are you? What does all this mean?" I blew on my coffee and took a sip.

"Just as you said, I'm Deborah Ann. I'm your wife."

I stood. "Sorry," I said. "I have to be going."

"You were born in West Virginia, went to Highland High School, marched in the band, played a little basketball and then dropped out of school. In the years that followed, along the way in your travels, you took a course in physics here, a course in creative writing there. Finally, you were awarded your bachelor of arts degree from Ohio University."

"How do you know —"

"I've traveled in time, Carl." She grabbed my arm so I couldn't leave. "I've come back to warn you — Oh, God, Carl, I loved you so much. I love you so much." She looked into my eyes. "Please sit down. Please."

What could it hurt? Besides everyone was staring, and I hated creating scenes. I nodded, and a nearly palpable aura of tension lifted from the old woman's body.

"Listen to me, please," she said. "Don't do it."

"What?" I felt exasperation. "What is it that I shouldn't do?"

"I said I was talking to my husband, at least all that's left of my husband before he fades away. Before you fade away."

"I — I don't understand."

"Live in the here and now, Carl. That's my message. Don't worry about the future. Live your life." She closed her eyes. "I'm doing this badly, but I must explain. There's a natural order to things, my darling. When we stick our noses in where they don't belong, the plan is destroyed. Worlds are destroyed. When you travel in time, you've made your decision and ended one alternate route of history. Just think of two roads branching off and one fading into the mist, never to be seen again."

"Are you trying to tell me that somehow I traveled in time or something?"

"I don't know if I can alter what already is, but I have to try." She reached out and touched my cheek. "Already you're fading away, just as I . . ." She pulled a gun from a purse she'd concealed on her lap. "For that other Deborah Ann, all the other Deborah Anns, I must do this." She pointed the gun at the empty chair and fired, but there was no sound. And I saw there was no gun in her hand.

"What is this?" I asked. "Am I losing touch with reality? Am I imagining so completely that —"

"I said I talked to my husband. He knew what I had to do." She glanced at the chair beside us. "He's already faded from existence, so I know I must be on the right track. I've changed things, set them right again, at least I hope so." She smiled, tears in her eyes. "Oh, Carl, don't you see, I've done it for us. I've made it possible for all those worlds with us in them still to exist." She gazed into my eyes, deeply. "May I ask you a favor?"

"I suppose," I answered only because she looked so sad.

"Don't fiddle around with what you don't understand. Someday perhaps, the human race will understand the meaning of time. But until then . . . live in the here and now. Don't let the fork in the road trail off to nothing."

As I watched, the woman's body seemed to fade and then come back. She swayed as if she were going to faint. "I did it for us, Carl, for every one of us who has a right to be." Her voice trailed to nothingness.

I must get home, I thought, and write all this down.

Lost in thought, I bumped into someone, splashing coffee on my shirt and pants. "I'm sorry," I said. "I'm sorry . . . Deborah Ann!" Oh, God, she was beautiful with that silken brown hair, those blue eyes. I glanced down. Of course, she wore a pair of gold tennis shoes.

"How did you know my name?"

I smiled and started to laugh. "Let me replace that spilled cup of coffee," I told her, "and I'll try to explain."

The major characters in a story should be unique so that the listener sees them as believable and interesting. There are a few exceptions, such as parables where the characters are not fully developed.

Similarly, the minor characters need not be well-delineated since spending a lot of time with them detracts rather than adds to the overall effect.

IS THE STORY TELLABLE?

Is your story simple enough that an audience can follow it easily? Many written stories have sub-plots, and this is fine because the reader has the story to look back on if need be. This, of course, is not possible for a listener. It is best if the story is unified around a particular character, that it have one protagonist who sets out to reach a certain goal. This most often means the story has a plot. All the action in the story should relate to the protagonist's either reaching or failing to reach that goal. Little Bit of Darkness wants to play in the light. This is because she's lonely and wants friends. Everything in the story contributes to this.

Everything that happens in the following story relates to Cecil's decision to help his relatives. He is the protagonist, who sets out on a particular course of action. The rest of the story shows what he does and finally what happens to him as a result. You also see what happens to his wife, but only in so far as she is tied to his course of action.

TRADEOFFS

When he awoke that night and sat up in his coffin, Ceece Harrington knew he was going to bite his great-

grandnephew's neck whether the People agreed with it or not.

"Alicia," he yelled, clearing the sleep from his throat.

"Yes, dear?" She was just sitting up, and he marveled anew at her beauty, just as he had nearly every evening for the past half century. Cheeks still rosy from last night's kill, she had eyes as brown as rich syrup and a body perpetually frozen at the human age of twenty-three.

Well, he thought, he wasn't so bad himself. Even though he was a bit older, a bit thick around the waist, he knew among their kind he was thought of as debonair — a playboy cut off at his prime.

Playboy, yes. He chuckled to himself. But cut off? No, sir. In another five years, he'd have lost his looks; his body would have thickened more than it already had. So unlike many of the People, he was glad for the change that had come about. He knew, of course, that nearly all of the People felt differently about the change, thus seeming to suggest that most of the human race would feel differently if they were to change. So he hadn't created any People. Nor had Alicia.

Had they remained as their old selves, would they have had children? He liked to think they would have. When he looked at his brother's children, and their children on down to the present generation, he felt a shiver of envy, the kind of brief shudder his mother used to suggest was someone walking over his grave. He laughed aloud.

"Am I failing to see some obvious humor?" Alicia asked with a hint of a pout. A pout, for God's sake. She was more than eighty earthly years old. Why would she still want to swell those cherry lips like a girl's? Well, it was only a minor thing after all, and in every other way, she'd always been more mature in outlook than he.

"No, my beautiful one," he said, "it's just good to be alive."

"Alive! Everyone knows your views, Cecil."

"Cecil, is it? Now what would make you mad enough to call me Cecil?"

"Ceece, then. Is that better?"

He crawled over the edge of the coffin, the outer shell covered in tarnished brass, the inside lined in pale pink satin with frilly pillows to ease a loved one on. Hell, he didn't care about the color. All he cared about was the comfort. It wasn't the easiest thing for one of the People to obtain a coffin, not at all like the old days when everyone still believed in them and gave them whatever they wanted.

"Well, Alicia, today's the day," he said, rising to his full height, brushing imaginary wrinkles from his trousers and coat. He'd learned early on to arrange his clothes just right and wake up with them seemingly as fresh as when he'd lain down. Of course, unlike a human being, once he lay down, he remained in the same position for the duration. And neither he nor any of the other People sweated or gave off those foul body odors he so much missed at first.

He stepped to Alicia's coffin, mahogany so rich it shone like burnished stone in the moon's pale light through the window.

"The day for what?" she asked as he helped her over the side. She patted her raven coiffure and smiled. "What adventure have you planned for tonight?" Her voice was too bright, too cheery.

"It's a horrible sickness," he said, "beyond the imaginations of anyone from our day and age."

"Now, Cecil," she replied, "we've been all through this. The People agreed —"

"Damn the People!" he bellowed. "Damn the People to hell!"

"A fine thing to say," she said. "Many think we're already there."

"Come on now, Alicia," he said, striding to the

cathedral-like window that faced San Diego's Fourth Avenue. "I refuse to indulge either you or myself in philosophical arguments." He turned to her. "My God, woman, you would allow these people to die? Your own great-grandnephew!"

"By marriage!"

"It's no joking matter. He and his wife and their little one are ill with this plague. By all that's holy, we've got to help them."

"Spouting theology, are you? Rather ironic."

"Jumping Jehosaphat, woman, can't a man even speak his mind?"

She walked to him and drew him to an ancient sofa against the far wall. "It's been condemned, don't you understand? We leave them alone; the People all agreed."

"And you agree too, do you?"

"Oh, Ceece." She closed her eyes and sat unmoving, bringing a stab of regret to his heart. When he saw her like that, it was brought home anew how he and she and the other People truly were separate from those whose pulses throbbed inside their breasts. For the most part, he agreed that the People could no longer be tied to what they once were. Yet he couldn't help feeling a tinge of sorrow at the passing of those who'd once been dear to him. At least, he mused, the closest ones had lived long lives.

Gradually, like the rest of the People, Ceece and Alicia, through necessity, had abandoned families and friends. Thank the saints, they'd at least had each other, unlike most People who transmogrified all alone.

Yet this disease, this virus, here now among those unchanged, was a thing apart. Striking men and women, orphaning little children, sick themselves, and left to die alone. How could you let such a thing go on?

"It's the little ones, Licia," he said. "They've had no chance at life."

"And you think by biting those little necks and

sucking out the poison you're going to save them. For God's sake, Ceece, would you condemn them to an everlasting perdition of darkness and fear?"

"Is it that bad, my love?" He knew that tears would be in his eyes if only he still could cry.

"I grant you, Ceece, we're luckier than most —"

"But they'd be lucky too, don't you see! Peter and Samantha and little Matthew!" He tried to smile. "I think I can save them."

"Cecil Harrington, you're a dreamer. You've always been such a dreamer."

"It's what attracted you to me."

"All right," she answered. "You really think you're smart enough to cure this thing before you make them —"

"Like we are? Creatures of darkness."

"Yes, my love, are you certain?"

He shook his head. "No, I'm not certain. But there's the possibility. The possibility that it might work. So we've got to try. Don't you see that if we don't try, we condemn them to certain death."

"But the People? What about the People and what they agreed?"

"You're afraid of them?" He smiled. "What can they do to us? Drive stakes into our hearts? We'd turn to bats and become too small. Burn us with crosses of silver? How, Licia? They can't touch those things themselves."

"Fine. All right," she said, "I'll go with you. I'll help you."

"Now, Alicia, I know you don't want to do this. And when I brought it up at the last meeting, I could see your reaction — the apprehension there in those lovely eyes."

"Yes, Ceece." Now it was she who went to the window, to stare into darkness and halos of street lights. Her back still to him, she spoke. "That day nearly fifty-nine years ago, when we repeated those vows, I meant what I said. 'Till death us do part.' And though some would argue with this, I agree with you that we aren't dead yet." She turned to him, the light of the street lamps lingering in her eyes. "When . . . when the change came, Ceece, do you know what worried me most?"

"No."

"That the change would somehow ruin our love. It didn't. Thank whatever powers there are, it didn't. How did Elizabeth Browning put it? 'To the height and depth and breadth my soul can reach . . . And if God will . . .' "

Throwing his arms around her, he drew her tightly against his chest. " 'I shall but love thee better after death.' " He kissed her. Then grasping her shoulders, he took a pace back. "Don't you see," he said, "I have to give them the chance."

"I know. That's why I'm coming with you."

"No, Alicia!"

"Look, old man, you've never won an argument with me yet. What makes you think you can win one now?"

"They'll know where we went," he answered. "The People will know."

"The People?" she said. "You realize I never liked anyone telling me what to do. Not my mama nor my papa . . . nor even you."

A cloud hid the moon, the street as dark as an unopened coffin. Quickly, Ceece drew Alicia up beside him. They stood outside the window of a tiny house where Peter lived with his wife and son in North Park. What would they think if they knew two vampires stood at their window? Two vampires Ceece had made sure they'd never seen.

Despite all his earlier bravado, he was frightened. Had he any right to let Alicia come with him? He shrugged. What's done is done, he told himself.

Beside him Alicia shivered.

He pushed up against the wood of the bedroom window. Ever so slowly, it moved. For the thousandth time he doubted what he was doing, doubted it would work. Yet if he was able to bring them to near transmogrification and then let go . . .

"Is everything all right?" Alicia asked.

He'd tasted the poison once — vile with a terrible sourness. Yet toward the end of the feeding, hadn't there been a difference? A lessening of the wrongness of it, as if a polluted river had begun to heal?

The People had accused him of sentimentality, of hanging on to things best forgotten, of intruding in places he didn't belong.

He agreed that except for the feedings, the two races should remain apart. He'd even admit he'd been wrong in keeping track of his family. The rest of the People, so far as he knew, didn't bother with the others. But now that he knew that his descendants —

The window gave way. Silently, he pushed aside the drapes and climbed up over the sill, lightly touching his feet to the floor. He turned and reached for Alicia, pulling her in beside him.

"I'll help you," she whispered. "So it will be more quickly done." Her voice was barely a whisper, but his hearing was keen.

"No need for that," he said.

"Shhh," she said, touching a finger to his lips.

He smiled and pointed to the near side of the bed where Samantha slept. "Only till you taste the difference," he said.

"Of course." She slipped to Samantha's side, while Ceece bent over Peter. It was quickly finished, and then he hurried to the baby's room.

Back outside, he took a deep breath. "If only it would work," he said. "If only we knew for certain."

"Yes," she answered, then chuckled.

"What is it?" he asked.

"Two of the People bringing life instead of death. How heretical!"

"I'm sure that isn't why the People object," he said. "It's a matter of contact, of violating established roles."

She took his hand. "Let's go home," she said.

They started down the sidewalk and stopped. "Oh, dear God, Alicia! I'm so sorry." It wasn't stakes or silver crosses. The People came toward them, carrying sabers and swords and all manner of knives. They formed a circle and slowly advanced.

Not all stories have a plot. (You will learn more about plot in Chapters Five and Eight.) One that doesn't is "The Disappearance of Billy Findlay," the tale involving Mr. Thomas. Yet everything relates to Mr. Thomas throwing the boy into the closet.

A story should have action and suspense to maintain an audience's interest. In "The Disappearance of Billy Findlay," there is action related to Billy's causing problems and in what the teacher does with him. Then there is suspense about what happened to the boy. This, of course, is never answered. But by then the listener realizes that the story has gone into fantasy, and that in the real situation, probably nothing much happened once the boy was released from the closet. The storyline is simple.

Part of being a storyteller then is being able to judge what will be acceptable to an audience.

The opening of a story should adequately set the scene, introduce the major characters and give the historical time of the story.

Let's take the opening paragraph of "The Flight of the Niños."

Manuel Ortega was twelve years old before he knew he could fly. One night he stood

45

at his bedroom window and simply spread his arms. He saw that the sky was filled with *niñas y niños*. He glided toward Eduardo Rodriguez, who was his best friend.

"You too, *amigo?*" Eduardo said to Manuel. "You are flying. I myself have never flown before. I find it a little bit frightening."

You know immediately that the story is a fantasy, that it takes place in a Latin country, and that the most important character is Manuel Ortega.

The second paragraph further sets the scene by telling the reader or listener that this is the first time the boys have flown, and that it is a frightening experience.

Or let's consider this excerpt from a story called "A Cowboy Parable."

The hangman pulled the black hood down over the man's forehead, over his yellowish eyes and scruffy black beard.

He was a killer, no doubt about it. Parker Johnson had stepped in front of him at the saloon, not even seeing him, and had ordered a drink. The man challenged him to a duel because of it. When Parker went for his six-shooter, the other man shot him dead.

There were those who said Parker deserved what he got, the way he beat his wife and kids, the way he broke bones and bloodied noses. Still, this man had no right to avenge such things. He was a drifter, some said a gunfighter gone to seed, maybe out to prove his manhood one last time.

It's easy to guess that the setting is the old west, that the killer, even though he is largely talked about to this point, is an important character, and that he certainly is not someone we would like. We can tell this by his looks and by what he has done. Further, we see that the story opens at a public hanging.

46

All of these things do not need to be stated explicitly but can be implied. Unless told otherwise, we can assume that any story we hear or read is set in the present.

Similarly, a story should contain any exposition or background necessary to its understanding.

In the excerpt from the story about the revival service in Chapter One, the narrator tells everything necessary to understand how the boy feels. He's at a religious revival service led by two evangelists whom he doesn't like because "they're horrible and ugly." Their description goes beyond the physical in that word choice and phrasing tell us how the boy feels about the two women. He had time to form this opinion because he was at church earlier when they spoke.

Or go back and look at "Tradeoffs," and see what you learn about the situation and the characters. You learn Cecil's feelings about family and how his opinions differ from those of the "People," whom we learn have set down rigid rules about noninterference in human affairs. This is what then leads to the conflict.

The language and style should be true to the story. Unless it were just for fun, you wouldn't tell a story that takes place in Elizabethan England using twentieth-century American slang. Nor would you use Elizabethan English in a modern story, except for certain unusual circumstances, such as time travel, reviving a dead historical figure and so on. Nor would you tell a highly exciting scene using long flowing sentences and flowery descriptions.

The story should have sensory imagery that is easy to grasp. Yet description that comes across as rich or beautiful in a written story can bog down one that is told. In "A Cowboy Parable" a few words of description — "yellowish eyes and scruffy black beard" — vividly show the killer's looks. A listener doesn't need much more than this to come to conclusions about the character.

Generally *avoid stories that have a lot of dialog.* If you do not, you may confuse the audience. In a written story, it can be confusing when there are no tag lines or attributions (such as "Tom asked," "Millie said"). But a reader has the option

47

of going back to figure out who has said a bit of dialog. The listener doesn't have this option. Of course, if you are a good actor and like playing different roles, you can make each character sound unique, and thus add to the audience's enjoyment rather than confusing them.

The story should be a piece that can easily be told in the allotted time. You'll learn more about this in Chapter Three. But the main rule to remember is not to speak so long that you begin to lose the interest of your audience.

The story should be appropriate for the audience. This will be discussed in more detail in Chapter Three. Yet when building a collection of stories to tell, consider the age group to whom you will be telling most of the time. Then choose stories that are suitable.

A story should not have tongue twisters or difficult pronunciations unless part of the humor is designed to come about because of them.

The characters' names should not be similar, like Jill and Bill and Will and Phil because this also becomes confusing. Avoid stories that have more than one or two unfamiliar or complicated names, such as might be found in a different culture.

As you learned in Chapter One, *a story should change the listeners in a positive way.* Will the audience be happier or more knowledgeable about something that affects them? Consider whether the story has something worthwhile to say and if it says it in an effective manner.

Finally, you need to *consider if the story is faithful to its source.* We can set "The Flight of the Niños" in a different culture, but it might lose something in the telling. On the other hand, you already learned that to remain relevant stories have to change with the times and culture. This is simply a consideration.

Certainly, some stories could not be changed from one culture to another and retain their meaning. A Christmas story wouldn't mean the same thing to a Buddhist as it does to a Christian.

ACTIVITIES

1. Which of the stories, "Who Are You and Why Are You Here?", "Tradeoffs" or "A Wag's Tale" would you prefer to tell? Discuss your reasons with the rest of the class.

2. What do you like about the story that opens the chapter? What do you dislike?

3. What is the theme of "Tradeoffs"? Of "Who Are You and Why Are You Here?" How did you come to this conclusion? Do you agree with the theme of each story?

4. Which of the stories in this chapter has strong characterization? Why? Which characters are weakest? Why?

5. Do you think the authors of the stories in this chapter did a good job in establishing a framework? Discuss with the rest of the class why you think each is believable or not within the framework.

6. Learn one of the stories in this chapter and tell it to the rest of your class.

7. Find a story not in this book and analyze it in terms of what was discussed in this chapter. Consider such things as tellability, characterization, language, theme, the story's opening and the use of dialog.

49

4

CHAPTER THREE

TYPES OF STORIES AND WHERE TO TELL THEM

Stories are told at many different locations for many different reasons. Here are some of the places. You can probably come up with more.

1. *Libraries:* They often have story hours for children. This is a good place to get started telling stories.

2. *Classrooms:* Lots of stories are told in classrooms. Tellers include the teacher, class members and visiting professional storytellers.

3. *Child care centers:* Many stories are told to young children by the teachers and sometimes by guests. This could be a good place to get started telling since many would welcome the chance for the children to hear new voices.

4. *Summer programs for children:* Many cities, usually in connection with the parks and recreation departments, hold summer programs of activities. Often these include storytelling events, sometimes by those participating and sometimes by guest tellers.

5. *Hospitals and nursing homes:* Often story hours, with guest tellers, are held in the children's wings of hospitals and sometimes in adult sections. There is often a weekly schedule of entertainment for people in nursing homes. This includes music, plays, storytelling and so on.

6. *Storytelling concerts:* Some towns and cities have regular storytelling events, often given at a local college or university. Sometimes this involves members of a storytelling organization or sometimes guest tellers who present a number of stories.

7. *Coffee houses:* Often there are nights set aside for readings or storytelling, perhaps once a week or once a month.

8. *Storytelling festivals:* Organizations such as NAPPS hold

national or regional storytelling events that last for several days. Here members have a chance to tell stories to others interested in the art.

9. *Radio:* Many public radio stations, for instance, have both local and national storytelling or reading hours. Sometimes these are regularly scheduled and sometimes to commemorate special events. This is an excellent place to gain experience in telling.

10. *Book fairs and conventions:* This is an obvious place to read or tell stories of all sorts. Often at such events there are rooms set aside for speeches and storytelling.

11. *Speeches:* Nearly every speech you hear includes anecdotes, jokes or stories, both to break the ice and to illustrate points the speaker wants to emphasize.

12. *Holiday celebrations:* At school and at community or religious gatherings, stories are told. This often is a good place to volunteer to tell your story, particularly if you are a member of the group holding the celebration.

13. *At camps and young people's organizations:* A big event at camps, for instance, is sitting around the fire telling ghost or other stories. Here nearly anyone who wants to has the chance to tell stories. At organization social events, stories are told.

14. *Various adult organizations:* Stories often are told as entertainment at senior citizens' groups or other clubs and societies. Often these organizations are happy to have storytelling programs, so this is a good place to gain experience in telling.

15. *Malls and street and craft fairs:* Often stories are told at special events or exhibits in malls. Storytelling also is often a part of the entertainment at street and craft fairs, sometimes at a particular booth or at a stage set up for the purpose of entertainment.

TYPES OF STORIES

Here are some of the types of stories and the sources for stories you can choose to tell.

1. *Tall tales:* These start out as if they are realistic but then

become more and more exaggerated. Often, a tall tale is told in first person, that is, the narrator pretends to be a character in the story. Often too, there are many stories involving the same central character, such as Paul Bunyan and Pecos Bill. This doesn't mean that all the stories were told or written by one person, but that once a colorful character was developed, the character belonged to everyone. The tall tale is a uniquely American type of folk story. Here is an example:

PECOS BILL AND THE RATTLESNAKE

Old Pecos Bill was the roughest, meanest, orneriest critter I ever set my eyes upon, not askeered a' nothin' nor nobody. That's why I always felt danged near invincible when him and me was on the trail together.

Like once't we was travelin' through Wyoming and it was gettin' on toward twilight. I don't rightly recollect how it was that him and me had lost our bedrolls, and didn't rightly know where we was gonna rest our heads. I suspect we dropped 'em when we leaped across the Grand Canyon, which sure was a mighty long jump.

But as I was sayin', it was gettin' on into wintertime and the nights was gettin' cold enough to freeze a man's blood to crystals right there in his veins if he happened ta slow down for more'n a minute or two.

Anyhow, I was frettin' about all this when Bill tells me not to worry.

"What we gonna do, Bill?" I asked. I mean we had barely finished our supper a' beans and lard fat when the wind started howlin' and it got so cold that the flickerin' fire just froze right up. I mean them there flames stopped in dead waver like some sort of artist or other had painted 'em on a canvas. Now I ain't never seen nothin' like this 'fore or since. But old Bill, he warn't worried one bit.

He set there a spell by that frozen fire, kinda like he was lost in thought. Finally, he says, "Bet this here wind's cold enough to freeze a coyote right in his tracks."

53

"You think so?" I answered, wonderin' a bit why he was concernin' himself with coyotes.

"If that there wind whips over us, we're gonna be frozen so stiff people will think we is statues. Why, we'd be so cold we'd never thaw out. They'd put us in a museum and call us some kinda splendiferous art."

"So what are we gonna do, Bill? I don't fancy myself in some dadblasted museum, my body froze stiff, my thoughts goin' round and round inside my head."

"Now don't you worry none. I think I done figgered out a solution to this here problem."

"Yeah?" I said. "And what is that, Bill?"

Instead of answerin', Bill stood up on his tippie toes and started in a howlin'. And durned if he didn't pull in so much air to let loose them howls that his belly expanded out four or five feet and broke the belt on his pants, which slipped down 'round his knees. He grabbed for 'em and gave me a sheep-like grin afore startin' in to howlin' all over again.

And then I look out and see ten or twelve pairs of eyes shinin' there in the dark. "Hey, Bill," I said, beginnin' to tremble, and not from the cold, let me tell you, "what you tryin' to do, make us coyote bait?"

"Jest hush now," Bill says and continues on with what he's adoin'. Except now the howls was mingled with barks and whimpers. And purty soon them coyotes come right up to us awaggin' their tails.

Bill looks over at me and says, "This is gonna be better'n any bedroll or quilt, just you wait and see."

The coyotes are comin' closer and closer, and Bill glances at me again and says: "We're gonna lie down nice and easy now, and I guarantee we ain't gonna feel the least bit cold."

And so we both laid right down on the ground, and them coyotes snuggled up close against us, warm as toast. One climbed under my head servin' as a pillow. And no matter how much the wind howled throughout the night, I didn't feel the least bit cold. Still I was a little worried when ol' Pecos Bill dropped off to sleep, 'cause who was gonna tell the coyotes what to do then? 'T'weren't me, that's fer sure.

But I needn't have worried 'cause them coyotes soon was all asnorin' like a bear with a chest cold. And then I musta dropped off to sleep m'self.

The next thing I knew the sun was comin' up real slow-like over the horizon.

Old Bill, he started into laughin'. "I 'spects the sun's durn near froze up too," he says, "and that's why it's movin' so slow."

One by one them coyotes waked up and wagged their tails. Pecos Bill stood up, and durned if his pants didn't fall down again. "Dadblast by gum durn!" he yelled and yanked them back up. Aholdin' on to them with one hand, he used the other to give all them coyotes a pat on the head before swattin' their rumps and sendin' them on out into the scrub brush and tumbleweeds.

"Dang," he said, "dang, what am I gonna do for a belt?"

Just then I saw this here rattlesnake stretched out by the fire, froze stiff as a stick. Ol' Bill, he noticed it too. "Just what the recipe called for," he says. "Come on, let's get that fire unfroze." He walked over to it, breaks off a couple of flames in his hand and breathes on them nice and gentle. I done the same. Then purty soon my hand begins to feel like I'm holdin' a new-baked potato. Real quick-like, I dropped my hunk of fire and seen Pecos Bill do the same. And afore you could count to one, that fire was ablazin' away like you wouldn't believe.

Then Bill picks up that rattler and starts rubbin' its body, creatin' a friction. And I knowed the rattler was thawin' out cause he started in ta rattlin'.

"Now, we'll have none of that," Bill says nice and gentle-like. And wouldn't you know, that snake up and stopped all his rattlin'.

So what does Pecos do but start threadin' him through the loops in his pants. And when he gets the snake the whole way through, he sticks its tail in its mouth and pulls it tight.

We gathered up our supplies and headed on toward Cheyenne.

And you know, the funny thing was that after that, every time I traveled into Cheyenne, I seen more and more folks sportin' rattlesnake belts. Course, they used only the skin. Years later ol' Pecos Bill told me that the snake had become the truest friend he'd ever had. Then one day its tail dropped out of its mouth, and Pecos knowed it was dead.

The snake had become so used to the pants that Pecos went to the general store and bought hisself a new pair and done buried the old ones with that poor ol' snake.

2. *Fairy tales:* Usually these are fantasy stories for children. The characters most often are magical creatures like elves, goblins and fairies.

3. *Fables:* These are short tales, most often with undeveloped characters, that point up a basic tenet or belief, expressed at the end as a "moral." The characters usually are animals. The best known writer of fables is Aesop. Following is one of his stories.

THE WOLF AND THE GOAT

One day a wolf spied a young goat feeding atop a high cliff where the wolf knew he couldn't reach him. He called up to the goat: "Be careful, or you will miss your footing. It would be better still to come down here. The grass is sweeter, and there is more of it."

"Thank you," the goat said, "but I do just fine here, and, if I came to where you are, it is you, not I, who would feed better."

Moral: The advice of an enemy is not to be trusted.

4. *Parables:* These are similar to fables in that their purpose is to teach a truth, a religious lesson or a moral principle using allegorical characters rather than real ones. In parables, the characters are types, and are usually not fully developed. Here is an excerpt:

PARABLE OF THE ADOPTED SON

There once was a wise man who had three sons, one of whom he had adopted after the death of his brother and his brother's wife.

The wise man knew that he was dying and called his three sons to his bedside.

"My time grows short," the old man said. "And I have decided to leave my fortune to the son who convinces me that he should have it."

"Certainly, Father," said his first son, "I should be the one to receive the wealth, since I am the eldest."

"But Father," the second son said, "I should be the one to receive your wealth since it is I who have cared for you and called for the physicians to attend you."

There was silence. "And what of you?" the father asked, addressing his newest son, the offspring of his brother.

"Oh, Father," said the third son, "I am not worthy to receive your fortune. Although you have treated me as a son and have legally become my parent, your other two sons, closer in blood to you than I, should receive your wealth."

5. *Ballads:* These are narrative, folk poems, written in short stanzas and with a simple rhyme and meter. They are lively and direct and have a lot of feeling. The form was popular in the middle ages, with the ballad often changing from one telling to the next. Of course, unless you're good at impromptu telling, you probably would memorize this sort of story. Often the balled is set to music. Examples with which you might be familiar are "Frankie and Johnny" and "John Henry." Following is an American version of an old ballad known throughout Europe.

THE HANGMAN'S TREE
Author Unknown

"Slack your rope, hangs-a-man,
O slack it for a while.
I think I see my father coming,
Riding many a mile."

"O father, have you brought me gold?
Or have you paid my fee?
Or have you come to see me hanging
On the gallows tree?
"I have not brought you gold.
I have not paid your fee.
But I have come to see you hanging
On the gallows tree."

"Slack your rope, hangs-a-man,
O slack it for a while.
I think I see my mother coming.
Riding many a mile."

"O mother have you brought me gold?
Or have you paid my fee?
Or have you come to see me hanging
On the gallows tree?"
"I have not brought you gold.
I have not paid your fee.
But I have come to see you hanging
On the gallows tree."

"Slack your rope, hangs-a-man,
O slack it for a while,
I think I see my true love coming,
Riding many a mile."

"O true love, have you brought me gold?

Or have you paid my fee?
Or have you come to see me hanging
On the gallows tree?"
"Yes, I have brought you gold.
Yes, I have paid your fee.
Nor have I come to see you hanging
On the gallows tree."

6. *Poetry:* There are many other narrative poems that tell a story, such as Ernest Lawrence Thayer's "Casey at the Bat." Usually, the teller memorizes poetry. Here is an example of a more solemn narrative poem:

THE SHIP
by Pat Cassady

Humid grayness hangs.
From a dingy, brick tenement
A scrawny six-year-old
Emerges,
Pauses a moment in the dreary doorway,
Saunters down several cement steps
To the wet sidewalk.
His grimy hand
Pushes a dirty-blond piece of hair
From a sweaty forehead.
He deliberately kicks a rusty, tin can
To make a clatter
Mingle with city noise.
He hesitates,
Turns, scowls at the brick building,
Glances suddenly from side to side,
Then quickly sticks out his tongue!
He shoves his hands into his pockets,
Turns to the gutter
And flops on the muddy curb.
A blue car streaks by,

Spraying dirty water on his jeans.
He looks down at them,
Leers at the disappearing car
And explodes a hateful "Damn you!"

A scrap of cardboard
Floats listlessly in the gutter.
He stops it,
Picks it up,
Shakes the water from it,
Turns it over in his hands several times,
And folds the corners
To make a tiny boat.
Holding tightly to one end,
He sets it on the water,
Pushes it downstream . . .
Pulls it upstream . . .
Pushes it downstream . . .
Pulls it upstream . . .
Pushes it . . .
"There y' are, y' little brat."
A sloppy, rough-voiced woman
Yells from a third-story window.
"What the hell y' doin' in that water?
Get in here!"
"The brat"
Slowly gets up from the curb
And kicks his ship
Toward the sewer.

7. *Ghost Stories:* These are stories, usually chilling and suspenseful, that involve ghostly visitations and supernatural intervention. Sometimes they are humorous, like those involving someone's daring to stay in a haunted house or a cemetery overnight.

8. *Animal stories:* These usually come from the folk tradition

and involve animals with human characteristics. Examples are "The Three Little Pigs" and "Chicken Little."

9. *Historicals:* These can be based on world, national, local or family events, and can show events in a wide perspective, such as a Civil War battle, for instance, or can tell about a specific person. Here are excerpts from two types of historical stories. The first is a tale about "grandaddy" getting the better of a con man. The second begins the tale of a real person, William Wells Brown, who didn't learned to read till he was nineteen and then became an attorney, a physician, a novelist and playwright, and a historian.

GRANDADDY AND THE LOST VIOLIN

I'm going to tell you a story about the time my grandaddy was out working the fields in Western Kentucky and this stranger come a walking down the road real slow-like. Grandaddy seen this man, all dressed in a black suit and hat, though it was the hottest day of summer. Grandaddy finished hoeing a row a taters and watched as the man, careful so as not to ruin the creases in his wool suit, climbed over the split rail fence separating the field from the old dirt road.

"Yes sir," Grandaddy said, "and what can I do for you?"

"Your name be Tom Carrothers?" the feller asked.

"You be right in that," Grandaddy answers. "Now tell me who wants to know."

"Well, my name be Arthur Smith, though most call me Art. I was hired by a Mr. Thompkins Fitzgerald to locate a fiddle."

"Must be an important kind of fiddle for this here fellow to hire you to find it."

"Mighty important, all right. You see, Mr. Fitzgerald used to live in these parts when he was just a little tyke, him now being a famous concert violinist and all. The toast of all Europe, if the truth be told. And this violin has a sentimental value to him, being his first and all."

61

Grandaddy wiped a hand across his forehead. "What has all this got to do with a poor old farmer man like me?"

"Well, it seems that Thompkins Fitzgerald was a favorite of your Aunt Sally's. She be your mother's sister, if I'm right."

Grandaddy got to wonderin' about the sense of all this but decided to play along and maybe catch Smith up in some sort of lie.

THE RUNAWAY

I'm going to tell you a story about a slave born in 1813, on a farm owned by Dr. John Young near Lexington, Kentucky. He was a wonder of a man, son of a black woman named Elizabeth and the farm owner's half-brother, George Higgins.

As was the case always in that time of shame, William, as the young boy was called, never was taught to read or write. You see, slave owners believed by keeping their slaves ignorant, there was less chance of their getting uppity and thinking they were as good as anyone else. So William spent his life working hard and receiving nothing for his trouble. Oh, his owner wasn't so bad; he treated his "property" pretty well. But financial troubles fell upon Young. And so he and his family were forced to move to Missouri. Here the land and people were different from anything William had known.

Young felt he had no choice but to rent William out to other masters, who weren't as "good" to his slaves as Young was. Well, these new masters sometimes whipped William so bad he must have wished he would die.

At the same time, things became worse and worse for Young, and despite a promise to Higgins never to do so, he decided to sell William outright.

Well, William loved his mama and couldn't stand the thought of being separated from her, perhaps never to see her again. So what does he do but persuade this fine lady to attempt an escape with him to Canada.

62

It was a dark night when they crept out onto the road leading north.

10. *Myths:* These are stories that deal with a legendary happening, usually involving a hero of some sort, and often growing out of particular religions. For instance, many myths involve ancient Greek and Roman deities.

11. *Fantasy:* These are similar to various other types of stories in that they are fanciful tales based solely in the imagination, and often involving unnatural events or creatures. The most common use supernatural elements. Both "Into the Light and Darkness" and "Tradeoffs" are fantasy because they involve nonhuman creatures.

12. *Legends:* These are stories that may be based on real people or not but which are handed down from generation to generation and generally accepted as historical. They sometimes involve the supernatural and most often have some basis in the life of a real person. For instance, there are many stories involving Johnny Appleseed. Other legendary characters are King Arthur, Robin Hood and William Tell. Often stories involving these legendary characters have come from a long oral tradition.

13. *Religious stories:* These can be based on holy writings or simply can have their basis in such writings. These are the sorts of stories you would find in religious magazines.

14. *Current events:* Often news stories and articles can provide the basis for stories to tell. Many nightclub or television comedians get their material from reading newspapers. Or you can take a newspaper feature story and tell it. The following is adapted from a newspaper account.

BURDENS

Mildred Simmons watched as Paul washed the dishes and set them carefully on the drainboard. She wished she could help; she hated to see Paul have to do so much. But she wanted to be sure things were neat and tidy for the children.

When Paul finished, he turned and smiled. "Well,

63

love," he said. "I guess that's it. Are you ready for your ride?"

"As ready as I'll ever be."

"Okay, then." He dried his hands on a paper towel and threw it into the wastebasket. "It's not too late to change our minds."

"No, the decision's made."

"Yes," he said. "Then there's no use delaying any longer." She watched his old, gnarled hands as they rearranged her feet on the footplates of the wheelchair.

She was damned useless, she thought, a burden. It wasn't fair to Paul; he was in terrible pain from the arthritis. Yes, what they were doing was right. She had a horror of being a burden; she knew Paul did too.

Oh, God, she thought, how the years had flown. It seemed only yesterday the two of them had met at a college dance. And here they were, fifty years later, facing the end.

Paul strode to the desk, opened the bottom drawer and drew out the pistol.

For the first time since they'd agreed, she had doubts. No that wasn't true. She'd written about her doubts in a letter to the kids. It was best though; they'd do it away from home. Strangers would find them.

15. *Shaggy dog stories:* These are extended jokes that usually end with a pun of some sort. For instance, there is one about a man "who is rough and tough and used to hardships."

The story tells about his wanting badly to become a sailor so he leaves his home in the midwest to travel to the Pacific Ocean. Along the way all sorts of misfortunes befall him. But each time, he comes out on top because he's "rough and tough and used to hardships."

Finally, he comes to California and finds work on a merchant ship. He is sent up the mast to repair the sails. He falls forty feet to the hard deck, his body smashed and bleeding. The other sailors gather around, afraid to touch him. But lo and behold, he pulls himself together and gets to his feet, his body magically healed. The reason: "Well, he was rough and tough and used to HARD SHIPS." The idea is to drag out these stories as long as possible, having the protagonist encounter one problem after another, until he meets his final foe.

16. *Humor:* There are many different types of humor including jokes, shaggy dog stories and narratives with silly situations. Here is one that relies on exaggertion or carrying a ✗ situation to the extreme:

LETTERS TO WHOLE WHEAT HAIR PRODUCTS
by Bill Jarosin

Dear Sirs:

I just got your package of Whole Wheat Hair Grow in the mail. Thanks for sending it so fast. I started using it last night and it made my head all tingly, so I know it's working, but my wife Jenny got mad at me this morning 'cause it ate a big hole through the porcelain in the bathtub. I rigged up a TV dinner tray outside the bathroom window — that works real slick. Jenny says it's like going to a drive-in restaurant where they used to hang hamburgers and french fries on your window. I even found room for the barbecue lighter and kerosene, which ought to make the towels and pillow cases stop smelling, since I won't need the linen closet no more.

So write real soon and tell me why your shampoo ate through the bathtub.

Sincerely,

Jerry Peterson

P.S. It also leaked clean through to Mrs. Finny below. She got real mad and told us her husband's a cop, but he's been dead three years, so don't worry.

January 31

Dear Sirs,

Thanks for writing back so quick with your Consumer

Information Booklet #26, "How to Repair Bathtubs With Asphalt." Your ideas worked great, but I had to go clear to Riverside for the roofer's cement, which dripped on Mrs. Finny too, until it got hard, but her husband's dead anyway.

I'm writing now, though, because something else happened. I was shaving yesterday, and had the Hair Grow sitting next to me on the back of the toilet. Well, my daughter Amy came in and before I knew what happened she had the cap off and took a big gulp of it. She burped this huge green bubble that grew and grew and pinned her to the ceiling. Jenny got the stepladder and we pulled Amy loose, but the ceiling bubbled up like Mom's cedar cabinet after I smeared it with paint remover. What should I do?

Sincerely,

Jerry Peterson

P.S. Still no hair growing, but I smell like that fancy aftershave from Sears Roebuck.

February 15

Dear Sirs,

Thanks for your Information Booklet #11, "How to Remove Children From Bathroom Ceilings."

I thinned your shampoo with high octane gasoline, just like you said, but you didn't tell me whether to use leaded or unleaded, and since the leaded nozzle's too big to get in the bottle, I had to use unleaded, but I sure know what it's like to have my car ping and knock when I use the wrong gas, and I wouldn't want that to happen to my head. So which should I use?

Sincerely,

Jerry Peterson

March 29

Dear Sirs,

I didn't get your letter yet, but since I need more help, I'm writing anyway.

I was at work this morning, leaning over a Chevy I was tuning up, and I reached over to grab the butterfly valve in the carburetor like I always do first thing in checking out a rough idling engine, and I bent my head down and a chunk of my skin fell right on the pulley that turns the flywheel, then flew out and hit the wall, just sticking there ten feet up above the Coca Cola sign. I made it to the hospital okay, and they fixed me up fast, but I felt kind of embarrassed.

I read the little instruction sheet later on but it didn't say nothin' about chunks of skin fallin' off. Is this supposed to happen?

Sincerely,

Jerry Peterson

April 20

Dear Sirs,

Thank you for sending Consumer Booklet #31, "How to Avoid Chunks of Skin Falling Off Your Head." I realize now I should have used leaded gas.

Also, I hate to keep writing, but I got another problem. Yesterday, after Jenny and me got a little amorous, she said my teeth felt fuzzy. I went to the mirror, and sure enough, I saw some thin white hairs all over my teeth. Is this normal?

Sincerely,

Jerry Peterson

P.S. I cut my gums up real bad shaving.

May 15

Dear Sirs,

I got your bottle of Hair Grow Tooth Fuzz Cleaner. My teeth feel great, and Jenny says it makes the oven shiny, too.

Sincerely,

Jerry Peterson

June 12

Dear Sirs,

I've started to notice fine black hair on the very top of my head, but every few days the patch moves to another spot on my head and nothing else grows. I have to wear a ski cap to work. Please write back soon.

Sincerely,

Jerry Peterson

P.S. I can feel the hair crawl around at night.

July 7

Dear Sirs,

Just got your Information Booklet #4, "How to Use the Hair Grow Staple Gun." Works fine, my hair stays put — but I'm worried it's growing too fast.

Like yesterday, I was in the bathroom brushing my teeth and looking at my head in the mirror when this big black hair shot right out from behind my ear and grabbed the towel bar. It wouldn't let go and started to wind up fast. The bar snapped loose and hit me in the face, but the hair kept winding tighter and tighter and I thought I was gonna lose my scalp again, but I yelled real loud and Jenny ran in with the electric meat knife.

Please send another booklet.

Sincerely,

Jerry Peterson

August 14

Dear Sirs,

Just like you told me, everything worked out just fine. We had a party and my friends were real impressed by all my nice, thick hair. I even got some orders for your shampoo. Please send thirty bottles.

Sincerely,

Jerry Peterson

September 2

Dear Sirs,

Got the shampoo, and passed it around a few days ago. Everything was okay for a while, but last night Jenny got up to get a glass of water, and when she turned on the kitchen light, there was this giant hairball making coffee and wearing Jenny's pink bunny slippers. Well, I woke up 'cause of all the screaming, but all I saw when I got there was a big hole in the screen door with hair all over it.

Then this morning, Harry, my neighbor behind me, calls and says he found hair in Sylvester, his cat's, bowl, who wouldn't come when he called him, and had I seen Sylvester? I said no, and then he tells me Joe Hopkins across the street heard something in his garage last night, and maybe that was Sylvester.

Please write real soon.

Sincerely,

Jerry Peterson

P.S. The neighborhood smells just like that Sears Roebuck cologne, too.

October 24

Dear Sirs,

Thank you for sending Consumer Information Booklet #96, "Making Bobby Pins Out of Cat Bones." I found it very helpful.

I don't think you'll get anymore letters from Jerry — he and Jenny and Amy are gone now, but my friends and I are having a good time drinking their coffee and going round and round in the washing machine.

Sincerely,

Jerry's hair

P.S. I met the lady downstairs today — we'll get along just fine. I like her husband, too.

17. *Literary or printed stories:* There are all types of printed stories which can be drawn upon and adapted for telling. You can find collections of them in any school or public library.

TYPES OF STORIES FOR DIFFERENT AGE GROUPS

Now that you have a good idea of the types of stories you can choose to tell, you need to know which types appeal to different age groups.

The very young: Children from two to five generally like stories that have particular patterns of sound and repetitions. They like rhymes and lullabies. Nursery rhymes are aptly named because they do appeal to kids of nursery school age. These include Mother Goose rhymes and chants.

> **Jack Spratt could eat no fat;**
> **His wife could eat no lean.**
> **So between them both, you see,**
> **They licked the platter clean.**

Young kids like repetition in stories: "Fee fie fo fum, I smell the blood of an Englishman. Be he alive or be he dead, I'll grind his bones to make my bread."

They enjoy stories that have a lot of activity, such as clapping, and a lot of movement. They like total nonsense because they find it silly and very funny. They particularly like these repeated throughout a story, as in the following excerpt:

MR. AND MRS. LITTLE AND MR. BIG

There was a little man who lived in a little house. Hi ho, fum dee oh, fiddle-ee diddle-ee dee.

He had a little wife and a tiny baby boy. Hi ho, fum dee oh, fiddle-ee diddle-ee dee.

One day a giant came along and asked the man and his wife for food. Hi ho, fum dee oh, fiddle-ee diddle-ee dee.

Because the man was so small and the wife was so

small and the baby was so small, they had not enough food for a giant who ate more in one meal than they did in a week. Hi ho, fum dee oh, fiddle-ee diddle-ee dee. The man and his wife bundled up their food in an old blanket and gave it to the giant. It wasn't even big enough to fit into his hollow tooth. Hi ho, fum dee oh, fiddle-ee diddle-ee dee.

Those in the primary grades: Children in primary grades like simple, highly predictable stories. They like audience participation, such as clapping and repeating certain words. They are more aware of what a story is than are younger children. Their attention span is limited, so a storytelling program for them should not be longer than about twenty minutes.

Children of middle school age enjoy folktales and myths. They have more an idea of what a story should be and will better understand the ideas behind the story and the conclusion. At this age children are more able to appreciate the way a story is told. They will be willing to listen for about three quarters of an hour before their attention wanders.

Young adults enjoy a larger variety of stories, including those from traditional literature and even excerpts from longer works. Their tastes are close to those of adults. The length of the storytelling program for young adults and adults is about ninety minutes, though there should be a break in the middle of the program.

Adults enjoy most types of stories, though, on a more sophisticated level than young children.

ACTIVITIES

1. Take one of the stories from this chapter and one you haven't already told from preceding chapters, learn it and tell it to the class.

2. Choose one of the excerpts from this chapter and use it as the basis of a story you finish creating. Then learn the story and tell it to the class.

3. Discuss with the class other places, besides those mentioned in the chapter, where you might tell stories.

4. Try to figure out other types of stories besides those mentioned in the chapter. Discuss these with the rest of the class.

5. Choose one of the categories of stories that appeals to you. Now choose a story of two or three minutes that fits the category. Learn the story and tell it to the class.

6. Go through the list of categories in the chapter and, with the rest of the class, discuss which types fit particular age groups. Why do you think so?

7. Investigate where stories are told in your community, other than in your own storytelling class, and report to the class how a person might go about telling a story at such an event.

CHAPTER FOUR

THE SITUATION, AUDIENCE, AND LOCATION

Before you tell a story, try to learn as much as you can about the situation, the members of the audience and the location, or you could be leaving yourself open to some unpleasant surprises.

THE SITUATION

The first thing you need to determine is the reason for the gathering and if the program has a particular theme, such as ghost stories for Halloween.

Or maybe the program will include stories from a particular country or culture — Arabian or Appalachian tales, for instance. Or maybe it's to celebrate Black History Month when you might want to use a story similar to "The Runaway."

Maybe an elementary school class is studying the Gold Rush era. Then you may want to tell a story that comes from that historical period.

You need to consider whether attendance at the meeting is voluntary or required since this may determine how hard you will have to work at gaining the audience's attention. For instance, how might you approach telling a story to pre-teens in a classroom and those in a scout meeting?

Think of as many situations as you can for each of the following stories. Why do you think they would fit these situations?

THE INSCRIPTION

I've never particularly liked Salvador Dali's work, so I don't know what it was that drew me to a small book, *Dali by Dali*, which lay on a table at the antiquarian book fair. Maybe I was simply clutching at any form of escape I could find.

73

I picked up the book and fanned through it back to front, stopping — by fate or chance? — at the flyleaf.

"David," a hand-written inscription began, "know that I am always with you. Wherever you go, whenever you need me, hold out your hand, and I'll be there." It was signed "Kate."

Though my friends have always known me as a man ruled by mind rather than emotions, I felt a sense of sadness, intensified as were all my emotions since my diagnosis.

I wondered if Kate's note had meant nothing to David? Else why would he part with the book? His relationship apparently was neither that of husband or boyfriend. A dozen questions raced through my mind. After a moment I put down the book, turned from the table and became absorbed in other displays.

Yet throughout the afternoon I was haunted by the inscription. Kate and David obviously had grown apart. But why? I hurried back to the table to examine the book once more, to try to gain a clue to the mystery. It was gone, the display half dismantled.

"Excuse me," I said to a young man filling a crate with books.

"Yes, sir?" I judged him to be in his early thirties, thin, with green eyes, blond hair and a tan acquired only through long exposure to the sun, a contradiction to his work. He reminded me a great deal of myself thirty years earlier.

"I saw a book here," I said. "I suppose it must have been packed or sold."

"Well, if it's packed, it's a simple matter —"

"Oh, I wouldn't trouble you with that."

He smiled, lines crinkling around his eyes. "No trouble. What is the book?"

"*Dali by Dali*. A small book with —" I broke off for the young man had turned deathly pale.

"That's impossible."

"No, I saw it. I was struck by an inscription written by a woman named Kate."

The young man stared as if in shock. "It was addressed to a man named David," he said.

"That's right. Then you know it."

"Yes, I know it, but I no longer have it."

"I'm sure that I saw —"

"If you'll excuse me." His tone became brusque. "I must pack my books. The fair will be closing."

"But if you have the book . . ."

"I haven't seen it in years." Color slowly returned to his face.

I felt bewildered. "How could I possibly know about such a book if I hadn't seen it?"

"All right. My name is David Farragut." He smiled, bittersweet. " 'Know that I am always with you. Wherever you go, whenever you need me, hold out your hand and I'll be there.' Did I get it right?"

"You did, yes."

"Let me finish packing," he said, "and maybe you'll join me in a cup of brew. There's a coffee house across the street."

We sat opposite each other, among dark wood, richly paneled walls. He held the earthen mug in both hands, as if to steady it. "Kate was . . . How do I tell you? When I needed her, she was there."

"Did you know her well?"

"I'm a skier," he replied as if I hadn't asked the question. "Or I was. I nearly made the Olympic team. But then it ended."

I waited for him to continue.

He laughed, staring me in the eyes. "You'll think I'm insane."

"Try me."

"There was an accident. I awoke in a hospital, in a body cast. She came to see me."

"You'd known her earlier then?"

"No. Suddenly, she appeared by my bed with the book you saw. *Dali by Dali.* 'Interesting work,' she said. 'Don't you agree?' 'Who are you?' I asked. She didn't answer.

" 'I've never seen anything like it,' she said. 'Not that I'm likely to in my line of work.' 'What is your line of work?'

"She smiled, dimples in both cheeks, complexion like . . . alabaster, I want to say, but it sounds so trite."

I chuckled. "Sometimes only the clichés will work."

He grinned. "Her hair was black and glistened in the sun through the hospital window. She held the book out to me. 'David,' she said, 'what happened to you on the slope was wrong.'

" 'I certainly agree,' I told her. 'But how do you know so much about me?' A smile lit up her face, mingling with the sunshine, a real light I mean — intense, golden, piercing. Yet neither blinding nor hurtful. I became engulfed in the light." He shrugged. "At least that's how I remember it."

"She affected you strongly then," I said, stating the obvious.

" 'I have a gift for you,' she told me, handing me the book."

"The Dali book?"

"Yes. I opened it, reached out to grasp her hand, I suppose, and found myself back on the ski slope, at the point just where the accident occurred. Only there was no accident. It was as if it had never happened. No, more than that. I realized beyond the smallest doubt that it never had happened."

"Hallucination?" I asked.

"That afternoon, when I returned to the room I

shared with another skier, there on a set of drawers by my bed was the book."

"But how did —"

"I don't know." His voice was filled with pain.

"What is it, David?" I asked.

"I loved her. More than I'd loved anything in my life. I'd been a selfish man. I thought only of my achievements on the slopes. Nothing else mattered . . . until Kate."

"You never saw her again?"

"I asked everyone in the village, even went to the hospital. Nobody knew her." He set down his cup. "I carried the book with me, as proof. And I changed. I stopped skiing; I wasn't as good as I thought. I began to spend less time focusing inward on my own desires, but rather outward. I became a different sort of man."

"It appears to me, David, that you no longer needed her."

He looked at me astonished. "Perhaps you're right. I never did reach out again, isn't that strange?"

"Not so strange if —"

"I've searched for a woman like her, unsuccessfully. But it is true, I never needed her again, not like I did that afternoon on the ski slopes."

"Do you like Dali?" someone asked.

I was back at the book fair. In place of David, a woman was seated by a cash box at the end of a table.

"Not particularly," I said.

She had black shining hair, skin as white as marble. Around her shone a golden light. "My name is Kate," she said.

"I'm Carl Morgan, a professor of linguistics at San Diego —" I broke off. "Sometimes I forget that's no longer true."

"You were good at what you did. You cared about your students."

I was shocked. "How could you know anything —"

She came over to me and picked up the Dali book. "Won't you examine this book again? It's a favorite of mine. I first became acquainted with it while waiting to visit a young man in Colorado. A skier. I had a few minutes to spare and wandered into a bookstore."

"Then the book is important to you," I said. "So why do you have it for sale?"

She picked it up. "Here. Please look at it once more."

I reached for it, opened it, my attention caught by an inscription on the flyleaf.

"Carl," it read, "know that I am always with you. Wherever you go, whenever you need me, hold out your hand, and I'll be there." It was signed "Kate."

"Please keep it," she said. "A gift."

"Thank you." I slid the book into the inside pocket of my sports coat. When I looked up, I stood alone on the steps outside my office at the university.

Had I been daydreaming? It happened more often now as the disease took over my being. I concentrated on the way my body felt and found no hint of that which had threatened me. Could this be so?

"Dr. Morgan," someone called, and I turned.

"Yes, Kate?" She was a student in a graduate seminar.

"Sorry to bother you," she said, "but I've become drawn to the works of Salvador Dali. So I was wondering if I might — It's far-fetched," she said. "But would it be possible for me to do my paper on the linguistics —"

"Of an artist's paintings?" I asked.

She blushed. "It is far-fetched, isn't it?"

"Not at all." I reached into my jacket pocket and withdrew the book, anticipating her response. "You might use this for starters. I won't be needing it any longer."

"Thank you, Dr. Morgan."

As she turned, the sunlight caught in her hair and if I hadn't known better, I'd have sworn it formed a halo.

BLACK HOLE GRANDMA
by Bill Jarosin

"It happened all of a sudden, near the iron moons of Cygnus: red, colossal, heavy, sweating, burlap monsters coming, sneezing, crawling — I was helpless, helpless!" Mrs. Brundy wheezed. Strands of long hair caught in her labored breath and flew like comets across the table.

Mrs. Seeley poured some tea. "Really, Martha, enough is enough . . . just because I only got as far as Mars." She put down the pot and blew on the tea to cool it.

"That has nothing to do with it," Mrs. Brundy snapped. "Why, it was like seeing a bunch of Jesuses dressed in white robes — except these were burlap, of course, and had long green hairy tongues — but they were just the same, just the same."

Mrs. Seeley sighed. "I admit the old space program certainly gave us some interesting assignments."

Mrs. Brundy nodded and leaned forward, her bulby nose blocking the teapot's rising steam. "Why, just yesterday I was telling Jody — you know, my daughter's little one — 'Jody, some day you'll fly through interstellar space just like Grandma did, through the rings of Saturn, past the Crab Nebula, maybe even into a black hole itself.' "

"Oh, Martha." Mrs. Seeley laughed. "That's ridiculous. I mean, gods are gods everywhere, but a black hole, now that's something else again."

Mrs. Brundy put her needlepoint down abruptly. "Well, just because *you* never went through one." She glared across the table. "And it wasn't easy being the first, either — monkeys and dogs are one thing, but it's a lot different when *you're* the one being squeezed down to the size of a thimble. Besides, everyone had been try-

79

ing for years to find a shorter route to galaxy M87, and I found it by accident. The best discoveries often happen that way, you know."

Mrs. Seeley looked up. "It was no accident, everyone knows that."

"That's not true, the trial proved it — it was evasive action. You'd do the same thing if big hairy creatures suddenly appeared in front of *your* ship . . . incredibly small, those black holes." She rubbed her elbow. "Took forever to stretch my cartilage back to normal."

Mrs. Seeley took a bite of cinnamon roll. "Well, if I had to take evasive action, I wouldn't go into a black hole."

"I didn't see it."

"Of course not, dear. But just suppose you knew those little sticky tongues would follow. Such a nice, quiet spot to bootleg a little vodka and some Levis. No light escaping, who would notice?"

Mrs. Brundy clicked her tongue. "Really, Zelda, and what were *you* doing, crawling around in argon fog on Venus? Word got around pretty quick how you were hobnobbing with those smelly rocks just to get your precious titanium."

"They were perfect gentlestones — didn't scrape an epithelial cell on my body. At least I got some practical results: couldn't roast your marshmallows all over this rug without titanium fibers in the acrylic pile, could you? Not even a string of goo, either."

Mrs. Brundy sighed and turned a browning marshmallow over with the toe of her shoe. "Well, we've all had to make compromises for the sake of science, haven't we?"

"I wasn't compromised dear, I was in love. Not like cavorting around behind the event horizon."

Mrs. Brundy turned red. "*I* did it for science. And look at what I accomplished: shorter routes to distant reaches of space, the study of new cultures, the expansion of economic trade."

"Yeah, now we've got a universe full of freeze-dried cheese and flash-frozen Jovian mugworts."

"Well, it sure makes dinner a whole lot easier. And big revenues for the Consortium, too." Mrs. Brundy reached down and pulled some colored yarn out of her sewing box. "Not to mention new techniques in cartilage repair."

Mrs. Seeley took another bite of her mugwort. "We *are* getting a little hotheaded, aren't we, Martha? How's your needlepoint going?"

"Oh, just fine; these marshmallows really *do* make the thread *so* much stronger." She turned her head and shot a long green tongue towards the carpet, snaring a marshmallow.

"True," Mrs. Seeley replied, "we argue about such silly things, and all around we're surrounded by wonderful new technology." She lifted her granite foot and crushed a cockroach below the table.

Mrs. Brundy nodded. "Have some more tea, dear."

How much time do you have or should you take? To answer this question, you need to consider attention spans, as well as whether you will be sharing the program with others.

The length ties in with the purpose of the meeting. Is this an awards banquet where you are providing after-dinner entertainment before the awards are presented? If so, you probably will want to choose a story that is short and humorous.

A story has to fit the occasion, the theme and the mood. All this is tied in with the purpose.

Even considering all the foregoing, you have a wide choice of stories or even types of stories to tell in most situations.

THE AUDIENCE

Try to figure out everything you can ahead of time about the audience so you can better judge the type of story to tell. You've learned that different age groups like different types of stories and that the occasion often determines the sort of story you elect to tell. But you need to figure out more about concerns of the audience. Will you be telling your story to members of a particular interest group? Suppose it's a meeting of the local business persons' association? How would a Fourth of July story you tell there differ from one you'd tell to a political group? Or could you use the same story with a different introduction?

Consider all the variables you think apply. Is the group made up of young women, middle-aged men or what? How would this affect your choice and presentation? What types of organizations do you think could effectively enjoy the following story? To which organizations would it not be effective?

FOR LOVE OF MISS WHIFFIN

No one could possibly consider Miss Whiffin pretty. She was short and squat with frizzy gray hair. Her lips were thin and constantly pursed, as if disapproving. But she rarely disapproved; she had, in fact, a great zest for life.

Even her students, the incorrigibles, the bottom of the tenth-grade barrel at Roosevelt High School, sat with angelically folded hands, haloes almost visible, eyes seemingly fixed in rapt attention as she talked about the beauty of *Ivanhoe* or diagrammed a sentence on the chalkboard. Yet as she performed the latter, she couldn't help but wonder, after thirty-three years of teaching, if diagramming a sentence was of utmost importance to the future lives of her students.

For the first time ever, Miss Whiffin, the perennial old maid, was in love. And the feeling was definitely not unrequited. Come mid-June, she would be married.

Yet as she walked along the hallway after class, she felt sad. School would be out in two weeks. The papers she carried would be among the last she'd ever grade. No more *Julius Caesar*. No *Silas Marner*. She laughed and clicked the fingers of her left hand in time to the beat of a nameless tune coursing through her head. She began to bounce, almost to dance.

Then she stopped. What would the students say?

What would Mr. Evans, the principal, say? She laughed aloud as she assumed a military posture and began to walk sedately, stiffly, properly down the hall.

"No more students, no more books, no more principals' dirty looks. No more students, no more books —" She marched in intricate patterns back and forth down the hall, faster and faster and faster.

Out of breath, she flung open the door to the teachers' lounge and collapsed on the paisley couch.

"For heaven's sake, Odelle," someone said. She glanced up to see Harry Benjamin, senior math, his brow furrowed in a frown. "What seems to be the problem?"

"Problem? How could there be a problem? It's a glorious day."

"Harrumph." He turned away.

Harrumph? Did people really say harrumph? She chuckled. Benjamin was a silly old coot. She laughed outright. He must be a good ten years younger than she.

"Miss Whiffin," Benjamin said, "if you don't mind, I'm trying to prepare for my classess." He sat at a small secretary desk. Ugly, ugly, ugly, she thought. Why they might have been brother and sister. She threw out her arms in acceptance. "All right then, Harry, work, work, work."

She closed her eyes. She'd never felt this way before. Mischievous, unrestrained. All because of John. She'd known him casually for years, but then one day in church he'd leaned across the pew till his face was inches from her ear. "Miss Whiffin," he said, "I hope you don't consider me forward, but . . ."

"What is it, Mr. Stoltz?" she'd asked.

"I wonder if you'd let me buy you Sunday dinner?" He held up his hand to forestall any answer. "Because, you see, the thought of going home alone isn't at all appealing."

She was taken aback and hesitated.

"Oh, I don't blame you," he said. "You a teacher, me a man who never went beyond eighth grade. I don't know what got into me."

"I'd love to have dinner with you." Briefly, she thought of the small beef pot pie slowly baking in her oven, of the papers she'd planned to grade, of the novel she was dying to read, and dismissed them instantly.

They drove to a restaurant at the edge of town, a family place that specialized in chicken. Miss Whiffin hated chicken, hated it with a passion.

"This isn't a fancy place," John said, "but I'm used to it." He lowered his gaze. "Me and Mary used to come here often." He smiled. "I don't know how well you're acquainted with farming, Miss Whiffin."

"Odelle," she said. "Please call me Odelle."

"Odelle, then. As I was saying, farming's hard work. It's all big business; not much room for the little fellows no more. I've had to work doubly hard. My daddy owned the farm. I quit school to help — I'm just babbling," he said.

"Please, there's no need . . ."

"What I'm trying to say is it wasn't fair to bring you here. With all the memories. Mary and I always stopped here after church."

She glanced outside, the November sun shining on crisp new snow. "Sounds like you were lucky to have her."

"The specialty of the house is southern fried chicken. Have you tried it?"

"No, I don't li —"

"You ought to; it's about the best I ever tasted."

Miss Whiffin's father had raised chickens. Her mother had helped when orders piled up. All Miss Whiffin could think about was the smell of feathers in scalding hot water. She picked up the menu. "I believe I'll have the ham," she said.

Afterward, in the car, John asked her if she'd like to go for a little ride. "Thought I might show you the farm."

"Out Old Town Road?" she asked.

"How did you know?"

She couldn't tell him she'd always known. Ever since she'd first seen him in church and asked who he was.

He started the motor. "It's not a big farm, eighty-some acres. It used to be more, but I sold to strip miners." He looked toward her and pulled out into traffic. "Some said I was helping to despoil the land."

"Why did you sell?"

"For the future. For Mary and the kids. For our dreams. They'd be somebodies, those kids. Not dumb farmers like me. Doctors or architects. Teachers or professors." She shrugged. "The older you get, the more you think of the past."

"Beautiful country," she said. "I don't often get out this way."

Rolling fields and hills stretched into the distance, bare-limbed trees scattered here and there.

John clutched the wheel with knobby hands. Thick wrists protruded from the sleeves of his pin-striped suit. They passed over a one-lane bridge. "Here we are," he said, "home sweet home."

A square-shaped house loomed at the end of a driveway opposite a faded red barn.

"Can I confess something?" His hands still gripped the wheel. Hers, in fur-lined gloves, lay one in the palm of the other on her lap. "I've wanted to ask you out for a long, long time. Near worried myself to death about it."

"I don't understand."

"You have so much education, what would people think?"

"I don't give a hoot what people think!"

He laughed. "Looks like I provoked a storm."

She folded her hands. "May I confess something?" She gave him a sideways glance. "You'll think me terribly immodest."

"I doubt it."

"I've been attracted to you for thirty-three years." Her heart pounded against her ribs like a bird caught in a box. "Though it's true, I never would have believed I'd tell you."

He patted her hand. "We'd best be getting back to town."

Miss Whiffin stood and poured herself a cup of coffee, opened a packet of sweetener and let is sift down into the bone china cup. She still hadn't read that novel she'd been looking forward to.

For a time she'd questioned what John saw in her, why he'd taken trouble to look beyond the exterior, but she accepted his love.

John was the one who wouldn't accept himself, his ignorance, as he called it. He refused to accompany her to school functions. Once she'd talked him into going to a high school dance she chaperoned. The entire evening he'd sat, shoulders tense, eyes downcast, beside the punch bowl.

To make it even worse for him, she taught an occasional course at the local community college.

The decision hadn't been easy — in fact the hardest she'd ever had to make. But she'd decided to give up teaching, something she dearly loved.

She took a sip of the coffee, poured the rest into the sink and rinsed out the cup. She'd receive a nearly full pension. John knew how much she loved her profession and at the end, just before she turned in her resignation, he'd tried to talk her out of it.

"Don't quit on my account," he'd said, as he stopped the car in front of her house on Sunday after church. He tried to joke about it. "I'm a dummy; I'll always be a dummy, that's just how it is."

"John, you're one of the smartest people I know."

"You've been teaching all these years, Odelle. You've told me again and again how much it means to you."

"You mean more."

He had no answer, and gradually as the days and weeks passed, he stopped mentioning it altogether. She wondered if maybe he'd accepted that her decision was final.

At the end of the day, she hurried outside. John would pick her up, and she'd cook him a pot roast, his favorite, at the small house she'd rented for the past twenty years.

After fifteen minutes she began to worry. He was always prompt. She ran home, a block and a half, and hurried to the phone. She dialed John's number and counted twenty rings. She slammed down the phone, rushed out to the garage and jumped into her old VW.

She made the eight miles to the farm in only ten minutes, yanked on the emergency brake and raced up to the house. An envelope, her name written in big block letters, was taped to the door. She hesitated a moment, then tore it open. Inside was a piece of lined paper.

"My dearest Odelle," it said. "I simply couldn't let you marry someone dumb . . ." She shook her head to clear her eyes. She crumpled the paper and pushed on the door. What had he done? The door opened easily. "John," she called. "John?" She raced from room to room.

The barn. Maybe he was there. She ran toward it. It took a moment for her eyes to adjust. No one.

She remembered the note. Outside once more, she smoothed it out. At first she was startled. Then she started to laugh. Tears mingled with the laughter.

"My dearest Odelle," it said, "I simply couldn't let you marry someone dumb. Without telling you, I got me a bunch of books and studied while you were at school. I took the high school equivalency exam.

"I'm going to college, a class or two each term, under a grant for senior citizens. I needed my birth certificate to prove my age.

"I tried to call, but they couldn't interrupt your class.

"You were willing to come into my world, and it was selfish to let you. I'll come into yours. Don't give up your job."

Miss Whiffin folded the note and stuck it into her purse. She'd call Mr. Evans; they hadn't hired a replacement yet. Then she'd go home and make the best darn pot roast John had ever tasted. She knew how these college kids liked to eat.

LOCATION

It is important to check out the place you'll be telling your story. Under ideal conditions, this should be in an area where there will be no interruptions and where there are no physical barriers between you and the audience.

This isn't always possible. If there are going to be distractions or the setting isn't ideal, it's better to know about this ahead of time so you can take it into consideration.

Maybe you'll be telling at a restaurant or a banquet where waiters are running back and forth, or at a shopping mall with a lot of pedestrian traffic.

There are other things to look for. Try to present your story where there are no distractions behind you and where the audience doesn't have to look into a bright light.

As you know, storytelling is an intimate art. If possible, you should be close to your audience to enhance the feeling of intimacy. Some tellers, particularly at story hours at libraries and with other small groups, prefer to have everyone sit in a circle. If the group is small enough, try to have eye contact with each member because this is a good way to make a listener feel involved.

If you are going to use special equipment, such as a tape or CD player to help set the mood or accompany a song a character sings, make sure whose responsibility it is to have to furnish and set it up — yours or the sponsoring group.

Anything you can do ahead of time to ensure that things will run smoothly will help you to give a better storytelling.

ACTIVITIES

1. With the rest of the class, make a list of as many different occasions you can think of where stories are told. Now discuss the types of stories you think could fit each occasion.

2. Attend a storytelling and report to the class on how well you think the storyteller did in checking out the place, the audience and the occasion ahead of time. Why do you think so?

3. Check out a place where stories either have been told or will be told. Is it an ideal location for a telling? What is good about it? What is bad?

4. Choose one of the stories in this chapter. Figure out an occasion, an audience and a place where you think it could be effectively told. If possible, actually present it there. If not present it to the rest of the class *as if* you were presenting it there.

5. Choose a story to tell to the class. It can be from the book, if you wish. Now learn and tell the story. Have the teacher and the class discuss how well you assessed the audience, the occasion and the place in your choice and in how you presented the story.

CHAPTER FIVE

ANALYZING THE STORY

Once you've analyzed the situation and the audience, you need to analyze your story to make sure you can communicate it to the best of your abilities.

Take steps in analyzing a story because the discussion of each step will, in part, relate to each of these.

DR. DEATH COMES TO ALL

Penelope Eddyns tossed *The Los Angeles Times* onto the oak dinette table and strode to the window.

There was little movement on the streets, few cars and fewer trucks. A visitor, not knowing the state of things, would be astounded at the sense of peace.

She closed her eyes for a moment and swallowed hard before striding across the narrow kitchen to pour herself tea. From the refrigerator she took a slice of sourdough bread, orange marmalade and butter. She didn't worry about cholesterol. Nobody did.

She sat at the table and slowly buttered her bread, thinking of Lewis. It had been decades — decades since he'd died. A normal person wouldn't think of a wedding anniversary after all that time. A normal person wouldn't live long enough to think of it.

Penelope was a hundred and thirty-four years old; Lewis had been dead for more than ninety years. And she was frozen in that time, her body remaining as it had been since just before he died.

She spread marmalade over the butter and placed the bread on a plate. She cut it into four equal pieces. Lewis would have laughed at that, the precision of her scientific mind carrying into her everyday life.

Poor selfless Lewis, begging her to try the drug on him first because he didn't want her to suffer dire side effects. She hadn't suffered side effects at all, so far as she could tell, but soon afterward, Lewis had contracted a virus and died.

She took a sip of tea, tasting of sassafras and birch bark. Even though religion was all but dead, it had shaped her life, a life she couldn't end willy-nilly, even though she wished it.

Her hand held steady as she raised the cup again to her lips. She'd been forty-four years old for decades now, at least in body. But her mind was old; it was ready to let go.

"Stop being so melodramatic," she chided herself. She chose one of the pieces of bread and bit into it with a fury that seemed to be her constant companion of late.

She and the others had thought the drug would end all suffering, would allow people time to follow their hearts. But it had become a curse.

For a moment, she stared at the china cup, part of a set cherished by her mother and nearly two centuries old. In an earlier age, that might have meant something. Everyone had such antiques now.

The drug had been cheap and easy to produce, so once the results were tested and retested, everyone was given it. Penelope and the others were heroes, at least for a time. After all, who wouldn't want to honor those four who'd made eternal life a reality?

But before too many years had passed, things went straight to hell. And now she lived in seclusion, not even in touch with the other members of the team. For a moment she wondered if they were still alive, then broke into laughter. Of course, they were still alive. Everyone was still alive.

She and the others, Roland and Samantha and Dmetri, had begun with the studies conducted by Gregor Mendel in the late nineteenth century. From there they'd progressed through the various stages of research and experimentation in gene therapy, beginning in the 1990s with the altering of T cells and the treatment of brain tumors, on through Weissman's work in the early twenty-first century. They'd had one goal in mind in developing the drug. It was to eliminate the few diseases still left and to stop the aging process.

They'd succeeded beyond their wildest dreams, except for an important side effect, not apparent at first — sterility. And no matter how Penelope and the others had tried, no matter how teams from the furthest reaches of earth had tried, they couldn't remedy the situation.

Adults were halted at whatever age they'd been when they took the drug. Children grew to maturity and froze as well, at fifteen or seventeen or eighteen.

There was no more need for toys, baby food, diapers, cribs, tricycles. Businesses went bankrupt. People became bored. For a time, the crime rate increased and then dropped off to nearly nothing.

There were suicides. People went to the mountains or had others take them and leave them there, as Indian tribes had done years earlier with feeble elders.

Yet now, more likely than not, those who by choice had been abandoned, hoping for death, found their way back. Their constitutions were such, their bodies so efficient, that few of them starved or were met by accidents they couldn't overcome.

People banded together for support, took sides; there were wars. Many died in explosions and gunfire. Those who were left came to the realization that war was immoral, and maybe even eternal life was too.

Penelope walked to the living room and picked up the phone, praying there were still enough Bell employees left to ensure that calls went through.

She dialed a long-remembered number and heard it ring, as at a great distance. "Humphries here," a voice answered.

"Roland?"

"Penelope! Is it really you?"

"I hope you don't mind my calling." She sat in the old rocker that used to be Lewis's, twisting the phone cord around her thumb. She'd been the one, after all, who'd demanded the team go its separate ways. Even back then, perhaps, she'd sensed the havoc the drug would cause.

"Of course not. It's good to hear your voice."

He was a handsome man. If it hadn't been for Lewis . . . No, she wouldn't think thoughts like that. It was disloyal to Lewis and invalidated her own life. "You might think I'm insane, Rollie." She hadn't called him that in decades.

"I doubt it."

"All the unrest. Do you . . . do you feel responsible? I don't mean you alone; I mean all four of us."

His voice was molasses and chocolate. "I wouldn't be human, Penelope, if . . ." She heard him take a deep breath. "Not most of the time, though. It wasn't our doing."

"Of course it was, Rollie."

"Surely, you don't believe that, Penelope."

She leaned back, the receiver pressed against her ear, the cord trailing from her fingers. "I'm sorry. I guess I'm feeling particularly low."

"Did something bring this on?"

"Lewis's and my anniversary. But that's silly. It was all so very long ago."

"You were in love."

"Yes, I was." She felt her eyes sting. "You never knew how I felt about you though, did you?"

There was a pause, uncomfortably long. She nearly hung up, but then he answered. "I was attracted to you, Penelope. Don't ever doubt it. But I had Dawn . . . and you had Lewis."

Strange, but she hadn't thought of Dawn. She'd somehow imagined Rollie alone all these years. "Stupid old fool," she muttered to herself. Then aloud: "How is she?"

"Went to the mountains."

"I'm so sorry, Roland. Is she —"

"She never came back. I can only hope it wasn't too difficult for her —" He expelled a sharp breath. "Yes, I blame us. I blame me, at least for my wife. Nobody is allowed to grow old gracefully. No one grows old!"

"The reason I called, Rollie . . ."

"Yes?" The voice was tentative, old in years if not in body.

"We've got to undo it. We've got to —"

"So many years, Penelope. Why now, after all these years? I talked myself into believing it couldn't be done, don't you see? I guess I knew we needed to try. But I pushed that away. Things would get better. The world would stabilize. Do you know what I read in the paper today?"

"The paper?" She was startled at the abrupt change.

"*The Times.* The Kevorkians? Did you read about them?"

"The Kevorkians?" Whatever was he talking about?

"Old physicians out of work. They've been holding meetings. Lots of people attending."

"Meetings? What kind of meetings?"

"I'm surprised you haven't seen —"

"Is it unpleasant? I try to avoid unpleasantness."

"Dear Penelope. You were always such a . . ."

"Pollyanna?"

"That isn't what I was going to say."

"What about these Kevorkians?"

95

"They have this group, this society, and it's spreading. Dr. Death, they call themselves. Look on page thirteen, the first section."

"I will." She wasn't so very much interested. She wanted to get back to the purpose of the call. "What I wanted to ask, Rollie . . . I mean, it's going to be hard, but the lab's still there?"

"It's still there."

"Everything would be outdated."

"The chemicals —"

"But we could start over again! I know we could."

"Perhaps. But where would we get supplies? The sources have dried up. There's no need."

"We know the composition —"

"Call Sam and Dmetri; they'd be better than I."

"You're not a quitter, Rollie!"

"You want to reverse it, don't you?"

"I've thought and thought."

"Physicians are supposed to preserve life."

"Physicians! We were medical researchers, Rollie. We didn't give a damn about preserving life except in the abstract. We wanted what all researchers want. To prove something. To make a great discovery. And, damn it, we made that discovery. Hell, if we didn't!" Losing control was the bane of a good physician, a good scholar. Her job was to remain impartial. "I'll do as you suggested, Rollie, and call the others."

She replaced the receiver and leaned back, phone in her lap. She was weary, so terribly weary. Yet her body was in its prime, for-goddamned-ever in its prime.

Curiosity got the better of her. She set down the phone and walked to the table. The tea in the pot was tepid. She poured a cup and picked up the paper.

SOCIETY OF DEATH
FORMED IN UPLAND

UPLAND — Physicians from across the nation are meeting today to elect officers for a recently formed organization called the Kevorkian Society, named for Jack Kevorkian, M.D., who in the late twentieth century was dubbed Dr. Death.

Until hindered by legalities, Kevorkian became known for his practice of helping those with incurable illneses or fatal diseases to end their lives.

Dr. Paul Livingston, spokesman for the Kevorkians, states that the group was founded at a meeting last June 8 in Upland, California, with chapters later formed across the nation and abroad. The purpose, Livingston claims, is "to attempt to remedy some of the despair brought about by having virtually eternal lives."

The group that began with a handful of men and women now includes two dozen chapters in the United States and abroad. According to informed sources, Livingston will meet later this week with the governors of California and eight other states to offer a proposal. "Our belief," says Livingston, "is that since death always had been unexpected, and since the general feeling is that eternal life on earth is wearing thin, we become enforcers of death, striking randomly, until the entire population of the world is extinct."

Another scatterbrained idea, Penelope thought. The only real answer was to bring back the biological aging process, to disaffect changes in gene structure and DNA. Only then could the world get back to normal.

She laid down the paper and called Rollie back. "Suicides, accidents, murders. We've got to get the world

97

back on course."

"The world, Penelope? That's an awfully big job for four people."

"Four?"

"I called the others. Sam and Dmetri. They're both interested at least in reversing sterility. They both agree it's a long shot, but what the hell? Can things get worse?"

"Can we reverse it?"

She heard a sigh at the other end. "That's the big question mark, isn't it, since we're not sure what caused it. If only we'd somehow known."

"Nature's way of protecing her resources."

"If everyone lives forever and doesn't age and still can produce children . . ."

"So when are we getting together?"

"You were never long on patience, once you made up your mind."

She laughed. "I suppose not."

"Well, neither was I. I arranged to meet tomorrow at the lab."

"Have you seen it? What condition it's in?"

"I haven't in years. I used to go there. See that it was kept in shape." His tone was self-deprecating. "I guess I saw it as a kind of shrine. So, eleven tomorrow morning?"

"Eleven it is," she said, replacing the receiver. They'd played at being gods once before. Maybe they could do it again.

***

She hadn't been out of the house in months except to buy groceries; there was no need, and she had no place to go. The friends she and Lewis had cultivated during their twenty years of marriage had gradually drifted away. She truly had become a pariah.

It was early spring, a hint of California winter still in the air. She grabbed a cardigan from the hall closet

98

and threw it across her shoulders. Deviating from her usual custom, she wore heels and a dress, pale yellow with a pattern of fall leaves. She wondered at her motives, if the dress was really for Rollie's sake.

She locked the door behind her and ran lightly down the steps. Not bad for a decrepit old woman, she thought.

She'd long ago given up driving, as had many others. There were few mechanics around anymore, at least not those who still were willing to work. Who could blame them or others who stopped working? Why would anyone want the same job for a hundred years or more?

The sun shone hot on her face as she stepped onto the sidewalk. A burst of roses and agapanthus bloomed alongside the house next door. At least someone still had a passion for gardening, she thought. Or was it simply a way to stave off boredom?

She was lucky; an empty cab rounded the corner, cruising slowly toward her. She raised her hand, and it pulled to the curb. She gave the driver the address.

He looked over his shoulder. "That's the lab, isn't it?" His face was pinched and red.

"Ummm." She supposed the address was still burned on everyone's brain.

"So be it, lady," he said. Once in the sparse traffic, he spoke again. "You aren't one of them doctors, are you?"

"What do you mean?"

"The ones with the drugs. Who developed the drugs, you know what I mean."

"Yes, I know," she said.

He headed for El Cajon Boulevard, passing the building where she and Lewis had lived while they both finished school at San Diego State.

"Well, are you?" the driver demanded.

It was such an innocent time back then. Who could

have forseen all the changes. "One of the doctors?" Why not admit it? she asked herself. Did it really matter? "Yes," she said.

"Well, doctor, I'm not one of them radicals who want you and the other three killed, you know what I'm telling you?"

"Yes," she answered.

"I'll take you there. But next time, I advise you to find another cab."

So that's how it was? Penelope thought as they glided through silent streets.

***

Even though she'd chosen to stay away from the others all those years, her step quickened in anticipation.

The building, standing on a back street near 70th and El Cajon, was an unpretentious gray stucco, with nothing to indicate that it was the site of the greatest change ever brought about by human beings and involving the human body.

Penelope glanced up and down the street, as if she expected to be stopped from entering. A couple, appearing to be in their mid-sixties, strolled by. She couldn't help but wonder if they were bitter about having their ages halted at the stage of their lives when joints became stiff and bodies refused to obey each command.

She shook her head as if to banish such thoughts. The door was locked, but she'd thought to bring her key. All those years, she'd kept it in a milk glass candy dish atop the piano, as if she knew she'd need it again.

Inside, she heard the faint sounds of a radio tuned to a talk show. Straining her ears, she realized it was an interview. "So tell me," the interviewer was saying, "do you think this scheme will be accepted? I mean, it's almost like an old-style comic book. Dr. Death, indeed."

She came in among the maze of tables running this way and that. It was so familiar, from the rows of glass beakers to the microscopes still placed on each table. It looked no different from when she'd left, except dustier and a little bit faded.

She turned at the sound of brisk footsteps. "Rollie," she cried, "it's so good to see you." He was a compact man, no more than five eight or nine, skin the color of wild honey, dark hair cropped short.

"Here, let me turn this off," he said, punching the button on a portable radio, cutting off the sound. He turned to her and smiled. "Ah, Penelope," he said, "I'd wondered if you'd changed."

"If I'd changed?" Of course, she wouldn't have changed.

"Not physically. But emotionally. If you'd grown bitter or cynical. It was your spirit more than anything else that kept us going."

"So it's my fault, is it?" she said, immediately regretting the words as she saw the hurt in his face. "Oh, Rollie." She threw her arms around him, buried her head in his chest.

"I love you, Penelope Eddyns. I always have."

She pulled back and smiled, seeing brown eyes glittering with too much moisture. "I know, Rollie, and I love you."

He chuckled, the sound coming from somewhere deep inside. "That isn't precisely what I meant."

"I know that too." She glanced toward the offices. "Are we the first ones here?"

"Samantha and Dmetri are stopping for lunch. Chinese. Remember how we gathered all the time in your office — because it had the largest desk —"

"And shot the bull?"

"Brainstormed, I prefer to think."

She smiled. "Surely, Wong's Golden Dragon isn't

101

still open."

"Oh, but it is. I've gone there occasionally; when the moon was right or something! Just to think of old times."

"Old times. We were so idealistic, heading toward setting the world on its ear." She tried to smile. "Little did we know . . . So any ideas?"

"What do you mean?"

"On changing the world back to what it was. On whether we should even try."

"I've thought about it," he answered.

The door opened, and Sam and Dmetri breezed in. "Penelope, Rollie." Straight hair as yellow as sunflowers, Samantha bore cartons smelling of rice and noodles. Her blue eyes glowed with an inner fire. She set down the cartons and flew to embrace Penelope and then Rollie.

"So good to see you both! Of course, I've seen Rollie occasionally, but never you, Penelope. It's so ridiculous to say you haven't changed. But it's true." She threw off a summer jacket and tossed it across a metal stool. She wore a white knit top and lavender skirt. "On so many faces you see the bitterness now." She fluffed her hair. "Sorry; I don't mean to get us all into a foul mood."

Dmetri stood behind her, unassuming, carrying the same quiet dignity Penelope remembered. "Dmetri," she said, "how I've missed you." He wore a faded T-shirt and khakis. She embraced him quickly and drew him close to the others. "How I've missed you all." And she wondered why in the hell she'd been so keen on self-isolation. It was stupid. What was she hoping to prove?

At first, they'd kept in touch. They'd been the toast of the country, of the world. The saviors; faces on magazines and the front pages of newspapers, interviewed for each news medium until it all began to turn sour.

"Is anyone hungry?" Sam said, laughing. "No, I haven't changed. Always eat enough for a horse and never gain an ounce."

Dmetri took Penelope's hand in both of his. A head taller than Rollie, he had prematurely gray hair and crinkly lines radiating outward from the corners of his eyes. The youngest of the quartet by a year or two, he was perhaps the brightest, the one who took each initial "ah ha" and carried it through to a logical conclusion.

"There's something we need to tell you, Penelope."

"Yes?" She frowned in puzzlement.

"Well, you see, it wasn't a deliberate deception. It's just that when you — Oh, God. When you —"

"Cut myself off from the rest of you?"

Dmetri stared at her. "Sam and I are married. Have been for the last . . . number of years."

"Oh." Of course, they would have been married. Even in the old days, Penelope could feel their love as a nearly palpable bond between them. "How wonderful," she said, feeling tears sting her eyes. Why, she wondered? Was it because of all the time without Lewis? No, that wasn't it. He was little more than a memory now, a memory slowly fading away. A sob caught her unawares.

"Are you all right, Penelope?" Sam asked. "We didn't mean to keep it from you."

"Of course. If it's anyone's fault, it's my own. I couldn't face the victors becoming the hated. I shouldn't have taken it out on you three."

"So," Sam said, "which of us feels that we've experienced enough of eternity?"

Rollie laughed. "An interesting way of putting it."

"We brought plastic silverware and paper plates." Dmetri pointed to the bags he and Sam had set on the nearest table. "What do you say we eat this food before it gets cold?"

Penelope and Rollie found a carton of paper towels and wiped off the top of Penelope's desk and the seats and backs of four chairs.

"Did anyone remember drinks?" Sam asked.

"Voila!" Rollie reached into the bottom drawer of the desk where he pulled out a six pack of cola.

The four of them passed the paper cartons back and forth, filling their plates.

"Did you have any trouble getting here?" Dmetri asked.

"No," Rollie answered. "Why?"

"Oh, it's this Dr. Death thing," Sam answered. "Dmetri and I got caught up the middle of some sort of rally — people on both sides of the issue."

"I didn't realize it had become such a big thing," Penelope answered. "I read the piece in the paper yesterday; Rollie told me about it, but —"

"I guess there are a lot of people who don't want to live anymore," Sam said, "and a lot who do. It's the usual clash, the thing that's been going on for decades."

"Dear God," Rollie said, "if only we'd stopped to consider what we were doing."

"You think we were wrong?" Sam asked.

"Yes, I do," Rollie answered.

"I do too," Penelope said. "Amoebas, paramecia, they were meant to live forever, but in a different sort of way, a way not meant for human beings. We've bogged down human progress, new ideas."

"So," Rollie said, "what do you figure we should do?"

"I thought it was decided," Penelope said. She turned to Rollie. "Aren't we in agreement that what we've done should be reversed?"

"People have been trying for decades," he answered. "We aren't the only genetic engineers in the world. But they've had no luck."

"But don't you think we have a step on them, Rollie? We were the ones —"

Sam looked from one to the other. She reached out and took Dmetri's hand, gazing into his face for a moment before speaking. "Dmetri and I are happy, at least for now. And I can't fathom when we won't be anymore."

"But the world is in a terrible state," Penelope argued. "Not only is there no longer progress, but many of the old technologies have been lost. Only a fraction of the population continues going to work. Society is falling apart."

"I don't think it's as bad as you paint it, Penelope," Dmetri said.

"What I dislike most," Sam said, "is not hearing the children. The world has become too silent. What if we could solve the sterility problem?"

"But within generations," Rollie said, "the world wouldn't be able to support the population. Just think, with no one dying, and kids growing to maturity within twenty or twenty-five years and having more kids. I'm sure you know all the arguments."

"We're all relatively young," Penelope said. "I mean, we were young when the aging stopped. We'd have years ahead of us yet."

"I'm ready for it," Rollie said. "I try to keep up pretenses. You three know me better than anyone does. I've always been an optimist. But this damn living isn't all it's cracked up to be. I don't mean I want to die right now. Ah, hell, we thought what we were doing was right. We didn't stop to examine the consequences. I remember when I was a kid, visiting an old neighbor woman with my mama. A woman named Mabel Cummins. Must have been close to ninety." Rollie's voice was soft. "She had a calendar up on her wall. And every day up to the present had a big red 'X' drawn across it.

"I was about seven, and my curiosity got the better of me. 'Ms. Cummins,' I said, 'why do all those dates have big red marks?' She stared at me, like . . . the question had paralyzed her. 'Well, you see,' she said after a moment, 'I'm countin' off the days till I die.' "

105

Rollie looked from one to the other. "I never understood that old lady. No, sir, I never understood her. Now I do."

"Rollie!" Penelope said. "That's a terrible thing!"

"Is it? I've been alone, Penelope. Alone after my mama and papa died when I was fifteen. Alone after Dawn went to the mountains. Early on, there was schooling and work to take up my time. And there were my friends like you and Sam and Dmetri. But there's nothing anymore. Hasn't been for years."

Penelope felt her chest being squeezed with his pain. "I love you, Rollie," she said. She felt her face flush, as she glanced at Sam and Dmetri and then back to Rollie. "I loved Lewis, don't ever think I didn't. But then he was gone, and, damn it, there were all those leftover restraints holding me back. Forgive me, Rollie. But where I was born, and when I was born, it was called apartheid. It's silly, and I'm sorry." To her horror, she burst into tears, feeling as fragile as a soap bubble out in the wind.

She felt a strong, brown hand grasping her hand.

Rollie chuckled. "I never expected to have an audience when I proposed."

Penelope looked up to see his gaze meeting hers. "Are you asking me to marry you, Dr. Humphries? Because if you aren't . . ."

"I sure enough am, Dr. Eddyns."

***

Later, the day after the wedding, Penelope and Rollie sat on the sofa. She turned to him. "I still haven't changed my mind," she said.

"Neither have I. Don't get me wrong; I want to spend a lifetime with you."

She leaned toward him and kissed him lightly. "A lifetime," she answered.

As the weeks went by, she and Rollie worked together in the lab. They were hindered at every turn. Almost nobody was doing experiments anymore, and lab animals were hard to come by. Supplies weren't readily available.

Sam and Dmetri half-heartedly helped at first till one morning they came in together. "We can't help you anymore," Sam said. "We're happy the way things are. But we wish you every success. Maybe if you find the key to changing things back like they were, people will have a choice. Maybe we can co-exist, the eternals and the mortals."

"Maybe," Penelope answered. And she found she thought it really might work. Anyone who wanted extra years or lifetimes could have them. When they got tired, the process could be reversed.

She and Rollie worked on, amidst growing unrest. The news media were filled with the doings of the Kevorkians. The *Times* reported that more than half the states in the United States and more than a third of the countries in the world embraced the idea, so that the Kevorkians were sanctioned. And where they weren't, they received tacit approval.

"Maybe it's a good thing," Rollie said one day. "Life is now uncertain. People never know when they'll be next, and that's the way it had always been from the beginning of time."

"It's too artificial," Penelope said.

Rollie squeezed her shoulder. "All of human life for the past ninety years has been artificial," he said.

"We're so close, Rollie." She reached for his hand. "Surely, if our lives had remained finite, we'd have come to terms with our feelings about one another before we died."

One day, the two of them, working side by side, began to observe the aging of a couple of rats, whose lives previously had been frozen at maturity.

Feverishly, they checked their notes, their records. "I think we're on the right track," Rollie said. "I don't want to be too enthusiastic, but —"

Penelope threw her arms around his waist. Only one other time in her life had she felt so elated, when their experiments had worked in prolonging life all those years ago. "A few more tests," she said. "And then we'll be ready to try it on . . ." On whom? she wondered. On herself? On Rollie? Now that it was within their grasp to bring an end to what they had once created, she felt that maybe she wanted to hang on just a bit more.

"I feel the same way," Rollie told her. "I see it in your eyes. Despite my spouting off about wanting to die . . . I guess I'm not really ready."

"That's too bad," a voice said.

Penelope glanced up to see that a man had come through the door carrying an old black doctor's bag. "I am one of the Kevorkians," he said. "I am Dr. Death."

THE BEAUTIFUL DRESS

The kids were already twelve and thirteen before I finished graduate school and took a job at a little college in New Jersey. So what with paying back student loans and finance companies to whom we'd gone into hock, things were awfully tight those first few years. We had to make every penny count.

Just before school started, Julie took Bobbie and Andrea shopping and by hitting all the sales outfitted them on a little more than three hundred dollars.

I'd had a tech assistantship in theatre, so all through grad school I wore grubbies and hadn't a tie or white shirt to my name. I had to hit the sales too. There were weeks of little more than packed peanut butter sandwiches I ate in my office for lunch and Hamburger Helper for dinner.

The second day of school Bobbie came home, refusing to wear her "ape" shoes.

Julie sat in the living room watching a PBS program on Zaire. I was at my computer in the alcove by the bay window trying to convert my notes on the acting book into interesting exercises.

"What do you mean?" Julie asked. She stood and snapped off the TV set.

Andrea, a year older, came in, tossed her books on the hall table and threw a disgusted look at Bobbie.

"Gorilla," she said. "They're Gorilla shoes. It says so right on them."

"That's a brand name, honey," Julie explained.

"Everyone'll laugh at me if they know I wear ape shoes," Bobbie said.

"You don't have a choice." I swung around in my chair. "We can't afford to buy others."

"I can't wear them." She turned and ran up the steps to her bedroom.

Julie turned to me. "It's true," she said. "There really is no money for shoes."

"Why can't she —"

Julie raised on her tiptoes and kissed my cheek. "I can see her side too," she said.

"She's being silly. Ape shoes, for heaven's sake!"

"In our eyes," Julie said, "it may look silly." She crossed to the window.

"What is it?" I asked.

"I told you once about how I felt wearing the outfits Mom made me. Different from the other kids' dresses." She turned back. "I can't make her wear those shoes."

"Okay," I said. "Maybe we can scrape up enough —"

"I don't think so," Julie said, more a definite statement than a point to ponder.

I thought of our weekly extravagance, an Entenmann's. Usually a cheese stollen. "If we cut out the Entenmann's and —"

"I won't insist she wear them," Julie said, "but we won't buy her new ones either."

"What'll she do?"

"She has last year's shoes."

"Are they still okay? Do they fit?"

"They're scruffy, worn down at the heels. But she hasn't outgrown them."

"Oh, God, Julie! Sometimes I wish —" I grimaced in frustration.

"Five years from now this won't matter," Julie said. "You'll make full professor by then, and we won't —"

"We won't have the kids," I said.

She stared at me for a moment, hurt in her eyes. "I've got to start dinner." She walked toward the kitchen. At the archway she turned. "Don't blame yourself," she said. "You weren't getting anywhere at the paper writing obits."

I started to protest, but Julie had already gone into the kitchen. I walked to the computer, a knot of sadness and doubt snarled up in my chest. Grad school had been an investment in the future. But a future without the kids. It would take years to pay our debts, years till I made a decent living. I stared at the blank screen.

***

We bought Bobbie a pair of shoes for Christmas. After the shoppng was finished, Bobbie announced that the eighth grade dance would be held Friday, the last day of school before vacation, and she needed a dressy outfit.

We agreed that this was important; it was the first time Bobbie had shown any interest in attending school functions. She'd always been a loner, able to entertain herself by keeping a journal, painting pictures, making things out of old aluminum cans.

Because Bobbie had waited till the last minute to

mention the dance, we had almost no cash we could spare, and our charge card was up to the limit.

We walked between countless racks of clothing. Then Julie spied this dress, and saw it was Bobbie's size. Made of a jersey-like material, the upper half was white with gathered sleeves, the bottom half the blue of a Mexican opal. It hung on the "Close Out" rack. The price tag read $18.95.

"What do you think?" Julie asked.

"I like it," I told her. "I think it's beautiful."

"Me too."

It was Thursday; the dance was the next day.

That evening when the girls came home from school, Julie handed Bobbie the dress. "Do you like it?" she asked.

Bobbie looked at us kind of funny and started up the stairs. "Bobbie!" I called.

She turned. "Yes, Dad?"

"Don't you like the dress?"

"I guess so," she said. She came back down and took it from Julie, then went upstairs.

"Oh, man!" I said, turning to Julie. "Couldn't she —"

"She'll be all right."

I shrugged and picked up the newspaper to read about the latest unrest in Eastern Europe.

It was a custom at our house in those years to have "fashion shows." Any time any of us obtained new clothes, as gifts or purchases, we modeled them for the others to see.

Andrea trotted down the steps. "What's wrong with her?" she asked.

"What do you mean?"

"I was going to ask her to model the dress. But she threw it on the bed and wouldn't look at me. If I got a new dress . . ." Her voice held hints of regret and resentment.

111

"I know, honey," I told her. "It isn't fair. But we can't afford —"

"It's okay, Daddy," she answered.

"The next dress that's bought at this house, it's yours."

She smiled, thirteen years old, with the poise of someone years older. "Can you believe Mrs. Kaplan giving us homework the last day before vacation?"

At dinner that evening Bobbie kept staring at her plate.

***

I had a late class the next day so didn't get home until almost six. "When's Bobbie's dance?" I asked. "Does she want us to drop her off?"

"She's not going," Julie said.

"What!" I crossed to the desk and put down my attaché case. Then I took off my outer coat.

"She's being silly, Dad," Andrea said. She'd been in the kitchen.

"What do you mean?" I hung my coat in the closet.

"It's the dress," Julie said. She looked tired, depressed. I was surprised; in the seventeen years of our marriage she'd seemed the eternal optimist.

"What do you mean?"

"She says it looks funny; nobody wears dresses like that anymore."

"It's a beautiful dress." I turned to Andrea. "Don't you think it's a beautiful dress?"

"I like it," she said, sounding less than enthusiastic.

I ignored the tone of voice. "I'm going to get to the bottom of this. Is she up in her room?"

"Yes, Dan, but please —"

I stormed across the living room and up the steps

two at a time. Julie's and my room was at the front of the house, the girls' room at the back. It was an old house, full of polished wood and patterned wallpaper. The door was closed.

"Bobbie!"

Yes?"

In that single word I read vulnerability, longing, a need for comfort. I ignored them. "Open the door!"

Slowly, the door swung inward. Bobbie stood there, a wild look in her eyes. Tears glistened in the glow from the hall light. Nearly as tall as her sister, she'd always been timid, unsure of herself. I was like that at her age.

"What, Dad?" she said, now defiant, yet still with that terrible vulnerability.

"What is this about your not going to the dance!"

"I can't," she said. I pushed on into the room. On the dresser, arranged from biggest to smallest, stood an array of Andrea's stuffed animals. Bobbie's lay heaped in the corner, along with dolls made from coke bottles and scraps of clothing, half-finished drawings and partially knit sweaters, beginning to unravel.

"Your mom and I spent good money on this. Money we didn't have. Don't you understand?" I picked up the dress from the back of the chair. "What's wrong with this dress?" I said.

"It looks weird. Everyone will make fun of me."

"It looks weird! Is that all you can say?" I thrust the dress toward her. "Take this and put it on!"

"No!" she screamed. "I can't. I won't. You can't make me!"

I grabbed her arm and forced her to face herself in the dresser mirror. "Just look at you," I said. "Behaving like a five-year-old."

She pulled loose and ran downstairs. "Come back here, Bobbie! I didn't say you could go."

She turned. "I hate you, Daddy. I hate you." She

113

grabbed her coat from the closet and ran outside.

"Where are you going? Where do you think you're going?" I pounded down the steps after her.

I heard her shoes clicking on the ice of the porch before the slam of the door nearly toppled the figurines in the window sill.

I looked down and saw I held the dress in my hands. Julie was in the kitchen, I guess. Andrea too.

I felt tears in my eyes, tears of frustration. What had I done by quitting my job and going back to school? A person tries to do his best, I thought and then . . . A sob tore my throat. I sank onto my desk chair, the dress in both hands. I grabbed it on either side of the neck and yanked with all my strength. Once it broke through, it split down to the waist. Once more I yanked, then again and again.

I buried my face in the dress, the dress that was now only rags.

The front door opened, and Bobbie came in. "Daddy," she said, seeing me in the alcove. She walked slowly toward me. I looked up, tears still forming prisms of light in front of my eyes. "I'll go to the dance," she said. "I want to go to the dance."

Then she saw the dress in my hands, that beautiful dress in my hands.

THEME

The first thing you should figure out is the theme. *Theme means the central idea or the "message" behind the story.*

In "Into the Light and the Darkness," you learned that this could be stated as, "Racial prejudice is wrong." The mother is reluctant to let Little Bit of Darkness go outside because she is afraid something terrible will happen to her, that, in effect, she will cease to exist. The character does, however, go outside, and once there, makes new friends.

So the theme might be stated in a different way: "Don't be afraid to make new friends." This still fits in with the idea that racial prejudice is wrong. Another way the theme might be stated is: "Friendships often take compromise." Little Bit of Darkness risked disappearing so she could make new friends, and then the friends were willing to "disappear" to be with her. You could probably state the theme in a lot of other ways, as well.

You might find a different theme in a story than your classmates do. That's fine, just so you can point to things in the story that back up what you say.

Even stories meant largely to entertain have something to say about life, something behind the humor. The theme of the Pecos Bill story could be: "Where there's a will, there's a way."

Often the theme can be stated in the form of adages or old sayings such as this one. This is because these are common beliefs or common premises, something most people believe in and with which they can identify. Examples are: War is wrong; everyone should be equal under the law.

Many stories have secondary themes, as well. One, in "Dr. Death," is similar to the main theme of "Into the Light and the Darkness." Penelope and Rollie are in love, even though they are different races — one white, the other black.

The primary theme or central idea for "Dr. Death" can be stated in several different ways. One, to paraphrase an old television commercial, is "Don't mess with mother nature." The idea that none of the scientists responsible for eliminating disease and slowing the aging process considered the consequences is never blatantly mentioned; it is suggested or implied.

You often need to "read between the lines" to understand what a writer means.

What are some other ways you could state the theme of "Dr. Death?"

In "The Beautiful Dress," the theme could be stated: Look before you leap. The father, out of frustration, tears up the girl's dress. In the meantime, she apparently has done some thinking and has decided that she will go to the dance. The father's action in destroying the dress was impulsive. The girl was impulsive too in immediately saying she wouldn't wear the dress. But there was a pattern established for this because of her refusal to wear the Gorilla shoes.

There are several secondary themes in "The Beautiful Dress." One could be: "Don't ignore the present in order to have a good future." In reading the story, you discover that the father used to write obits at a newspaper. Apparently, he and his wife viewed this as a job with no future. So he quit and went to graduate school. In the long run, this might prove to be better for the family, except that the kids would be on their own before the career change paid off. Of course, this secondary theme really is just a re-statement of the main theme, "Look before you leap."

What other themes and secondary themes can you find in the story?

STRUCTURE AND ORGANIZATION

There are various ways in which a short story can be structured. The most common is for it to have a plot.

The Plotted Story

A plot involves the meeting of two opposing forces. Stories are interesting because they deal with characters who encounter problems or situations with which we can identify. Our interest is maintained because we want to know how things turn out. The plot keeps us in suspense.

The Protagonist and the Antagonist

The two opposing forces are the protagonist and the antagonist. The former needs or wants something, and the latter tries to keep him or her from getting it. The protagonist is the "hero" of the piece, the one with whom we identify.

The protagonist is almost always an individual — whether animal, human being or other entity. The antagonist can be an individual, though often it is a force, such as social or economic conditions.

In old movie westerns the protagonist was the good guy who went after the criminal who had shot up the town. It was a simple struggle between the two men who represented opposites, good and evil, sheriff and criminal.

Most stories, however, are not this clear-cut. In "Dr. Death Comes to All," the protagonist is Penelope Eddyns, but there's really no one person or even a group of people who oppose her. So what then is the antagonist? It seems to be the "status quo," the way things are. The world is stagnating; there is little progress in any area, and most people no longer work. Some become so bored that they "go to the mountains," that is, they try to commit suicide. But even that is hard.

Penelope recognizes that the state of the world she and the other scientists were responsible for creating is not the ideal everyone thought it would be. The story says that life is more interesting when we face the unknown or unexpected. Therefore, Penelope decides to contact the other scientists to see if perhaps they should reverse what they've done. This then is the problem.

Part of the struggle is deciding whether or not to do anything about the status quo. Part is in trying to find a way to make people mortal once more. The status quo has created dissatisfaction, as evidenced by the Kevorkian Society. But the society itself is not the antagonist.

The antagonist may be the protagonist's environment, the forces of nature, or even a condition within the mind, and is shown largely in the central character's relationships with others.

In "Tradeoffs" the protagonist is Cecil, the antagonist the "People," that is, the other vampires. Cecil decides to defy the People and go ahead and try to cure his relatives of a plague, never mentioned by name but most certainly the AIDS virus. In the ballad "The Hangman's Tree," the protagonist is the young man about to be hanged, while the antagonist is the "force" that condemned him to die for some reason we never learn. In "Pecos Bill and the Rattlesnake," a very simple story, the opposition is much more direct than in many other stories. Of course it is nature, which in many ways is trying to defeat Pecos Bill and the narrator of the tale.

In "The Beautiful Dress," the antagonist is "economic conditions."

117

The Inciting Incident

The inciting incident is the point at which the balance is upset. A question is raised that has to be answered. Will the protagonist be able to restore a balance or not?

The story begins with a situation in which there is a balance of sorts, or when the balance recently has been upset. In "Dr. Death," there was a balance after Penelope and her fellow scientists eliminated disease and death. Some time later, however, people become disenchanted with the way things were. There is no clear-cut beginning for the opposition. Rather, it has been a gradual thing.

In "Into the Light and the Darkness," the struggle or opposition begins when Little Bit of Darkness decides she wants to play with the children who are outside in the light.

So there is a difference. In "Dr. Death," the balance was upset ahead of time; in "Into the Light" it was not, although the factors for the opposition already were there in the mother's distrust of the unknown.

The Rising Action

The inciting incident introduces the rising action during which the protagonist's problem is intensified and continues to build. The suspense increases. Will the progatonist triumph or be defeated? The suspense, the struggle and the conflict continue to escalate until the action can go no further without something irrevocable happening. If you were to diagram the plot, it might look like this:

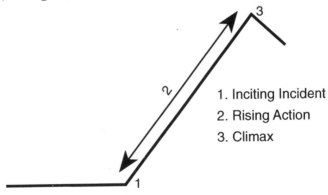

1. Inciting Incident
2. Rising Action
3. Climax

Turning Point and Climax

The point at which the irrevocable happening occurs in a story is called the turning point. This is when the protagonist knows he or she will win or lose the struggle. *The actual point at which the central character wins or loses is the climax.*

Occasionally, the turning point and the climax are the same; at other times they are separated. In "Dr. Death," the scientists discover a way of reversing what they had done. This is the turning point. The climax is where a member of the Kevorkian Society shoots them. In other words, in this story the protagonist loses; she is defeated by a segment of the society that is taking things into its own hands. Penelope and the others find one solution; the Kevorkians have found another. This is more complicated then, than is Pecos Bill meeting the forces of nature head on and defeating them. In "Dr. Death," the status quo is what stirred up both Penelope and the Society; both are reacting against it.

In "Pecos Bill," the action is direct, the confrontations exact. In this story, and in many others, except those that are most simple, the action does not build in a straight line to the climax. Instead there are a series of minor complications or crises that still are part of the overall problem.

For instance, in "The Creosote House," (Chapter Eleven) the first complication occurs almost immediately where Mr. and Mrs. Gravely argue about what he has done to the house. Then Mrs. Gravely dumps dishwater on her husband's head. Then she tells him that she used an animal hit on the road to provide meat for dinner. Each of these seems to be solved or at least ended, but you know that the underlying conflict has not been solved. What finally solves it is the realization on both the characters' parts that although they can't stand one another, they also cannot live without each other.

In "The Hangman's Tree," there is a complication that ends in momentary defeat for the man being hanged when his father refuses to pay his fee. There is another crises when the mother arrives and the same thing happens. The story ends, however, when the man's true love pays the fee. In this case, the action does not continue to build to a climax. Rather it rises and falls, rises and falls, like the figure on page 120.

Sometimes these minor problems seemingly are resolved, only to intrude again and complicate the rising action. Except in simple stories like "The Hangman's Tree," each minor crisis somewhat alters the direction of the story. Odelle feels she is too ugly but then accepts that John doesn't notice this. John feels too ignorant or dumb and so is uncomfortable at the dance. Because of this, Odelle decides to quit teaching. Resigned to never again entering a classroom, she discovers John's note. Then she hurries to get her job back. All of these complications and crises stand in the way of Odelle's and John's being happy together. In this story, of course, much of this occurs before the opening.

In "The Beautiful Dress," the first complication is Bobbie's not wanting to wear her "ape" shoes. This is solved, although the underlying problem — the family's having little money — is not.

Most often each new complication is introduced by one minor climax or resolution and ended by another. Still the rising action continues to build.

Even in scenes where there appears to be no conflict, it is inherent. Penelope in "Dr. Death" is at home not really taking any physical action; yet she is remembering and feeling bad. The feelings continue to build within her until she calls the other researchers.

Most often, rather than proceeding in a straight line, the plot of a story could be diagrammed something like the figure on page 121.

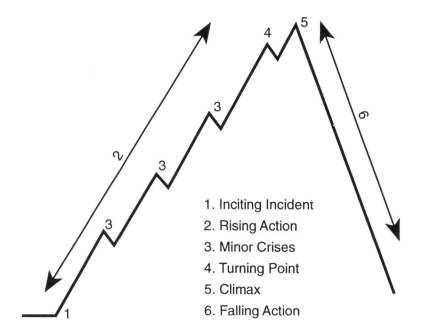

1. Inciting Incident
2. Rising Action
3. Minor Crises
4. Turning Point
5. Climax
6. Falling Action

Every scene in a story should relate to the underlying conflict or problem.

The protagonist can either win or lose in a struggle, but for the story to be believable, he or she always has to be a direct part of it. It wouldn't be believable to have a protagonist who is only "acted upon," where someone else steps in and solves the problem. If this happens, the story will not be believable. Of course, if the story is largely for fun, this may be okay.

Action involves a give and take. You say "hi" to someone, and he or she responds. If you argue with someone, you can expect an argument back. The same holds true for the characters in a story.

The Falling Action

After the climax comes the falling action, which shows the result of the climax, how things will be for the characters from now on. John will get a college degree and Odelle will go back to teaching, a "happily ever after" ending. Penelope will die; the status quo will be about the same, except that the Kevorkians will keep on killing people. Much of the falling action is implied, as in "Dr. Death." We know Penelope will be killed, but the world will remain pretty much the same. This is implied, not directly stated. Pecos Bill and the narrator get to Cheyenne. The falling action tells us that the world returns to normal, except that afterward snakeskin belts are popular and Pecos Bill keeps the rattlesnake as a belt and a friend. The falling action, in effect, ties up loose ends.

Plotlines

In all stories, *there are some lines, often referred to as plotlines, that are vital for the audience to hear in order to follow what is happening.* It can help to go through and mark the important lines, so you can try to make sure the audience hears and understands them. Of course, when you actually tell the story, the lines may be changed somewhat, but still you will have the important ideas in mind. Here are the most important lines through the beginning section of "The Beautiful Dress."

> **The kids were already twelve and thirteen before I finished graduate school and took a job at a little college in New Jersey. So what with paying back student loans and finance companies to whom we'd gone into hock, things were awfully tight those first few years. *We had to make every penny count.***

> **Just before school started, *Julie took Bobbie and Andrea shopping and by hitting all the sales outfitted them on a little more than three hundred dollars.***

> **I'd had a tech assistantship in theatre, so all through grad school I wore grubbies and hadn't a tie or white shirt to my name. I had to hit the sales too. There were weeks of little more than packed peanut butter sandwiches I ate in my office for lunch and Hamburger Helper for dinner.**

> **The second day of school Bobbie came home, refusing to wear her "ape" shoes.**

Julie sat in the living room watching a PBS program on Zaire. I was at my computer in the alcove by the bay window trying to convert my notes on the acting book into interesting exercises.

"What do you mean?" Julie asked. She stood and snapped off the TV set.

Andrea, a year older, came in, tossed her books on the hall table and threw a disgusted look at Bobbie.

"Gorilla," she said. "They're Gorilla shoes. It says so right on them."

"That's a brand name, honey," Julie explained.

"Everyone'll laugh at me if they know I wear ape shoes," Bobbie said.

Even in a story that has no plot, you should figure out the most important lines or the high points.

Episodic Structure

Some stories, like "Chicken Little," or "The Hangman's Tree" are episodic. This is, *they don't really continue to build but are just a series of complications which may or may not bring about a resolution of some sort.* Pecos Bill also is episodic; it doesn't really continue to build. Neither does the solving of one complication lead to another. Pecos Bill breaks his belt and uses a snake as a replacement. Pecos and the narrator are freezing, so they sleep with coyotes. The fire is frozen, so they thaw it. The story is fun and good entertainment, but it does not follow a traditional plot line.

Thematic Structure

Sometimes stories are written around a certain theme, and this is what provides the interest. For example, in Bill Jarosin's humorous story, "Letters to Whole Wheat Hair Products," there is an elementary plot of a sort in which the situation builds from one complication to another. But we really don't get to know the characters, and the story ends in an utterly bizarre manner. More important than plot or characters is the idea around which the story is built — a customer trying to get satisfaction from a company that has sold him a bad product. This is a type of shaggy dog story that is funny because it is something to which people can relate. Nearly everyone has bought a defective product or one that didn't work. This is carrying the idea to the ultimate extreme.

Miscellaneous Structures

Sometimes a story is organized geographically or according to space. For instance, the Three Little Pigs build a house of straw at one spot, out of wood at another and out of brick at a third. Not much difference occurs in what happens at the different locations, except that in the last the wolf is defeated. If you were telling a story about your family, for instance, you might talk about when you lived in Ohio and then Indiana and then Illinois.

Another type of structure, particularly for a personal experience piece, would be a topical (topic by topic) arrangement. In Chapter One, the grandfather started collecting newspapers. Then maybe he started collecting scrap metal. Then maybe he started collecting used appliances. Each topic is treated and then pretty much dropped to go on to another topic.

Often there is a combination of structures within a single story. As mentioned, Bill Jarosin's "Letters" has an elementary plot. So does "The Three Little Pigs," though in the former the theme is more important than the plot progression, and in the latter, the geography is more important as a way of showing a progression of events.

THOUGHT CENTERS

When you analyze a story, you need to determine the important words and the important word groupings or thought centers, in much the same way you figured out plot lines. A thought center is a complete image or idea, but not necessarily a complete sentence.

In the following, taken from the opening paragraphs of "Dead Man's Corner" by Ann James Valdes, the various thought centers are italicized.

> 1) *Ellen imagined* the 2) *current conveying*
> a *corpse* and 3) *depositing it,* like a 4) *dog with*
> a *bone, at her feet.* The 5) *shriveled face* had 6)
> *Jeremy's square jaw,* his 7) *long nose,* his
> ... She 8) *dropped the plate* she was drying. The
> 9) *glazed brown clay broke into four pieces.*

Figuring out the word groupings is another way of help-ing you see what words or phrases are most important. In pointing out the word centers, skip over the unimportant words.

CHARACTERIZATION

You need to analyze your characters and to figure out anything important that will help you present them more effec-tively. In stories designed to be told, characters are often less complicated than in written stories. Sometimes they are types rather than individuals. If this is the case, you do not need to do a lot of character analysis. Generally speaking, *the more important the characters, the more detailed the analysis.* For instance, you would spend much more time analyzing Little Bit of Darkness than you would the other children, who are not so nearly well developed or are not so important as individu-als to the story. Characters, such as David in "Flight of the Niños," often are only devices to explain what is happening or to provide background. In this story, Manuel and Señor Viejo are much more important. But you do need to understand where all the characters fit into the overall story.

Here are some of the things you might try to figure out about them.

a. Where is the character from? How does this affect feelings, thoughts and attitudes?

b. How old is the character? How can you effectively present a person this age? If the person is younger or older than you, how should you go about portraying him or her?

c. What can you tell about the character's environment, geo-graphically, historically and economically? What about so-cial status? How does all this affect the type of person he or she is?

d. Similarly, what have been and are the major influences on the person's life? Sometimes this is easy to determine because the entire story relates to an issue important to the person. Sometimes, you can only infer specifics about the character.

e. What are the character's personality traits? How can you tell? How do the traits affect how the person comes across in the story?

f. What are the character's motives and goal? What does the person hope to accomplish, both in the story and in life overall? In "The Hangman's Tree," the character's goals for the length of the ballad and for his life are the same — to be saved from hanging. In "Dr. Death," Penelope wants to find a way to reverse the cure for disease and aging. That's her goal in the story. Her life's goal is to be able to know she can die, if she so chooses. In "The Dress," the father's immediate goal is to be able to buy adequate shoes and clothing for his kids. Overall, it's to have an improved life; that's why he was willing to go into debt to attend graduate school.

g. Is the person likeable? Why or why not? How do you feel about the character? What makes you feel this way?

h. What sort of relationship does your character have to the others in the scene? How do you know this? Why do you think there is this sort of relationship? How do the characters feel about each other? Why do you think they feel this way?

i. What emotions does your character feel during the story, and how should you go about portraying these emotions?

You will interpret a character much differently than will anyone else. That's fine, so long as you are consistent with what is written in the story. You can infer as much as you like or add on as much as you like if this goes along with what is already there, and if it doesn't detract or take away from it. If you built up Andrea's role in "The Beautiful Dress," you probably would be taking away from the basic story, the central theme. She is important to the story, but she should not overshadow everything else.

126

UNIVERSALITY AND IMMEDIACY

Any story that you tell should have universality. It should have meaning for your audience; everyone hearing it should be able to relate to it. As mentioned, in "Letters," Jarosin dealt with a common experience. Many people can relate to a family's having little money and having to carefully budget their money so there is little or none for extras, as is the case in "The Beautiful Dress."

In many stories, it's the characters that the audience most relates to — Penelope in "Dr. Death," Grandaddy in "Grandaddy and the Fiddle," and so on. This is not usually the case with parables, myths or fables. Rather these contain principles, truths or morals to live by. We can't relate well to the characters in the "The Wolf and the Goat" because they aren't well developed. We know nothing about them, so we can't care very much about them. But we can relate to the theme of not trusting our enemies.

Some stories have immediacy, as well as universality. That is, they deal with here and now issues such as street gangs and drugs. Often we can relate more readily to this sort of thing because it is something we know or have seen firsthand.

Each story that you choose should have a universal or immediate appeal. That is, it should have meaning for your audience; it should be something they can care about.

SYMBOLISM

Symbolism simply means that one thing stands for or means another. It is a device to condense and compare. Folktales, those that have been handed down from generation to generation, have characters and situations that stand for something else.

In "Dr. Death," the Kevorkian Society symbolizes people's dissatisfaction with the way things are. The society stands for all people who want to change back to the way it used to be.

"Who Are You and What Do You Want?" is filled with symbolism. In one interpretation the old woman can be viewed as a symbol of a story idea that the narrator is getting, rather than as a visitor from the future. In "The Beautiful Dress,"

Bobbie's refusal to wear the dress is a symbol of all the frustrations the father is feeling. The pastry, the Entemnann's the family buys each week, is a symbol of what they have lost and what they hope to gain. It's the extras that make life worthwhile.

It's a good idea to try to discover this sort of symbolism in any story you want to present, so you can be sure to present it truthfully.

There are other types of symbolism, as well. Two common types, used as comparisons, are metaphors and similes. The first states that something *is* something else; the latter says that it *is like* something else. For example, in "Dr. Death," Penelope describes Rollie's voice as "molasses and chocolate." This is a metaphor, meaning his voice was smooth or steady and the tone rich. This also is a way to condense, rather than having to describe in detail, and it's more memorable too. A simile would say, "Rollie's voice is like molasses and honey."

IMAGERY

Imagery is any word or group of words that has sensory appeal, that relates to one or more of our senses. These include the usual five — hearing, sight, smell, taste, and touch. But more than that, there are the senses of movement, heat or cold, balance, hunger and pain. Imagery is important in stimulating the imagination, in bringing about a blending of an audience's and a storyteller's own personal experiences.

In "The Beautiful Dress," there are a variety of images:

1. *Cheese stollen* — applies to taste, smell, seeing.

2. *Scruffy and worn down at the heels* — sight, feeling of shoes on the feet, maybe even balance if the heels are badly worn.

3. *Made of a jersey-like material, the upper half was white with gathered sleeves, the bottom half the blue of a Mexican opal* — refers to feel (jersey-like) and the way it hangs, to sight (looks and color), to feel again in the gathered sleeves.

4. *Trotted down the steps* — movement, sound.

You need to figure out and emphasize the imagery for the audience because it is important in their perceptions of the characters and the setting. It makes the piece come alive. You might want to go through a copy of the story and mark the imagery.

PREDOMINANT AND SECONDARY MOODS

What feelings do you want to convey to the audience with your story? The predominant mood is the most important, the one the audience most feels when the story is over. In "The Beautiful Dress," it might be a feeling of sadness because of how the situation has affected both the father and the daughter. Or it could be pity for them both, or irony at the situation. Throughout the story are other moods, a longing for things to be better, frustration that finances are so bad, a sense of loss in knowing that by the time the debts are paid the two girls will be on their own and so on. You need to figure out the moods and where they change so you can portray them for an audience.

You might figure out different moods than others do. That's okay if you can back up what you think and present it convincingly.

PARAPHRASE

You should be able to sum up the important parts of your story in three or four sentences, and you should be able to paraphrase the entire piece. This is to make sure you understand each of the parts and are getting the major points. Of course, if there are things you don't understand, words of which you don't know the meaning, look them up.

ACTIVITIES

1. Discuss with the rest of the class what you think the central idea or theme is for: "The Flight of the Niños," "The Inscription" and "Black Hole Grandma." Do these three stories have any secondary themes? If so, what are they? Why do you think so?

2. Analyze the plot or structure of: "Who Are You and What Do You Want?" and "Into the Light and the Darkness." What are the high points of each?

3. Do you think there is universality and/or immediacy in

"Pecos Bill and the Rattlesnake?" What makes you think so? How about "The Hangman's Tree"?

4. What symbolism do you find in "The Wolf and the Goat"? Explain.

5. Point out and explain any imagery in "Letters to Whole Wheat Hair Products."

6. In a paragraph of no more than half a page, write out and read to the class a synopsis of "Dr. Death," "Tradeoffs" or "The Inscription."

CHAPTER SIX

ADAPTING STORIES

If you choose a story from a source other than your own experience or creation, you most certainly will want to change it to make it yours.

ADAPTING YOUR STORY

Often stories contain elements with which the teller just isn't comfortable. Some stories should be simplified or shortened. A good point to keep in mind is that a story should begin as close to the climax as possible. That is, don't have a lot of details that can merely be suggested. There sometimes is a difference between written and spoken language, and since the story will be spoken aloud, you will want to make it as natural as possible, that is, natural to the narrator, not necessarily to the way you normally speak.

Here are some specific changes you can make:

1. Simplify the characters or the plot. Particularly if you choose a "written" story as opposed to one that is meant to be told, you may want to cut out characters that aren't important, and you may cut out some of the traits or background on the others.

2. Stories often have secondary plots that you may choose to cut in the telling. This is true of a lot of "written" stories. It may be confusing to an audience to try to remember two or three subplots, and it may detract from the major plot. However, you need to be sure to keep the atmosphere and background in order to be true to the original intent of the story. In "Tradeoffs," for instance, if you cut the part about the relationship between Cecil and his wife and concentrate only on his trying to help his nephew, you might risk changing the tone and intent too much since part of what "Tradeoffs" is about is the importance of family.

3. Often in a told story, you can cut out a lot of description. It is better to have a few sharp images than long passages of description — which are beautiful to read silently, but

131

which can bog down a story.

4. Particularly if you are telling stories for children, be sure to retain repetitive words and phrases, or even add some that aren't there but could be without destroying the intent of the writer.

5. If you are telling a story to children, you may want to spell out or emphasize what is only implied in the original story, as opposed to implying rather than stating some things for a teenage or adult audience. It is implied that Little Bit of Darkness is lonely, for instance, but you might want to tell kids more explicitly that this is so.

6. Young children recognize more "heard" words than written ones. They can better infer them from context. Still, be careful not to use a lot of polysyllabic words that they wouldn't understand.

7. As suggested in an earlier chapter, you may want to make folktales or traditional stories more applicable to contemporary times. That is, you may want to make the characters and setting more specific and contemporary. You may want to give them a more modern vocabulary. You might do this sort of thing, for example, with certain fables.

8. You can rearrange the plot so there is a clear sequence of events. "For Love of Miss Whiffin" is told largely in flashbacks or "thinkbacks." The "present" really is just the end of the school day, Odelle's waiting for John, going to his house, reading the note and so on. Everything else has happened much earlier. To make certain the story is clear for an audience, you might want to begin it when John invites her to Sunday dinner.

9. You may want to change some of the dialog to narration to condense the story or to avoid having to portray the characters. On the other hand, if you like to portray characters, you may want to retain the dialog and even add more. Your goals should be enjoyment for both you and the audience. Whatever you feel comfortable doing is the right thing, just so you don't stray too far from the original story.

10. If you are telling a story that takes place in a past age, be sure you remain true to the language. Don't have one of

King Arthur's sword-wielding knights tell the bad guy, "Hey, man, I'm gonna cut you up good."

11. You may want to change the point of view. This means whose head the listener or teller is inside, or whose perspective is used. For instance, we see "The Beautiful Dress" through the father's eyes. If you were a female telling the former, you might want to change from first person point of view, that is, "I" to "third person."

   You would then change: "The kids were already twelve and thirteen before I finished graduate school" to: "The kids were already twelve and thirteen before Peter finished graduate school." Or you might choose to tell it from the wife's point of view: "Our kids were already twelve and thirteen before my husband finished graduate school." You wouldn't want to change it to Bobbie's point of view since this would change the focus from monetary concerns to peer acceptance.

12. You may want to include audience participation. There are some stories that need clapping (Peter Pan to make Tinker Bell real) or other sound effects. One that uses a lot of sound effects is "Jungle Safari," in which the listeners rub hands together to sound like walking through tall grass, pound on their chests to simulate walking across a bridge, and so on.

   Any time a person is actively involved in a story, he or she is listening. Audience participation is a good way to keep the listener involved.

   There are a few "don'ts." Don't change a well-known story unless you're specifically doing it for fun. Otherwise your audience, particularly if they are young children, may contradict you. Second, if you tell an authored or written story, be sure you have the author's permission to do so.

   Following is a story that was written to be read silently. So you probably would want to adapt it to tell aloud.

BENEATH THE ICE COLD MOON

The moon splashed puddles of silver on the dented lids of garbage cans lining the curb. Although the temp-

erature hovered in the fifties, Millie shivered and grabbed Arnie's arm in both her hands.

"What the hell's wrong with you?" Shadows hid his face.

"It's dark," she said. "Only the moon and the street-lights —"

"It's nighttime, for God's sake. What's gotten into you?"

"I'm sorry."

He slapped her hands away and strode on ahead. She tried to keep up.

They'd been together a year and a half, and she was beginning to think it might last.

She'd met Arnie just after getting off the Greyhound bus, huddled in a corner of the depot, her possessions stuffed into two plastic bags.

"Hey, little girl," he'd said.

When she didn't answer, he came up to stand beside her. "You ain't afraid of me, are you? I don't bite." He laughed uproariously, like he'd said something real funny.

She looked up and smiled.

"That's better. Bet you're hungry." He was skinny with a brown beard on the verge of looking scraggly. Hair tied in a ponytail reached to his collar. He was an older man, at least twenty-six or twenty-eight.

"I ain't ate in near three days, since two days after boarding that Greyhound bus in Wheeling, West Virginia."

"Wheeling," he said, taking her arm. "Why, missy, I'm from right next door in East Liverpool, Ohio. Left there to join the Navy."

He bought her dinner at a greasy spoon, and it was the most natural thing in the world that they go to his room at the Pacific Hotel a couple of blocks away. She thought right off that she loved him, but later knew she didn't 'cause of the kind of things he did.

She wasn't raised to be no criminal, no dope pusher. Not that Arnie used the stuff himself. She was glad of that, though he drank rotgut whiskey and cheap wine just like Pap did. And just like Pap he beat her, sometimes so bad she couldn't do nothing but lay all huddled in bed.

He was way over six feet; she was skinny too but just five foot and half an inch. People on the street called them Mutt and Jeff. She didn't know what that meant until someone told her they was two characters in an old comic strip.

One thing about Arnie, no matter how bad it got, he never forced her into whoring like other men often did to their women.

She wished things was different, that Arnie had a regular job, that they lived in a house, instead of a fleabag hotel with hardly no space to turn around. And she wished she wasn't so dumb and that she'd gone beyond seventh grade.

But that wasn't her fault. Mam and Pap had made her quit school and go to work doing whatever she could. Taking in washing, helping neighbors with their canning, sometimes working in the box factory, even though she was underage. And if the money wasn't enough for Pap to stay drunk and Mam to smoke and hack her way through each day, they beat her till her whole body was covered in welts and scars.

That's why she'd run away, though it took long enough. She was near sixteen when she had the sense to begin burying money in a tobacco tin by the old gate post each time she got paid.

One time when Pap was drunk and Mam was snoring in front of the black and white TV, she stuffed all her things into grocery bags.

She had a choice of North, South, East or West. She'd seen a movie once that showed the beaches by the Pacific Ocean in California. She remembered how pretty that looked, prettier than any place she could imagine. She was a week from being seventeen and that's where she headed.

***

The soft light spilling on streets and buildings created shadows of ghosts and demons. At first Millie wasn't sure if she was seeing another woman or not, a woman a year or two older than she was. Light caught the woman's eye as she glanced toward Millie and carefully laid a bundle between two garbage cans.

Her hair was as black as the lumps of coal that spilled from the trains speeding through the mountains where Millie had lived. The woman rose up then, nodded and hurried around the corner.

"Arnie!"

"What the hell is it now, woman?"

"Don't talk that way to me." She grabbed his hand and held it so he couldn't shake loose. "That bundle," she said. "It moved."

"What?"

"I think it's alive."

"You're nuts, that's what I —"

"No! Listen." The cry was unmistakable. "It's a baby, Arnie. A little baby." She ran toward the sound, grabbed the bundle. It was a newborn or near to it, face scrunched up and waiting to cry.

"Put it back," he said. "It ain't no concern of ours."

"We can't." She'd never stood up to him before, and she was scared.

Millie spied the woman in the alley, her face turned toward them. The woman stared for a second, then turned and ran. Arnie took off after her.

In a minute he was back, huffing and blowing. "She was here. I heard her running, and then there was nothing."

"Maybe she hid somewheres."

"Didn't have time, and there's no place to hide."

"I guess that's that," Millie said, smiling, thinking they could keep the baby. She wanted it so bad.

"We'll take it to the police," Arnie said.

"No, Arnie, we'd just get in trouble." She glanced up toward the sky as a bat winged its way across the moon. She shuddered and pulled the baby more tightly against her.

"Maybe you're right! Maybe we could . . ."

For the first time since she'd met him, he sounded unsure. "Ain't got no choice, Arn. Gotta take it home. It'd die out here alone. Starve, most likely."

"Don't be getting ideas," he said, taking her arm, leading her down toward F Street. "We can't keep no kid. Anyhow what kind of life would he have with us? Hell, Millie, you know we ain't much better than beggars and vagrants. Besides —"

"Ain't he sweet? Ain't he just the sweetest little thing you ever saw?"

"Ah, hell, woman, you don't make no sense."

That was wrong, she thought. She was making real good sense. They'd have a baby to love, a baby that bound them one to the other. Despite Arnie's words, she'd seen a softness to his face when he looked on the little thing.

"Come on," Millie said. "We'll go home and see if he needs changed. We can use . . . What can we use, Arnie?"

"Pillowcase?"

"And we gotta get some milk. A baby can't live without milk."

I don't like where this is heading, Millie." They turned west. "I'll see you home and go get the milk."

"And a bottle," she said.

"All right, and a friggin' bottle."

"And a nipple."

"For God's sake, Millie, I ain't that dumb to buy a bottle without no nipple."

***

The baby was a boy, and his diaper was dry. But he wouldn't stop crying. Millie heated the milk in a quart pan on the hotplate, poured it into a bottle and screwed on the cap. She shook a few drops onto the inside of her wrist as she'd seen others do. It didn't burn, and it didn't feel cold, so she guessed it must be okay.

When the baby, whom she'd already begun to call Arnie J for Arnie, Junior, took the first few drops into his mouth, he began to scream.

"It's okay, it's okay," Millie said, turning toward Arnie. "Can't you do something?"

He reached for the baby.

"Steady his head," she told him. "Have you ever given a baby a bottle?"

"Nah."

"Maybe we're doing something wrong."

The baby was so tiny it fit into the crook of Arnie's elbow, its legs not reaching halfway to his wrist.

"Give me the bottle." He sat on the edge of the bed.

The baby stopped crying, but his eyes darted frantically back and forth. Millie was surprised. She didn't think newborn babies could see that well.

Arnie gently stuck the bottle into the baby's mouth. Arnie J began to suck. In no more than a moment he screamed and threw up.

"For God's sake, Millie, I can't put up with this crap."

She grabbed a T-shirt and hurried to the bathroom at the end of the hall. She hated to go there alone. Drunks hung around, and often as not, someone was shooting up. Now, thank merciful God in heaven, the door stood open, the room empty. She hurried in, turned on the rusty tap and held the shirt under lukewarm water.

138

The baby was asleep over Arnie's shoulder. Millie dabbed at the curdled spit up.

"He stopped crying as soon as you left," Arnie answered. He looked down. "You're a good little feller, yes, you are."

A lump inside Millie's chest gave way to a feeling of joyfulness. Arnie liked the baby.

"But we're going to have to do something about him."

"What do you mean?" The lump was back.

"Christ, Mil, how can we keep him even if we want to?"

She eased down beside him on the sagging mattress. "He won't be any trouble."

"All babies are trouble."

Tears made a rainbow in her eyes as she reached for him. "I won't give him up!" She'd always wanted a baby. Something to love. She'd had a cat once, an old scraggly tom with half a tail. But her daddy beat her half to death when he caught her sneaking it milk.

"This is important to you, Mil, I know that — though I don't know exactly why." He stood and pulled off his shirt. "Let's see how you feel about it in the morning. I doubt you'll be getting a hell of a lot of sleep."

"Thank you, Arnie."

He kicked off his shoes and jeans. A half smile touched his lips as he crawled behind her and slid under the covers.

Millie reheated the bottle and tried to feed little Arnie. He cried and turned his head. Twice some of the milk must have slipped down his throat. He spit it up and howled. He clamped his lips so tight that Millie couldn't force the nipple inside. Exhausted, she lay on top of the bedspread, the baby resting on her bosom. She thought of her old tom, and how Pap had kicked him so hard he couldn't walk no more.

Arnie J didn't sleep, he didn't eat, and he never wet his diaper. It wouldn't take long before he starved, Millie thought. Then she remembered when Mam talked about how Cousin Harold couldn't keep down his milk. What had Aunt Carla done?

She sat up abruptly. It was some sort of substitute. "Simulate." No. Something like that. Sim-u-lak. She'd go to the drugstore near Horton Plaza. They stayed open all night.

She glanced at Arnie, sound asleep, spittle leaking from the corner of his mouth. In her purse, she had a five dollar bill he didn't know about, money she'd kept for a rainy day. She giggled. Maybe this was as rainy as it would get.

Should she take the baby with her? No, there might be questions, particularly if Deborah Ann was working. Often Millie went into the drugstore at night just to stare at all the pretty things. She and Deborah Ann would talk.

Millie didn't like to lie, but if Deborah Ann was there, she'd say something about needing formula for the baby of a friend.

Arnie J was whimpering quietly now, so she laid him up against Arnie. She grabbed her fluffy pink sweater, opened the door and slipped into the hall. She didn't like going out alone, but she did it often enough when Arnie was drunk. Rather that than a beating.

There was a stillness to the city, the streets empty, the only sound the sputtering of a neon sign above a Chinese restaurant. Her shoes clacked on the pavement as she fled up the sidewalk and around the corner toward the drugstore.

Suddenly, someone stood before her, a woman with dark hair over her shoulders and skin as pale as bleached linen. She stared into Millie's eyes for a moment and then scurried away.

Millie shivered. She could swear it was the woman who had left the baby by the curb. "Hey you," she yelled, angry now rather than frightened. She wanted to ask the woman why she'd abandoned a poor helpless baby. She was nowhere in sight.

Millie jerked open the door to the drugstore and scurried on in.

"Help you, Millie?"

She jumped a foot, and turned to see Deborah Ann. "God, you scared me."

"Sorry." She was about Millie's age, tall with blonde hair caught in a clasp behind her head, and big boobs. Mam had made fun of Millie's dishwater hair; Pap had teased her unmercifully for having no tits. Well, she had tits, all right, but not much else. It didn't seem to matter to Arnie.

"Deborah Ann, I got this friend who has this teeny tiny baby. He gets sick when he tries to drink milk. I thought maybe there was something —"

"Doesn't she know what the baby needs?"

"I guess she does, all right. But she's gone overnight and asked me and Arnie to keep the little one."

"What gets into people?" She took Millie's arm. "Come along, hon. I'll show you what we have." She led Millie to the infants' section.

"I — There are so many kinds," Millie said.

Deborah Ann pointed out the two that sold the best.

"I ain't got money for both," Millie said, "and I'm scared I'll pick the wrong one."

Deborah Ann leaned close. "Give me what you got, and I'll make up the difference. I couldn't stand to let the poor thing starve."

Millie raced out the door. Suddenly, someone stepped out in front of her. "Is . . . is the baby all right?" she asked.

"Now you lookee here!" Millie said.

The woman bared her teeth like a dog gone mad in the August heat.

Millie jerked back. "Oh, my God, oh, my God!" They weren't teeth, at least not all of them.

"Is my son all right?"

"He's not all right." She was furious. "There's something wrong, and I'm trying to fix it. He spit up his milk."

Suddenly, the woman sobbed and raced off into the darkness.

"Come back," Millie said. "Come . . ." No! Why would she want the woman back? Arnie J was hers. The cans of formula tight against her bosom, she ran down the street so fast her lungs felt afire.

She hurried inside and back to the room. Arnie still slept, the baby just where she'd placed him. His eyes, like black beads, caught the moonlight.

Millie hurried to the bathroom for water, came back and mixed the contents of a can. She warmed it and scooted across the bed on her knees to put the bottle into Arnie J's mouth. He opened wide and began to suck. Then he choked and gagged till Millie thought he might die.

"Oh, Lord Jesus in heaven," she said, "what am I going to do?"

She mixed the other formula, but it didn't help. She held the baby snuggled against the side of her face, her tears running down his cheeks.

She laid him on the bed, pulled down his little suit and checked the disposable diaper. Still dry. When she tried to fasten it again, the tabs were too worn out to hold.

She dug around in her purse and found two safety pins. She stuck them in her mouth, took off the old diaper and folded the pillowcase to make it fit the little body.

She tried to stick in a pin, but the cloth was thick. She jabbed again right through the cloth and into her finger. "Ouch!"

The baby let out a piercing scream. "Shh," she said, grabbing him up heedless of the blood on her thumb. "Shhhh." She tried to smooth down his hair. Quickly, his tongue shot out and licked at the blood.

"Oh, sweet Lord," she said. She couldn't let Arnie know! He'd make her give the baby away.

The woman had had fangs. For the love of Holy Jesus, she'd heard about such things but thought they were just old tales to scare the young. Idly, she stuck her thumb into the baby's mouth.

"What the hell's going on?" Arnie stared at her.

She turned away so he wouldn't see. "What — what do you mean?"

"He's some kind of monster." She didn't answer. Isn't he?!"

"He's a . . . baby . . . Arnie."

The baby let out a snarl, releasing Millie's thumb.

"Look at him!" Arnie said. "Look at him." He swallowed hard.

"I —"

"A baby that young can't have . . . teeth."

"Teeth!" She looked at him, at the two tiny fangs.

"He's a vampire! Would you believe it, a friggin' vampire!"

"He's a baby, Arnie. A little baby."

"I'll kill the son of a bitch." He leaped out of bed and struggled into his pants.

"No!" She jumped up, ran into the hallway, pounded down the steps and scooted on outside. Holding the baby close, she raced up the street. Suddenly, the woman was there once more.

"Out of my way!"

"Stop!" the woman commanded. "Stop."

She kept on running, and then someone screamed.

She turned to see the woman's face buried in Arnie's neck, blood dripping to the sidewalk.

"Nooo!"

Arnie's face relaxed, took on a look of joyfulness.

That's better," the woman said. She stepped back. "Much better." She beckoned to Millie. "Come here."

Millie shook her head.

"I won't hurt you."

"How can I trust —"

"My baby. I wouldn't hurt my baby."

"You abandoned him."

"I had to." The woman cried in great wracking sobs. "I'm a vampire. I didn't want to be, but I had no choice. I was pregnant, ready to deliver. That's when it happened. It was just after dusk when this young man appeared at the door. He told me he'd been in an accident; he was all wounded and all cut up. I invited him inside." She looked Millie full in the face. "He said he needed nourishment, needed to call a physician."

"Why are you telling me this?"

"He'd been attacked. Back in the mountains of North Carolina as he lay in his . . . resting place. They were trying to kill him. But he awakened in time and escaped. He flew the whole way here to the edge of the ocean, as far as he could get. If I'd known . . ."

"I'm sorry," Millie said, taking a step toward the woman. "It's true then that a person can become —"

"What I am? Yes. I made the mistake of inviting him in. And this was what happened. Oh, God, I loved my husband. We were happy. But it was nothing compared to this. Do you understand? Though the young man did it to me, I love him. But I love my baby too. The young man thought — His name is Boris. Boris thought, and so did I, that maybe the baby would be . . . normal. He convinced me to . . . give him up."

"So you left the little mite, hoping someone would

come along."

"Yes."

Millie glanced toward Arnie, a dreamy look on his face. "What about —"

"Your friend?"

"He's taken care of me."

"Beaten you too, I'd guess, by the looks of it."

"That ain't your concern."

"Since you were good enough to care for my son, I'll spare your man." She reached for the baby. "We'll let him drink his fill; it can't be much."

"Oh, God! What will happen to me then? What will Arnie do if he remembers, if I let you —"

"He'll remember all right, but you wouldn't deprive the baby of his nourishment."

Millie bit her lip so hard she could taste the saltiness of her blood. "All right," she said.

"My name's Serena, what's yours?"

"Millicent. People call me Millie."

"Such a beautiful name." Serena smiled, ruby liquid coating her teeth. "Hold him," she said, placing the baby in Arnie's arms, the little face beside the already opened vein in his neck.

The baby cooed contentedly. Serena turned once more to Millie. "Thank you for taking care of my baby. To tell the truth, I'm grateful he isn't normal. Now I can keep him with me always."

Millie sobbed. "I never had anyone to love before." She glanced at the baby, greedily sucking. "Arnie is . . . security. He never loved me, and if the truth be known, I never loved him."

"There are times I'll want another to care for him when the blood lust is on me." She reached out as if to stroke Millie's hair. "You can't go back to Arnie, not after this. I'll give you everything you need, if you let me."

145

"Arnie won't be too weak . . ."

"He'll be weak for a day or two, unable to help himself."

"He won't become like . . . like you and Arnie J?"

Serena laughed. "Is that what you call him?"

Millie's face flushed.

"You must tell me your decision."

"I love the baby, more than anything else in my life. But Arnie needs me. I know he needs me."

"Are you sure?"

"He needs me, and Blessed Jesus help me, I need him too."

Serena took the baby from Arnie.

"May I hold him one more time?"

Of course."

Millie took him into her arms, bent her head and kissed his forehead. When she looked up, she saw that the rainbows were back in her eyes. She handed Serena the baby. "Come on, Arnie," she said, "we'd better go."

As they walked back home, two bats, one of them very small, crossed the face of the ice cold moon.

When you tell a story, you often have the option of reading it or memorizing it. If that is the case, you might want to just leave "Beneath the Ice Cold Moon" as it is. It is, however, a long story, so you may want to figure out how to cut it. If so, you need to decide how to do this.

ACTIVITIES

1. Take one of the stories you've read up through this chapter and adapt it for telling. Keep track of the things you changed and write them out. Then present the story to the class. Afterwards, discuss with the others the changes you made and why you made them.

2. Find a story to tell to young children. Now figure out some

audience participation activities that you could use with it. Adapt the story and tell it to the class. It should be about two minutes in length.

3. Find a very short story, such as one of Aesop's fables. Using the same moral, set the story in modern times and make it at least twice as long. Tell it to the class.

4. Choose one of the longer stories in the book. Cut as much from it as you can and tell it to the class.

5. As a class:
   a. go through and discuss the sorts of changes that you might want to make in "Beneath the Ice Cold Moon" in order to tell it effectively.
   b. on your own then, change this story (or if you prefer, leave it as it is) and tell it to the class.
   c. discuss and compare the different ways in which the story was told.

Part II:

Developing Original Ideas

CHAPTER SEVEN

IDEAS FROM EXPERIENCE

Sometimes it might be more fun to tell a story that you've made up, rather than one that already is written. An advantage is that since the story is yours, you probably will remember it more easily.

Almost anything can trigger an idea for a story. Ideas come to us all the time, but we often squelch them almost before they reach our conscious minds. To create and tell your own stories, you have to gear yourself to look for and consider ideas.

Sometimes, of course, the ideas we get are not worth developing, but it's better to be able to look at and examine them first before abandoning them. Since ideas are fleeting, get into the habit of carrying pen and paper with you all the time so you can write them down when they come to you.

Sometimes ideas come to us without our consciously searching for them, and that's fine. But there are many "tricks" to stimulating the imagination. Some follow.

FINDING IDEAS

Ideas usually are triggered by an experience we have. Something we see or hear or read often starts us thinking and imagining.

As young children, probably all of us have been told to quit daydreaming and get to work. But when you are looking for ideas to develop into stories, you should daydream. Ideas can come from any experience. The following story came from knowing a woman with mental problems and wondering what this must be like:

THE OLYMPIAN

Carolyn was fifty-eight years old when she decided to train for the Olympics. Already she'd had successful

151

careers as a dancer and a television writer.

After she'd danced her last ballet and written her last TV show — a series that never got off the ground — she returned to the same house she'd grown up in, the yard turned to mud, the paint peeling now that her mother was dead, her father made a vegetable by alcoholism and a series of cerebral accidents.

She sat on the front porch in a scuffed wooden chair. It was a warm day in winter, poinsettias blooming in pots alongside the neighbors' porch.

The idea had come to Carolyn early that morning. If she trained for the Olympics, all her needs would be met.

She'd always been considered beautiful, and that certainly couldn't hurt her chances for a gold. She'd never cared how she looked, so long as she was clean. Simply because it was easier, she wore her hair shoulder length. Dark red, the color of autumn leaves, it spread like a shawl over back and shoulders, complementing her honey-colored skin and warm brown eyes.

It amused her that other women always envied her looks, as if she'd been responsible for them herself. She'd never cared about fashion, a fact the members of her various dance companies and the TV people attributed to eccentricity.

Only lately, though, she'd packed dresses and slacks in boxes and taken to wearing loose fitting sweatpants and unmatched shirts, pulled from her father's drawers to somehow keep him close. She laughed to think that a bonus was the disguising of unseemly bulges. As a dancer, she'd watched her weight. As a writer there'd been too many nights of acid-burning coffee and dried out sandwiches to put on pounds.

Then she'd come home to look after her father, a mound of human flesh whose only forays out of his bedroom had been in search of cheap whiskey. Carolyn pursed her lips at the thought that she sometimes needed a drink as much as he.

All that would change when she went into training. The booze would go, the black coffee, the greasy foods bought at local chain restaurants because she had no inclination to cook and no idea how.

Maybe it would be the Winter Olympics she'd enter, she thought. She'd become a downhill skier. Closing her eyes, she visualized herself at the top of a treacherous slope gazing at toy cars below.

Yet she hated the cold and the snow, despised trips to the mountains. It was foolish to think of skiing. She'd become a gymnast. The Sisters at Saint Aloysius had praised her athletic abilities, her tumbling and cart-wheels.

If she were in training, her necessities would be provided. Since they'd decided to open the Olympics to professionals, maybe she'd even get paid.

The air turned chilly and darkness descended like the soft blankets Daddy piled one by one on her bed when she was a child and suffered fever and chills.

Oh, she'd make him so proud when he saw her there on the podium, bowing her head to receive the gold.

She stood, a smile on her face, a feeling of strength in her legs and arms as she picked up the chair and went inside. Tomorrow, she thought, she'd find out how to go about starting her training.

Her father's room was on the first floor, a cubbyhole she'd shared with her sister as a little girl, her sister who'd been married for thirty years and had three children.

Carolyn had never been able to visualize herself a wife. She loved children, but she'd turned down all the young men who'd approached her. They were nice, all of them, but none could match her father. "Oh, Daddy," she said to herself, "why did you never feel proud?"

What could she expect? He came from a strict Catholic family; Carolyn's upbringing had been strict, as well. But she'd rebelled; she'd had such dreams.

She never closed her father's door; she wanted to be sure to hear if he called out to her day or night. The dim hall lamp cast shadows, revealing only the mound of his body under piles of quilts — quilts brought from the old country, made by Daddy's grandmother, stored till last year in cedar chests.

She'd rigged a rope between eucalyptus trees, stretching it taut to hold the quilts and air them out. At the end of the day, she'd lovingly placed them on Daddy's bed, yanking the dingy blankets out from underneath.

She thought to go straighten the covers, but he seemed to be breathing easily now. And he ranted at her so often of late, calling her unspeakable names.

She went on upstairs to brush her teeth. Pulling the brush from a holder shaped like a grinning cat, she turned on the faucet. She recoiled in horror. They'd gotten to the water supply again. The gasoline fumes attacked her eyes and the sensitive lining of her nose, burning, itching. She dropped the toothbrush and ran for her bedroom.

***

The flannel nightgown had belonged to her grandmother, a harsh woman filled with words of God's vengeance, of souls bound for perdition.

As she lay staring at the papered ceiling in the pale light of the moon, Carolyn wondered why she'd dug out those nightgowns. Why wear anything belonging to a woman who'd whipped her unmercifully with a razor strop after a boy had touched Carolyn, had torn her middy blouse innocently in a football game when she was ten.

Suddenly, Carolyn had an unsettling thought. She couldn't be free to train. Why had she thought she could? What would become of her daddy?

***

Just as the sun began its uneven dance up the sky, Carolyn leaped from her bed. Today was the day, she thought. Today she'd join the gymnastics team.

She shucked the nightgown, ripping the flannel under the arms as she hurried to pull it off. Maybe today the water would be okay. Cautiously, she turned on the faucet. Just a hint of gasoline. She'd brush her teeth and even risk a shower.

Suddenly, steam gushed out of the sink. It hissed in the bathtub, spewed up from the toilet. Carolyn jumped backwards, raced to the bedroom, pulled panties and bras and socks from drawers, sweatpants and shirts from the closet.

On the floor of the closet lay a stack of shopping bags, left over from somebody's Christmas. She pulled out two with pictures of Santas, two more with red-ribboned wreaths.

She wouldn't take time to pack a suitcase; she had to get out of the house. She had to find the training center and talk to a coach. She had to hurry because she couldn't live here any longer where turning on the water could result in death.

Hastily, she dumped her clothes into the bags, keeping only what she'd wear. She hurried to the secretary desk in the corner, brushed papers and pens and notebooks in on top of the clothes. Frantically, she opened drawers to find all her precious papers — her high school and college diplomas, her automobile insurance policy, now expired.

That was everything important, she thought. No, wait. Her jewelry — her bracelets and rings and chains and watch. She grabbed them from her dresser and threw them into the bags.

She yanked on her panties and socks, her sweatpants and shirt. With dismay she realized she'd forgotten her bra. No matter what the young ones thought, a woman had to wear a bra. As fast as she could, she drew it around and fastened it in back. No one would notice; no one would care that she hadn't taken time to put it underneath the sweatshirt.

She ran from the room, bounded down the stairs, saw that her father still slept. Good, she thought. He'd be all right now; she was certain. Softly, she closed his door. She'd go make the team; that was the thing she had to do first. Then she'd come back. She'd take him with her; they'd buy a big house and hire a butler and cook.

She ran toward the door, then came to a sudden stop. Maybe what she was doing was wrong. Maybe . . . maybe she should call the International Olympic Committee. She glanced at the phone. No! She couldn't take time.

She'd better grab a coat and sweater. Evenings could be cold. She set down the bags, pulled a ragged brown cardigan from the closet and tried to stuff it into a bag. It wouldn't fit. In frustration, she kicked the closet door and immediately was sorry. That would wake Daddy, and he needed his sleep.

The sweater bunched up and barely fit over her sweatshirt. She grabbed a camel hair coat that had once been Daddy's and slipped into that as well.

Heaving a sigh, she picked up her bags, squared her shoulders and walked out the door.

She didn't know where she was going, but it didn't matter. She'd get there. All she had to do was keep walking. Keep walking, keep walking, keep walking. Daddy would be so proud.

Among all the ideas we conceive, there are bound to be some that excite us, ideas we know can be developed into interesting stories.

Part of getting and developing ideas is being sensitive to other people, to yourself and to things around you. What do you see that you like? Why? How could you use this in a story? What bothers you about any situation? Use this to develop a tale in which your central character takes what you dislike and changes it.

Many of the stories you've read so far in the book came

from personal experience — the one about Mr. Thomas, "Grandaddy and the Fiddle," "Revival Meeting," and so on.

Of course, how you develop the story depends on your interests. If you like science fiction, you may want to develop ideas in that direction. The following came about after driving along Balboa Park, a big expanse of land that houses the zoo, theatres, and many museums in San Diego.

MUTANT

The car began to grumble and dip, and Pierre felt a jolt of fear. He was passing the jungle, a green tangle of choking vines and undergrowth, the place where grotesque mutants lived.

Pierre hated the drive home alone at night, and to make matters worse, the full moon showed pale yellow beyond smoky clouds. This was the worst of times, a night of insanity when sleeping beasts began to stir, when hideous beings rose to stalk the night. Or so the legends said.

War had nearly decimated the earth; Pierre's grandfather talked about how lucky a small minority was to escape, at least till the mutations became apparent. The worst fled to the jungles of Balboa Park, once a zoo and cultural center for the city of Diego. Yet everyone to a degree had abnormalities.

The car coughed and slowed, nearly crashing through its cushion of air. Damn mechanics anyway. They'd assured him the car was fine, just a matter of adjusting the timing.

He'd always tried to be careful. As a police inspector, he knew the dangers that could befall a lonely traveler. Strangely enough, he'd never seen the creatures that inflicted the torturous deaths on those who ventured too close to the jungle. Even though there seemed to be an unvoiced agreement about each group keeping to its territory, citizens sometimes strayed. Usually, it was teenagers out to prove their bravery.

Pierre had seen throats ripped open by fangs or

bodies cut in small pieces, most of the parts dragged off. He gripped the steering wheel. Only a mile or so till the worst was over, till he was away from danger. Headlights illuminated the path before him, a road now cracked and nearly overgrown. If only he hadn't decided to take the short cut. But he'd been delayed and had promised this time that he'd be home to see his twin sons' soccer game, played against a school up north in the City of Angels.

He began to sweat. He glanced right, toward the jungle only yards away, creeping ever closer to the road that no one would dare fix for fear of attack.

A clanging began, and the car spit fitfully. Pierre's fingers formed bands around the steering wheel. His jaw ached with tension. He started to rock back and forth, as if the motion would somehow propel the car forward. With one last gasp, the motor died.

***

Milt Johnson opened his eyes and stretched. He sighed deeply and sat up. Now the change would begin, the change to power. Feelings of strength flowed through his body. He held his hands out and saw them sprout coarse hair. The fingernails narrowed, hardened into claws. Pads formed on his palms and fingers.

As blood surged within him, he ran from the sleeping cave, tore off his clothes and sniffed the powerful odors around him — must and decay, mixed with animal smells. It was good to be alive. He threw back his head and howled at the moon.

***

The worst had happened, and Pierre had to accept it. The decision made, his breath came easier. He glanced around to see if there was anything important he should take with him. There wasn't really. He loosened his seat belt and climbed out. No one would ever risk coming back for the car. He'd simply abandon it.

He hadn't been in this particular area of town for a couple of years, and things had deteriorated. No one knew how to keep the jungle contained. He shrugged. He wouldn't have to travel far on foot, and he was in good shape. He ran or biked each day, swam a couple of times a week. He slammed the door shut. Maybe he'd be lucky and make it.

***

Milt lived for the nights of the full moon. In his alternate state, huddled with the others in hollowed out caves, he hoarded his strength for times such as this.

***

Pierre trotted along the asphalt, keeping up a steady pace. Thirty-four years old, he'd worked hard to overcome his handicap and gain his appointment as the youngest police inspector on the Diego force. Everyone was handicapped to a degree, and many simply gave in to it. But not Pierre; from the time he was a child, he aimed at the police force, determined to let nothing stop him in achieving his goal.

He glanced toward the jungle, wondering what horrors lurked within. Intellectually, he could feel sorry for the beings who lived there. As the histories told, his people and the jungle inhabitants had sprung from common stock.

Pierre denied the aching of his joints, the pain caused by each additional step. In no more than two or three minutes, he knew, he'd be past the jungle. He'd make it, maybe not in time for his sons' soccer game. But there'd be other games. He listened to the plop of his feet.

***

Milt had never known another kind of life. Folktales had it that beyond the jungle only "normals" lived. He knew they weren't completely normal, but not so altered as he and his kind. Yet Milt enjoyed the diversity among his family and friends. By unspoken agreement, they never preyed upon one another, but upon descendants of the zoo animals. The ultimate satisfaction came in stalking and killing the occasional outsider who ventured too far from safety.

159

The only differences among those outsiders, Milt believed, was their size. Among Milt's kith and kin, there was more uniformity, which, despite the diversities, prevented bullying. Yet with each generation they seemed to be growing smaller.

All these thoughts went through Milt's head as he raced toward the road at the edge of the jungle.

***

Pierre began to tire. Still, with each lagging step, a shot of adrenaline pumped through his system, spurring him forward once more. Up ahead he could see the lights of Diego, kind and protective. No jungle creatures ever ventured there. It was theorized that they feared all light except that reflected by the sun hitting the moon.

Throat parched, sweat soaking his clothing, breath coming in heaves, Pierre shucked off his suit coat and let it fall behind him. It would be a great expense to replace, but his life was worth much more.

***

Milt paused and sniffed. The scent was stronger now. The hackles rose on his neck, and he growled deep in his throat. He cocked his head to listen. Someone was running, coming closer and closer.

The lust for blood was all-consuming. He'd eaten nuts and roots in his other form. It had been a month since he'd tasted blood. He could imagine his fangs ripping and tearing, and the liquid fire spraying his muzzle and face. He'd bury his nose in warm flesh and gorge till he was filled. Then once he changed back, he'd hack the body to pieces with sharpened stones and drag it back to the cave for the others to finish.

If he waited in the thicket at the near edge of the road, the normal wouldn't see him. He'd be concentrating on escape, on getting back to his family. Milt felt a wrench of sadness. He had family too. But there was no comparison. If he didn't kill the normal, he and his family could easily die of starvation.

160

The closer the footsteps came, the faster Milt's heart pounded till he felt his arteries would burst. He felt a stab of excitement. The normal had come into sight. Milt and his family would feast. He gauged the time and leaped.

***

Pierre stumbled and twisted his ankle but kept on running, despite the needles of pain. Yet something was wrong because he kept slipping. When he finally reached the lights of town and knew he was safe, he pulled off his shoe, a gigantic oxford as befitted his fourteen-foot body. On the bottom, squashed against the sole was a tiny animal. Pierre shook his head in puzzlement. It looked almost like a dog.

There are many ways to stimulate your imagination.

DAYDREAMING

Certainly everyone has daydreamed what it would be like to be an outstanding athlete or musician or movie star. Use this as the basis of a story. For instance:

MOVIE STAR

I was sitting in Schwab's Drugstore when this guy came up and sat beside me. He was a dark little man with a two-day growth of beard and beady, bloodshot eyes. "You don't know it yet," he told me, "but I'm going to put you in pictures."

"Sure, Mack," I said and turned away from him, concentrating on my cherry coke. I'd heard cherry cokes were popular at the time the first movie stars were found in Schwab's.

"Hey, I'm not kidding," he said. "Have you heard of . . ." And he mentioned two big stars. Now I mean big, like sumo wrestlers.

"Yeah," I said, "I heard of them. So what?"

"Well, I made their careers, and I can make yours."

I wanted to believe this jerk, but I couldn't get past his broken shoelaces, missing button, frayed collar.

"Oh, well, I don't have to look like this," he said. There was this puff of smoke, and sitting beside me is this handsome man, a surfer dude. Tanned and blond, muscles bulging in all the right places.

PAST EXPERIENCES

Many storytellers talk about their early lives. An example is the following, taken from the beginning of a piece called "The Farm in My Mind."

My grandfather's farm in the 40s was a magical place — a kingdom unto itself. I loved to roam through the sugar woods up behind the barn that blew down and collapsed in upon itself or to play in the grass of the rolling fields.

The house itself was a wonderful building. At my own home bare bulbs hung from the ceiling to cast the shadows from furthest corners. In Grandpa's house glass lamps with thick wicks burned orange in the half-darkness.

Three stories high with an attic, the house held treasures beyond compare — two pump organs, a spinning wheel and a maze of bedrooms. Some had doors nailed shut; others I rarely saw. Yet I imagined Dad's fifteen older brothers and sisters occupying the iron beds with the homemade comforters.

Grandpa, a widower, slept in the room on the right at the top of the first flight of stairs; my uncle John, unmarried, slept in the room on the left. Grandpa's room held nothing personal. John's smelled always of camphor.

Carl Catt based "Night Walk" on a summer job he had while attending college. Here is an excerpt:

I left the highway and walked up the narrow road leading into the woods. The trees were huge. Their branches interlaced overhead. It was like a cool tunnel, a refuge . . . .

Ahead of me lay ten miles of narrow blacktop meandering through the woods, dead-ending at the park. I tossed my small canvas bag into the air and ran, fantasizing a football as I caught it cradled in my arms. There were lots of cars coming out of the park, but none were going in. It was late afternoon. "Stupid ass," I said, "I'll never catch a ride this time of day."

It was getting darker and there was no moon. The tree crowns over the road left a scattering of small dead branches. Even though the air was cool, I heard crickets. Soon there were thousands of them screeching like demons in the night. It kinda scared me. I loved it.

I recalled a trip on the road weeks ago with Ralph and Leon, two campers from a small college in Maryland. One night we drove to town to see a double feature. It was after midnight when we left the highway and started up the narrow blacktop to the park.

I was flabbergasted by all the snakes on the road. A few had been hit by cars and thrashed about on the pavement. Some of the undamaged snakes stared into the headlights. They were blinded, I supposed, because they too slithered about aimlessly. Ralph swerved side to side, running over the snakes. Two or three times we stopped to look. Some could still raise their heads a few inches and strike at us, but they couldn't wriggle off the road. The sound of their quivering rattles riveted me with fear. That night Ralph killed over twenty snakes, eleven of which were rattlers.

Ralph said that on cool nights, snakes, being cold-blooded animals, like to move onto roads because the blacktop stays warm long after sundown.

My thoughts of snakes and friends faded as I saw the flat spreading branches of an old white pine up ahead. In the near darkness, it was like a huge layered sculpture. To my side was a hemlock with its drooping twigs silhouetted against the sky. In spite of the darkness, it wasn't difficult to follow the road. There were openings between many of the trees, making a path of lighter darkness. I was laughing to myself about *lighter darkness* when I stepped on a stick. If I tripped and hurt myself, I'd be all alone five or six miles now from either the park or the highway. I hadn't seen a car for more than an hour.

The ride up the road with Ralph and Leon that evening flashed across my mind again when I stepped on another stick. Suppose it had been . . . a flash of fear engulfed me. I was suddenly sweaty, cold, shaking. I stopped, couldn't move. The next step might be on a rattlesnake. Soft, giving somewhat, rolling under my foot like a rope — a thick rope wrapped in soft cloth. But it wouldn't be a rope. It would be alive.

When you want to develop ideas for a story, simply let the memories flow. For instance, think of your first day in fourth grade. What sort of person was your teacher? Did you like this person? What made you either like or dislike him or her? Answer the questions and then tell about it.

What has happened in your life that frightened you as much as Carl Catt was frightened? How can you build this into a suspenseful story? What has made you very happy? Sad? Angry?

There are techniques you can use to stimulate the memory. Look at your belongings. What about that toy you've saved all these years? Why did you save it? Why is it important to you? What about the present your grandmother gave you when you were just a little kid? You've kept it all these years? Why? By looking at the things you own, they should remind you of circumstances involved with them. Then these can become stories.

For example: "When I was twelve, my grandmother gave me a silver fountain pen with a gold clasp. I could use it just to take notes or do homework, but then when I wanted to, I could have it draw wondrous pictures and write magnificent stories that then became real."

Examine things in your house and do the same with them. What about the clock on the mantlepiece, or the old sofa in the extra bedroom.

You can do the same with places. Describe them and then develop a story from the description: "I always hated to pass the house next door; it frightened me somehow. I know that's silly, but it looked so big, so ominous as if . . . I don't know. It was three stories tall, painted grey and seemed to somehow lean toward the sidewalk. Grandpa told me it had been built when he was just a kid, six or seven years old. Even then, people were afraid of it. And maybe there was good reason."

OTHER PEOPLE'S LIVES

You can create stories using neighbors, friends, relatives, teachers or anyone else. You might want to stick almost totally with what happened, or you can go into fantasy, similar to what was done with "The Disappearance of Billy Findlay."

There are many ways to approach a story about others. You can do it from memory, from what you can observe, from stories you heard the person tell, or even by interviewing him or her.

The following excerpt is from a longer piece, *Because of Romek,* which came about after James D. Kitchen interviewed David Faber, a man who survived several concentration camps during World War II.

One night, all of us were sitting around the table Romek and I had carried home from an empty apartment downstairs. Suddenly, we heard footsteps on the stairs which came three flights straight up from the street.

"It's the Germans!" Romek said. "Quick! Hide!"

Sonia was the first to step on the chair, climb onto the wardrobe and scramble through the hole. The other girls were right behind, then Mother and I. Romek hurried in after us and pulled the picture into place.

We heard a crash, then the sound of footsteps and a rough voice.

"Nobody here!"

"They're hiding! Look, the window's open." This one sounded younger.

"Under the roof like the ones we found yesterday."

We held our breath and listened to them climb out the window. Their boots scraped on the tiles.

Mother gripped Romek's arm.

"Where's Papa?" she whispered. "Why didn't he hide with us?"

Romek groaned. "There wasn't time, Mama," he said. "He hid under the roof."

"Oh, my God! They'll kill him!" Mother's voice shook. We heard tiles breaking and sliding.

It often helps to try to view the world through the eyes of another person. How are his or her perceptions different from yours? Maybe you can even write about how the two views come into conflict.

Of course, you can examine past historical events or

persons, as was done with "The Runaway," the story about William Wells Brown in Chapter Three.

NEWSPAPERS AND MAGAZINES

As you learned earlier, you can get ideas from reading about contemporary events. "Dr. Death Comes to All" came about after newspaper stories began to appear about the real-life Dr. Kevorkian helping terminally ill and suffering patients to die. Professional writer/performer Charles Kray once said that he develops all his ideas from reading the newspapers.

CONCENTRATING ON STORY TYPES

You learned there are many different types of stories that can be told. One way to get ideas is to look at different types and work backwards in creating a story to fit the category.

For instance: "Once upon a time in a kingdom atop a high mountain lived a beautiful princess who had never seen another human being."

Obviously, this sort of beginning can be developed into a fairy tale.

Or you might want to take a character from folklore and develop a story around him or her:

Paul Bunyan could eat more than any man I'd ever met in my life, and, believe me, I've met some big eaters. But like I was sayin', none could compare to Paul.

Once when I was loggin' way up in the Yukon, I remarked to Paul: "Paul," I said, "I got me an idea." He looked at me sideways but didn't say anything. We was right in the middle of eating breakfast, hotcakes, sausage patties so wide around they covered the whole tin plate, big hunks of French bread. Already had eaten twenty of them patties, thirteen stacks of hotcakes, stacked sixty cakes high, eight-and-a-half loaves of bread covered in three pounds of butter and five quart jars of blackberry preserves. This ain't even considerin'

the eighteen pots of black coffee and ... Anyhow, that should give you a right good idea ...

You can do this sort of thing with any type of story you think you'd like to tell.

DREAMS

You should get into the habit of keeping a pen and paper beside your bed so that you can record your dreams. Sometimes we dream whole stories, other times situations that can be developed into stories. Like ideas, dreams are fleeting. If you don't write them down immediately upon waking, chances are you won't remember them.

It can help to read before you go to sleep because this stimulates the imagination. In that time just between being awake and being asleep, you often will find yourself carrying the characters and the situation in the story you've read into new problems and adventures, which you can use in your own stories.

Sometimes just before we fall asleep, we see images behind our closed eyelids. The next time this happens to you, put these images into a story.

STREAM OF CONSCIOUSNESS

When you want to come up with an idea, just begin writing anything that comes to mind. For instance: Once in a forest by a big spring there lived a young man who had a pet toad. One day as he was walking to the spring, the toad leaped up onto his shoulder and said, "Hey, man, why do you always go to that dumb spring every day?"

"Funny, you should ask," said the young man. "Every time I go there I see this beautiful creature in the depths of the pool."

MISCELLANEOUS METHODS

There are many other ways to try to get ideas. One way is by using *word association*. Start with any word and keep on saying the next word that comes to mind: cat, mouse, dog, bark, tree, leaves, roots, growing, acorn, and so on. Then try to use a few of these words in a story: One day my cat was chasing a mouse around and around a tree, tearing the ground away from the roots. All at once there was this loud bark, like it was made by the biggest dog in the world. The cat and mouse both stopped running. "That's better," said a voice every bit as loud as the bark.

Another method is by looking at a photo or a painting and imagining yourself a part of it. Then tell a story about your life or what is happening.

In the next chapter you will learn ways to develop characters for your stories.

ACTIVITIES

1. During the next week, keep track of your dreams. Then choose one from which to tell a story. Discuss the idea with the class and have them give you suggestions on how you might develop the story.

2. Tell the class a three- or four-minute story based on someone else's life. This can be someone you know, maybe a neighbor or a relative.

3. With another class member, come up with a historical person upon whom you could base a story. Figure out what in the person's life might be interesting to tell. Now develop a story based on this and tell it to the class. How do your stories differ from each other's? Discuss with the class why you think this is so.

4. Divide into groups of five or six. Then do word association, each of you coming up with a different word. Now individually begin to develop a story using at least three of the words on the list. Meet with the group in two or three days and tell the story you developed because of this.

5. Develop a two- or three-minute story based on something of yours that you've had for a long time, such as was done with the silver pen. Tell the story to the rest of the class.

6. Take one of the story beginnings from the chapter and develop the rest of the story. It should be two or three minutes long. Tell the story to the class.

CHAPTER EIGHT

CREATING CHARACTERS

Character, as you learned earlier, often is the most important element of a story. In fact, it sometimes *is* the story. This is true, for instance, in "The Olympian." And even though a story may not be simply a character study, like Carolyn is in "The Olympian," character often determines a story's other elements. In "Mutant," Milt Johnson acted a certain way because of what he was — a werewolf. There would have been no story, at least like this one, if Milt had just been a tiny person and if Pierre had been normal size.

This means that you can begin with one particular trait, such as a man's being a writer ("Who Are You and Why Are You Here?") and see what develops. Because he is a writer the character will act like a writer. What will he do? Well, obviously, he daydreams stories and characters.

You and your audience will usually remember the characters before anything else in a story — except those in parables or similar stories where the message is most important.

How can you make your major characters interesting and memorable? First, they have to become real to you.

There are a number of ways to develop a character.

Begin With Someone You See

The next time you go out in public, observe someone you don't know. Later make a list of as many things as you can remember about the person. Then write a description, trying to include everything you observed, but adding other traits or emotions, as well as giving reasons for the person's behavior, based on what you saw. Suppose you see a character like Carolyn from "The Olympian." You observe that she is dressed strangely, with many layers of clothing, and she's carrying several shopping bags, that she is nice looking, has long auburn hair and so on. Ask yourself why she looks this way? She's obviously a street person. Why? Maybe she is mentally ill. In what way? Perhaps she's paranoid schizophrenic. Was she always this way? Probably not. So what was she like before this? Well, she had careers as a writer and as a dancer. In other words, she was successful. How does this affect her now? She feels a longing still to be a success. Taking into consideration that she is mentally ill, what sort of goals does she have? Well, they are unrealistic, weird. She wants to be an Olympic athlete. What about her early life? Her family? She has a domineering father, who is difficult to please, and so pleasing him becomes more important to her than anything else. She never has pleased him, though she keeps trying even in later life.

Continue the questions until a credible character begins to emerge. Once you have finished your description, place the character in a scene. Suppose you've developed the writer in "Who Are You and Why Are You Here?" Where would you place him? Maybe he's taking a break from writing and has stopped in at a coffee shop. Being the sort of person he is — a writer — who would he meet there? Well, maybe he took a break because his writing wasn't going well, and he knows that often ideas come to him when he doesn't try to force them. He writes science fiction and is interested in quantum physics. So he imagines a character, perhaps based on a real person he's seen in the coffee shop.

When you develop a character this way, put him or her in a situation in which there is conflict. Carl Catt's character in "Nightwalk" is placed in a situation in which he becomes terrified. Why? Because he's seen a lot of snakes in the area and because he's alone.

Often, it can work well to place the character with someone else immediately, either as a partner against a common foe — "Pecos Bill and the Rattlesnake" — or against another person — Carl Catt's "The Creosote House."

The Type of Story Sometimes Suggests the Characters

A story can suggest the sort of characters to be included. You need a bigger-than-life hero like Pecos Bill and Paul Bunyan for a tall tale. Part of the work may be done for you already with certain types of stories since often you are working with characters already established.

For most stories, however, you need to consider what you can do to make the person unique. For instance, in a ghost story, what can you do to make your ghost different? Maybe instead of frightening people, he is frightened of them. How does this affect him? Well, the other ghosts always make fun of him. What does he do to make them like and respect him instead? You often can simply ask yourself questions about your characters and then come up with answers.

Characters Sometimes Suggest Other Characters

Just as the writer imagined Deborah Ann in "Who Are You?", a character you start with often suggests other characters. Maybe your central character is overly concerned about her appearance. Why? Maybe years earlier, when she was a young girl, an older cousin made fun of her by constantly telling her she was ugly. Maybe it was just because her family was poor, and she didn't have nice clothes. Suppose she's now married and spends hours every day choosing the clothes she'll wear and putting on make-up. Since this is a significant trait, you'll want to show how it affects her and those around her. Place her in a scene with her husband. He doesn't know how she feels and becomes very impatient.

How does this in turn affect her? What emotions does she feel as a result? It's logical that she feels hurt and resentment. She feels that nobody understands. Yet the fear is irrational because the husband doesn't know about the cousin. As you continue asking questions, you can see that there are many possibilities for developing a storyline. There can be conflict between the husband and wife and conflict with the cousin who now is a successful beauty consultant.

Or you may find that one of the characters you developed as a result of working with the original character is more interesting. This could be the husband's story. He loves his wife but can't stand to live with her because she drives him crazy taking all the time to get dressed and constantly needing reassurance. He talks about it to his best friend, who, in turn, becomes another character in the story.

173

Setting Can Suggest Characters

A setting, real or imaginary, often brings characters (as well as other elements) to mind. Suppose you start with a deserted warehouse you see every day on the way to school. Until recently, it had been empty, trash littering the grounds around it. Now all at once it's cleaned up, and the windows are painted black. Every time you pass, you hear nonverbal sounds — grunts, screams, wild laughter — as well as yelling. What is going on? Who is inside this place, and why did they fix it up? You sneak back after school and peer through a crack in the door. Suddenly, someone grabs you from behind. Who is he? What is happening? What will this person do to you?

It's a man dressed entirely in black. "What are you doing here?" he asks. You try to explain that you're curious. He lets you go and explains that he's a movie director, and the warehouse is being used to film a movie that takes place in Italy in the twelfth century.

Since you are so frightened, he offers to take you inside and introduce you to all the other characters. But there's something funny going on. You think that no make-up could be so good. The griffin really is a griffin, and not an actor made up to resemble a mythical beast. The same is true for the woman who has snakes for hair.

"Don't jump to conclusions," the director says. He explains that yes, the creatures are real, but they aren't like they've been portrayed. Medusa is a kindly grandmother, for instance. Yet she and the others need money to live in the modern world, and the only way to do it is to exploit the legends about them.

You haven't turned to stone, so you finally believe what the director is saying; he's Medusa's great-grandson, by the way. Because of all this, you have a theme: People should not be stereotyped as all bad or all good. The characters and their circumstances suggest a theme of prejudice. Often prejudice exists because people assume certain things about other classes of people.

These people and their relatives, equally as "monstrous," are starving, and this movie is their last chance to buy food and shelter. But they really don't have enough money to keep on renting the warehouse or buying props or even film. What can you do to help them?

Nirmala Moorthy and her husband for a time lived in Africa, which inspired the following story, which also is an excellent character study.

THE BEAST WITHIN

They called him Freddie the Ferret because of his ability to ferret out the news. Once he went after a story, he never gave up. In appearance he was more of the weasel. There was a furtiveness in his manner, a touch of the inquisitive in those quick darting glances that appeared to see in all directions at once; and something uncanny about his intuition that kept him one step ahead of the competition. His real name was Frederick Foss, and he worked as a crime reporter for a leading newspaper in Los Angeles. He had won a Pulitzer for investigative journalism, and had several lesser awards to his credit.

The case that brought him to Nigeria was an insignificant one in terms of news value or headlines, but it would bring him $20,000 if he managed to recover the daughter of a wealthy Beverly Hills real estate broker. Last seen in Lagos, the capital of Nigeria, about five months earlier, she had lived for a year in Enugu, making a study of local tribal customs for her Ph.D. thesis in anthropology. She was officially attached to the University of California in Los Angeles.

Her last letter to her family back home had been written nearly four months earlier, before her proposed field trip to the eastern states to "live in the villages and learn firsthand about the people." Doris Fletcher was not a sociable person. She had many friends in Enugu, but since she met them only infrequently on account of her field trips, her disappearance went unnoticed for almost two months. Her landlord, anxious to receive his monthly rent, made the first complaint to the police. The police informed the American Embassy in Lagos, ques-

175

tioned Miss Fletcher's landlord, gardener and houseboy, made copious notes, and closed the case after three months. The only important fact that they unearthed was that Doris Fletcher's chauffeur, George, had also disappeared.

Miss Fletcher's parents came to Nigeria and searched for her for weeks, without any result. She had vanished without a trace. The only clue they could give the Ferret was her diary, found in her house with the rest of her belongings. The last entry in it, dated June 20, the day after her return from Lagos, said: "Tomorrow my safari begins, and I don't know where it will end. The next two weeks are going to be pure hell — and sheer excitement. George will drive me to Port Harcourt. If I'm lucky I'll find Anton Fournier, manager of one of the Elf oil refineries; the only person who can guide me, tell me where to go."

Wherever the Ferret went, he drew a blank. Nobody really seemed to care. Everyone was polite, cooperative and helpful. The police in Lagos gave him access to the files. Fred discovered that approximately forty-five people were missing in Lagos alone in any given year. In Port Harcourt the number was seventy-five. The police had done their best.

"Insh'allah!" they said. "Miss Fletcher will return of her own accord."

The officials at the American Embassy were sympathetic, but they had no information. Doris Fletcher, the anthropologist, and George, the driver, had disappeared off the face of the earth. Since the jeep that Doris had bought had also vanished, Fred inferred that she had actually left for Port Harcourt. He decided to call on Anton Fournier.

First he went looking for George's wife, Sarah. She had a liquor store in a shantytown market on the outskirts of Enugu. She looked like an amiable hippopotamus. She sat in front of her store, with her enormous behind daintily balanced on the upturned aluminum bucket, her bovine stare fixed on the ground. Her fat, dimpled hands were in constant indolent motion, adjusting her printed wrapper, fiddling with the spotted handkerchief tied around her head. She spoke no English, and his repeated questions attracted a crowd of onlookers, who seemed to vary in age from two to eighty. They appeared to have nothing better to do on a Monday morning than to stand around and stare at him.

Then he saw a little old man who came burrowing out of the crowd like a gopher. He was dressed in a crumpled, gray-brown suit which was at least twenty years behind the fashion. He spoke perfect English, swallowing the vowels in the manner of educated Englishmen, and translated what Sarah had to say. George had probably run off with another woman, she said, her eyes opaque and expressionless as blobs of mud. He would, when he tired of the hussy in a couple of months, as he always did, return to her and their six children.

"She is not financially dependent on her husband, you see," explained the old man. "In Nigeria, women always support themselves and their children. She is prepared to wait and see." He beamed at Fred as if to say that this was exactly what everyone should do.

The old guy must be a retired school teacher, thought Fred inconsequentially.

Anton Fournier turned out to be another dead end. He lived way out in the bush, near the oil refinery.

"Doris Fletcher?" He peered at Fred like a bewildered rabbit, while his prominent front teeth accentuated the likeness. "Are you telling me the police haven't found her yet? She went east, towards the Cameroons. Maybe she crossed the border. The patrols are so slack, you can do that in a hundred places!" His pudgy fingers twitched nervously on his plump belly. "You should go back to Lagos and ask your embassy to contact the Cameroonian police. If they get onto her trail, Miss Fletcher can't go very far, don't you agree?"

"No way!" said Fred. "You've seen her. That means I'm getting somewhere. I can feel it in my bones. I'm close now, very close." His thin pointed nose twitched with excitement, like a bloodhound on the scent. He could hear the crackle of crisp dollar bills — 20,000 of them.

"I suppose you should look around in the villages." The Frenchman sounded hesitant. His myopic eyes blinked behind his gold-rimmed spectacles. For a moment there was an uncomfortable silence while he went through the agony of decision, and his mouth opened and shut several times like a fish sucking algae off the glass wall of a tank. Then: "Maybe I can help you," he said. "There are no hotels here. You can stay with me, and I'll give you my jeep to drive around." Suddenly he sounded enthusiastic. "I live alone. Except for Miss Fletcher, you are the only white person to come here for years. Sometimes I miss having company."

Anton Fournier lived in a little bungalow with a well-maintained garden. There was a whole acre at the back devoted to fruit trees and vegetables: eggplants, carrots, tomatoes, lettuce and the ubiquitous okra. "We have the best paw-paw in the world," boasted Anton, "and my mango trees might produce stringy fruit, but you'll have to admit they are sweet."

Fred's one-week stay gradually extended into three, and he barely noticed. From dawn to dusk he combed the swampy countryside with Emmanuel — Anton's assistant — as driver, guide, and interpreter. As they drove along the frequently water-logged roads, they saw villagers holding up giant lizards or baby crocodiles for sale.

"Bush meat," explained Emmanuel. "We eat them here!" Besides this, the villagers eat fish, yam and cassava. Their poverty, malnutrition, and vulnerability to disease, was obvious.

Fred's evenings with Anton were a gourmet's delight. Sebastian, Anton's cook-houseboy, was a superlative chef. Fred invariably ate too much.

"We Frenchmen have the priorities right, don't you

think?" said Anton. "We know that food is the most important thing in life." After dinner they usually sat out on the verandah, under a crimson canopy of bougainvillea blossoms, sipping their brandy and savouring the cool night breeze. Anton regaled him with stories of local customs, tribal rituals and black magic. He had lived in Nigeria for twenty years and spoke the Ibo dialect like a native. Some of those years had been spent in the company of a native woman, a Beninoise, who had died in childbirth. Anton spoke of her with great fondness.

But of Doris Fletcher he did not have anything good to say.

"Never trust an anthropologist, *mon ami*. They make trouble wherever they go," he declared. "They go poking and prying into other people's affairs, and then they write books about them. Miss Fletcher wanted to learn everything about a whole race, a whole culture . . . about generations of history, in just a few weeks! She was a rapacious vulture picking at dead flesh — a nibble here, a bite there, and then she would bare the bones for the world to gaze in horror and disbelief!" Fred stared in surprise at his angry host. For a split second the rabbit had turned into a wolf.

Sometimes Anton spoke of his youth in France. He had no family there now.

"It does get lonely here," he said, "but this is my home now. I can never think of going back to France again. I just wouldn't fit in anymore." His pink lips trembled with distress. "But I have everything I need here. I fish. I hunt. I have a nice house and a good cook . . . What more can a man need?"

"But don't you feel cut off from civilization? You get your newspapers and letters about once a month! You've no idea of what's going on out there in the world, do you?" Fred's voice rose. "Why, I'd die of the blahs . . ." He stopped in midsentence, silenced by the violence of his own reactions. For a moment there he had lost his cool! He had shouted at Anton, that poor little slob who had been so kind to him.

The time had come for him to go home, Fred decided in the morning, as he shaved and showered. He stood before the mirror and pulled at the flab around his middle. He had eaten far too many of Sebastian's pies and souffles. He had lost that ferrety look: he was becoming a jelly-belly — like Anton?

"I think I'll go back to Lagos tomorrow," he announced at breakfast. "I don't seem to be making much of a headway here."

"Tomorrow is Sunday, a holiday for me. Why don't you come out with me for a change, maybe you'll find something?" Fred agreed. He could leave on Monday.

This time they drove northeast, towards the border, the only region he hadn't yet scoured from A to Z. The orange sky was turning indigo when they arrived at the village. There was an air of festivity about the place. A group of young men danced about a bonfire to the rhythmic tap-tapping of the drums. There was something different about this village. The laughing children who rushed out to greet them seemed healthy and well-fed. The young girls covered their mouths with their plump hands and giggled among themselves. Fred grinned and waved at them.

As they got down from the jeep, Anton turned to look at him. His eyes were huge blue pools of regret behind his bifocals.

"I hope you understand, Fred," he said. "I told you to go back, and you wouldn't listen. It's your own fault, really!"

The villagers were close now, surrounding them. As they smiled and looked him over, Fred noticed that their front teeth were ground to sharp points.

"Once you've tasted it, you can never give it up," Anton was actually pleading, asking him to understand. "You become addicted. The meat has a sweet and sour taste, like no other. And the stew they make from the bones . . . you didn't know what you were eating, but you said it yourself, Fred . . . you said you'd never tasted anything like it!"

Fred stood still. Fear held him rooted to the spot.

"You'll never get away with this." His voice came out as a strangled croak. He was the rabbit now and Anton the ferret. "They'll come looking for me!"

"They won't find your body, Fred," said Anton gently. "No one can file a murder charge without a body. What remained of Doris and her driver, when we were done, was so little. There was hardly anything left for the crocodiles. Her jeep was more of a problem. It took six men to sink it in the swamp."

BUILDING CHARACTERS

What sorts of things should you figure out about your characters before you begin your story? These are the same things you learned earlier when analyzing an existing character. There are five broad categories: 1) physical characteristics, 2) background, 3) attitudes and beliefs, 4) patterns of behavior, and 5) dominant traits.

These are all related. A person's educational and family background affect attitudes and behavior. A man who had to quit school and go to work to help support his family will view life differently than if he went to a prestigious prep school and on to college before taking a position in his father's firm.

When planning a character, you need to take all these five areas into consideration. What are the physical characteristics? A person who is very tall and one who is very short may feel they are misfits. But their stature will affect each differently.

What physical traits stand out for each of your major characters, and how do they affect personality, attitudes or relationships?

Background involves such things as where a person grew up. A woman from a tiny town in Mississippi will view many aspects of life differently than will a woman who grew up in

Los Angeles. Religion or the lack of it will affect a character's outlook, beliefs and personality. You need to take into consideration anything important in a character's background that makes the person behave in a certain way.

Some people are pessimists, others optimists. How do they behave differently in a similar situation? How does a person's attitude affect being the butt of a joke?

What are the strongest traits a person has? These are identifying traits; if people who exhibit these traits were to change, friends and acquaintances would find it hard to accept. As a storyteller, you need to point up the most identifiable traits about your characters so they come across clearly to the audience.

Suppose you come up with an idea for a character you like? What are some ways you can begin to find out more about the person? Suppose the editor of your school paper asked you to write a profile. How would you go about doing it? The most logical way would be to interview the person.

The Character Interview

There's an acting exercise called the character interview. It has three rules:

1. You cannot plan anything ahead of time.

2. You cannot answer as yourself but rather as a character who is beginning to take shape.

3. All the answers have to be consistent. For example, a person cannot be both outgoing and introverted.

A person agrees to be "it," and other actors ask questions until a character emerges.

Even though this technique started as an acting exercise in which someone agrees to be questioned, you can do an entire interview yourself, playing both roles, or you can do it in class with one person agreeing to be interviewed and the rest of the class asking random questions. In either situation, simply let the questions and answers flow. For example:

Q: What's your name?
A: Ron Silvers.

Q: Where are you from, Ron?

A: Right here, what do you think? Like I'm going to leave or something.

Q: You sound angry.

A: So what?

Q: I just wondered why.

A: Aw, hell, it ain't your fault. My buddy and I was gonna take off, go out to California, and maybe on to the South Pacific.

Q: Why didn't you go?

A: His mom found out.

Q: How old are you anyhow?

A: Fifteen.

Q: Where do you live?

A: Oh, well, can't you see, it's this magnificent mansion. A hundred rooms, thirty-five bathrooms. Get serious!

Q: It sounds like you don't live in such a nice spot.

A: The slums, okay? I want to get out.

Q: What would you do if you left?

A: My buddy and me formed this group, you know?

Q: A musical group?

A: Hey, man, what else?

Q: Why do you want to leave?

A: Just look around you. Drug dealers, kids gettin' killed in drive-by shootings. Like my brother Tommy.

Ron comes across as a credible character who wants to escape a bad situation. So what does he do? What happens to him? Maybe you can put him in scenes with other characters to try to find out.

The character of the girl in "Beneath the Ice Cold Moon" was developed using the character interview. Look back at the section that begins, "They'd been together a year and a half, and she was beginning to think it might last" and ends, "She was a week from being seventeen and that's where she headed." Pay attention to all the background information provided about her.

You can even take an existing character, one that you're

trying to put into a story, and ask questions to make the person come across more clearly.

Q: Medusa, why did people get such a wrong idea about you?

A: Well, there was this guy who liked me, but I didn't like him. We'd dated a few times before I found out how selfish he was. I broke up with him. He started to tell people . . . well, you know.

Q: He started spreading stories about you, you mean?

A: Yeah, about how if people just looked at me, they'd turn to stone or something. Puh-leese!

Q: That didn't happen then?

A: Are you serious? I mean, sure, sometimes I don't like all these snakes hissing and rattling — it drives me nuts. But can I help it?

Q: Can you?

A: I guess if I wanted to kill 'em all, I could. But that wouldn't be very nice. They have a right to live too.

Q: So what you're telling me is that you're a pretty nice lady.

A: I try. And I *was* married. My hubby passed on. He was mortal, and they just don't live as long as we do.

Q: How long —

A: We were married fifty years. That's it, a mere twinkling. And now I have to spend the rest of my life alone.

Q: Why's that?

A: Let me ask you something? Would you want to marry someone like me?

Q: Well, look —

A: Come on, admit it. All these damn snakes sticking out of my head. Real romantic, huh? Real conducive to a good relationship.

There are a number of other ways to develop your character.

Focusing on a Significant Trait

You can start building a character by listing a personality or physical trait. Suppose that you decide to develop a character who is a worrier. What does this mean? Well, let's suppose the character's name is Katie and she worries about everything — her job, her kids and even whether her husband George is going out with other women. She can never be sure, so she questions his every action. One night he can't take any more of this and slams out of the house abandoning her and their two kids, a three-year-old girl and a one-year-old boy. What does she do then?

Word Association

A similar way of developing characters is word association, the same device you used earlier to come up with words around which to build a story. This time, however, start with a physical or personality trait and write down the next words that come into your head. Suppose you start with "blonde." Then go on with "attorney," "distrustful," "kind," "athletic," "married," "anorexic," "intelligent."

Keep going until you have ten or twelve traits. Now take four or five and use them as the foundation on which to build your character. Add whatever you wish to what you already have. There are a number of ways you can proceed from there. For example:

1. You can begin by writing a paragraph or two of description using the traits.

> **Judy Thompkins is an attorney with a large firm. Very bright, she's blonde and athletic. She trusts no one, including her husband. Despite this, she is a kind person who at one time in her life was anorexic.**

2. You can use the same traits but put your character into a setting.

> **Judy Thompkins leaned back in her desk chair at the law firm where she works. Although she was intelligent, people seemed to view her as an airheaded jock. She'd been a distance runner in college, obsessed with her weight, so much so that she became anorexic. She's also blonde, which adds to the empty-headed image she feels people must have of her. Although she**

185

genuinely likes people and can be very kind, she can't bring herself to trust anyone. She feels other people are interested only in her good looks.

3. You can immediately put your character in a scene of conflict.

Judy Thompkins, junior partner in Smith, Reynolds and Blair, the biggest law firm in town, leaned back in her chair and closed her eyes. A new client was stopping in to see her, and then she was going to lunch with her husband. She dreaded both meetings. She was sure the client felt he was somehow stuck with her, and she'd decided she would tell her husband Tom that she wanted to call it quits.

4. You can put two characters together, where the second character is suggested by the first. Just keep in mind that the basis of most stories is conflict.

Judy Thompkins looked up from her desk to see Ralph Fox entering her office. She'd never met him before, but she knew he was one of the most influential men in town. One of the senior partners had specifically asked her to meet with him. She didn't know why.

"Mr. Fox," she greeted him, forcing a smile to her lips.

He was sixtyish, with silver hair and slender hands. Right away she resented him. He was rich, while she'd had to work for everything she'd gained in her life.

"Judy Thompkins," he said, "you may wonder why I requested seeing you."

You're darned right I do, she thought, but wouldn't give him the satisfaction of saying it.

"I have a deal for you."

"A deal?" Apparently, he thought he could pull something over on her. Most men did. Because of her looks, they seemed to think she was an empty-headed bimbo.

"That's right." He touched the back of a chair. "May I sit down?"

"I suppose so, Mr. Fox," she said. "But maybe we should get this over quickly."

Fox laughed, which surprised her. "Bob Reynolds told me you were a little feisty."

"Feisty!" How dare he?

As you see in the way this developed, there is immediately conflict, though it is inside Judy's head. So far no one is really opposing her, though she thinks they are.

You can take two characters you developed independently and put them together having a conversation. Let's take Ron Silvers, the teenager who wants to escape his situation. The second character is Judy. Since one of her traits is that she's kind, she does some legal aid work. Why would the two of them come together? Suppose that Ron is accused of trying to get even for his brother's death.

JUDY: So, do you want to tell me what happened?

RON: I don't know. I really ... I mean, why do you care about me? *(He looks her up and down.)* I mean, you're a rich lady. What am I to you?

JUDY: Look, Ron, just accept that I want to help, okay?

RON: I guess so. I ain't got much choice.

JUDY: So, right up front, Ron, did you do it?

RON: No, damn it! I didn't do it.

JUDY: Why are you so angry?

RON: Okay, I'm not angry. Does that make you happy?

Keep in mind all that you already know about each character and proceed from there. It should be easy for the reader to spot that Judy really wants to help and that Ron questions why. You could then develop this into a story where two people from different backgrounds, both mistrustful of the other, learn to trust and to see the good qualities in each other. Because of this, their lives are changed in positive ways.

It doesn't matter how you begin developing your story. Just keep in mind that the kind of person a character is can suggest situations in which to place him and other characters with whom he can react. It's easy to suppose, for instance, that Judy, the attorney, comes into conflict with someone she doesn't trust. The lack of trust finally starts affecting the other person. So you have situation and tension, as well as other characters.

Once you assign a person's traits, you may want to delve into the reasons behind them. What caused Judy to become distrustful? Maybe she came from a broken home and each parent played her against the other so that she becomes a pawn, rather than a person to them. They simply use her without showing that they care about her at all. Subconsciously, she begins to feel that she is unworthy and so overcompensates by going on the offensive with everyone.

Begin With Attitudes and Beliefs

How does the character view the world? Is she kind or mean? Let's say she's kind. In fact, she's a sucker for every sob story she hears. She's always giving people handouts. How do her family and friends react? Are they glad she's always this way and do they support her in this, or are they tired of doing without because of her generosity? Figure out why she's so giving. Maybe she feels guilty for not buying one of her kids the bicycle he wanted, even though she could well afford it. Maybe she grew up during the Depression and had to do without a lot of things, and as a result feels that kids shouldn't be given everything they want. And maybe shortly after that her son became terribly ill and died. Now she's trying to atone for this.

Even though you couldn't possibly include every facet of a character in your stories, the more you know about each one, the more convincing the person becomes for the audience.

Allow the processes to work for you. The best reward is that if you use any of these methods, you need never again be stuck for a character, a plot and utlimately a story to tell.

ACTIVITIES

1. Go to a department store or mall and observe someone you see there. What sorts of things can you tell about the person by the way he or she talks, walks, gestures? What sort of mood was the person in? Why do you suppose this was so? Take what you observed and add to it. Then on this basis, put the character in a scene with someone else.

2. In turn, go around the room listing character traits. Now take four or five of the traits and develop a character. Put the character in a scene with someone else, and then tell the scene to the rest of the class.

3. Decide on a type of story you'd like to tell, maybe a myth or a tall tale. Now develop a character to fit the type of story. Describe the character to the rest of the class.

4. Think of a setting — perhaps a building or an empty piece of land you pass on the way to or from school. Now think of the type of characters you might find in this setting. They can be realistic or fantasy (like Medusa, for instance). Put these characters in a situation then and tell the rest of the class about it.

5. Have several people in class agree to be interviewed, following the three rules listed for a character interview. Do several interviews in class. Each should last thirty to sixty seconds. Now take one of the characters and place him or her in a scene that has conflict. All this should be based on what came out in the interview. Next take two of the characters and place them together in a scene.

6. Develop a three- to four-minute story based on one of the exercises. Tell the story to the class.

CHAPTER NINE

PLANNING THE STRUCTURE

Once you have the elements of a story in mind, the next step is to plan the plot or structure.

THE STORY LINE

There are several ways of planning a story. One is the outline. This shows the exact progression, so that you can tell if the story moves ahead logically and that each complication or episode leads directly into the next and proceeds logically toward the ending.

For each division you include the characters involved, the location, the time and a description of what happens, in this form:

I. Opening Scene

   A. Characters:

   B. Location:

   C. Time:

   D. Any special conditions:

   E. Progression of the action:

      1.

      2.

      3.

      4.

Here, for instance, is the beginning of an outline of "Mutant," which is easy to break into different scenes or crises because the story switches back and forth between Pierre and Milt's points of view.

Mutant

I. Opening Scene

   A. Characters: Pierre.

   B. Location: Driving along Balboa Park in Diego.

   C. Time: Sometime after dark.

   D. Any special conditions: It's after a nuclear holocaust where everyone has some degree of abnormality.

   E. Progression of the action:

     1. Pierre is driving home.

     2. His car begins to stall.

     3. Pierre worries about what happens to people caught out late in the park.

     4. The car becomes worse.

II. Second Scene

   A. Characters: Milt Johnson.

   B. Location: Inside Balboa Park.

   C. Time: Nighttime as Pierre is driving past.

   D. Any special conditions:

   E. Progression of the action:

     1. Milt begins to change form.

     2. Changed now, Milt howls at the moon.

III. Third Scene

   A. Characters: Pierre.

   B. Location: Still outside Balboa Park.

   C. Time: A few minutes later.

   D. Any special conditions: Pierre's car has stopped; the park has deteriorated.

   E. Progression of the action:

     1. Pierre accepts the situation.

     2. He leaves the car.

You would do the same type of thing for a story that is not plotted.

Pecos Bill and the Rattlesnake

I. Opening Episode

   A. Characters: Narrator, Pecos Bill.

   B. Location: Wyoming.

   C. Time: Probably the 1880s, evening near twilight.

   D. Any special conditions: Very cold; inadequate bedding; the fire is frozen.

E. Progression of the action:
1. Narrator is fretting about the cold.
2. Pecos tells him not to worry and ponders what to do.
3. Pecos mentions coyotes.
4. Narrator talks about what will happen if they don't get warm.
5. Pecos again says not to worry.

II. Second Episode
A. Characters: Pecos Bill and the Narrator.
B. Location: Same.
C. Time: A little later.
D. Any special conditions: Same.
E. Progression of the action:
1. Pecos starts howling. His belt breaks.
2. Pecos feels sheepish about this, but keeps on howling.
3. Coyotes start to appear; narrator is worried.
4. Pecos reassures narrator again and continues to call the coyotes.
5. The coyotes come closer.
6. Pecos tells the narrator to lie down slowly.
7. The coyotes gather around and snuggle against the two human beings.
8. The two men and the coyotes sleep.

III. Episode Three
A. Characters: Same.
B. Location: Same.
C. Time: Early morning.
D. Any special conditions: Still cold.
E. Progression of the action:
1. The sun, probably partially frozen, rises slowly . . .

Each time there is a change of location, time or characters, there is a new scene or crisis.

When you do this sort of outline, be sure to include anything important to the story, such as character's ages and occupations. Let's try outlining a new story, one that was suggested by characters in the last chapter.

Untitled Story

I. Opening Scene
   A. Characters: Narrator; Patrick, fourteen years old.
   B. Location: A warehouse that was abandoned and now has been cleaned up, the window panes painted black on the inside.
   C. Time: About 7:45 a.m.
   D. Any special conditions:
   E. Progression of the action:
      1. Patrick is on his way to school. Not for the first time he notices a formerly abandoned warehouse now is occupied and wonders what is going on.
      2. Patrick sneaks up and tries to see inside.
      3. Someone grabs him from behind.
      4. The man asks Patrick what he's doing there.
      5. Patrick is scared; he explains he is just curious.
      6. The man says he's a movie director, and says he'll let Patrick watch filming for a bit and meet the actors.
      7. Patrick sees that the actors are "real"; they are mythical creatures. He tries to leave.

II. Second Scene
   A. Characters: Patrick, the director, Medusa, Griffin.
   B. Location: Inside the warehouse.
   C. Time: A few minutes later.
   D. Any special conditions:
   E. Progression of the action:
      1. Medusa calls to Patrick.
      2. He turns to look at her.
      3. She explains that the creatures he sees are not bad; they've just gotten "bad press" over the centuries.
      4. Patrick feels sorry for them.
      5. Medusa says she doesn't turn people to stone; the Griffin says he's a good family man.
      6. The director says that they are making the movie as a way to live, but they're almost out of money.
      7. Patrick says he'll try to help them.

This is a good way to plan your story because it forces you to think exactly where you're going and what is going to happen from beginning to end. It also is a good idea for you to determine the characters' motives and list them either before or at the end of the outline. As you know, characters may have different life goals or motives from those in the story. Yet in the story, the motives most often contribute to the life goals. Even motives in different scenes can be different. For instance, in the story about the warehouse, we find that the creatures are making a movie to get money to support themselves and their families. Patrick's overall goal might be stated this way: Patrick wants to help his newfound friends and their families to survive. His goal in the first scene, however, is: Patrick wants to discover what is happening in the warehouse.

Let's take "Mutant" because the goals of the two characters are important. They also are to survive. But they go about this in different ways. Their goals therefore are:

Pierre wants to make it home safely.

Milt wants to get food for his family.

Do not be afraid to revise the story and change it. You may find that some things you originally included really are irrelevant. Or maybe some of the characters aren't really necessary. Then cut them. On the other hand, you may find that you have to go back and put some things into the story so the action progresses more clearly. Of course, when you tell the story, you also may want to change it further.

If you prefer, you can write out a brief paragraph that summarizes the story before you go into a more detailed outline. You may want to begin with background information, including special conditions necessary for telling the story. For instance:

"Mutant" takes place after a nuclear holocaust. All the people are mutants to a certain degree, although those who have changed the most keep to Balboa Park in what was once called San Diego, but is now just Diego.

The story will have just two characters: Pierre, a so-called normal and Milt Johnson, who lives in the park with his family and periodically changes into a werewolf.

When the story opens, Pierre is on his way home from work. He has taken a shortcut past the park in order to get home in time to see his sons play in a soccer game against another school. However, his car starts to die just as he's passing the park. This scares him because he's seen what terrible things are done to people who are caught by those living in the park.

Continue with this until you have the entire story summarized.

A third method is to write a sort of skeletal version of the story using actual dialog or narration. For instance:

Millie and Arnie are walking down the street in San Diego. Although it isn't cold, Millie shivers.

"It's dark," she says. "Only the moon and the street lights."

Arnie is disgusted with her. She thinks about the time they first met when she had arrived in San Diego with no money and only two plastic shopping bags of belongings. He'd come up to her and asked if she was hungry.

"I ain't ate in near three days," she tells him, not since she left Wheeling, West Virginia.

Try the three different methods with your stories, or do a combination of the three methods to see which works best. Or maybe you will even want to develop your own method. The only important consideration is what is most comfortable for you or what works best.

As you're planning the story, remember that the characters are working toward a goal, and everything in the story either has to explain why they are going toward the goal or has to have them actually moving toward it. In more realistic stories, something in the characters' background has pushed them toward an action.

In other words, a character is pulled toward the goal while

being pushed toward it by his or her background. Due to certain experiences in the character's background, the person behaves a certain way.

For instance, Cecil and Alicia in "Tradeoffs" behave more politely toward each other than many contemporary couples might. And even though Alicia certainly has a mind of her own, she believes that a wife should be solicitous of her husband. Cecil has a strong sense of family and so has refused to abandon his descendants. He is "pushed" by this trait developed in the past while being pulled toward curing his nephew and his family.

Because we know certain background information about the protagonist and the other important characters, we expect them to behave in certain ways. We know from folklore that Pecos Bill is bigger than life, that there is no problem too great for him to solve. We know that Ceece Harrington can be killed by having a stake driven into his heart because this is the way tradition tells us that vampires "die."

In a way this sort of background information is foreshadowing. We know that because Manuel Ortega doesn't want to leave the earth and Señor Viejo wants him to, that there will be a confrontation between the two. We know that the dissatisfaction of the people in "Dr. Death Comes to All" will cause some sort of confrontation. The audience anticipates this.

But more so, there often is more obvious foreshadowing when a teller deliberately tantalizes the audience or hints at something that will happen. For example, when the narrator in "Night Walk" is frightened of snakes, you know he has to encounter snakes or at least limbs of trees that make him think they are snakes. If Catt had simply dropped the idea of the snakes after mentioning them, it would be misleading the listener.

If the storyteller has a character hiding something under the mattress in one scene, then this thing that is hidden has to play an important part in the outcome of the story. Let's look at the foreshadowing in the following.

DEAD MAN'S CORNER
by Anne James Valdes

"Did they tell you about the dead man?"
Delfina asked as she rinsed the dishes in the
***apantle*, the stream flowing through the gar-**
den.

"Dead man . . . here in the village? In
Amatecalpan?"

"*Si, Señora Ellen*. Right here." A plump
finger pointed to the stream.

Ellen imagined the current conveying a
corpse and depositing it, like a dog with a bone,
at her feet. The shriveled face had Jeremy's
square jaw, his long nose, his . . . She dropped
the plate she was drying. The glazed brown clay
broke into four pieces. She picked up a shard,
stared for a second at a painted yellow flower,
and threw the piece in the water until the flow
carried it away.

You know immediately that the dead man will play an important part in the story, and soon you know that Jeremy will too.

Foreshadowing also means pointing up character traits that do not seem completely germane at first but will become important later on. We see the seeds for a certain behavior early and see these seeds grow later. For example, if somebody becomes angry at a little thing early on, you know that this anger will play an important part later in the story. As a teller developing your own story, you have to be aware of this.

Pecos Bill isn't worried early on about the cold, so you know he can handle any problem that comes up. The fun and interest is in the exaggeration, the sheer fantasy of how he accomplishes his goals.

Often after you've plotted or planned a story, you see where you might plant an earlier clue to a happening or a character's behavior. If so, go back and revise your outline.

THEME

At the beginning you also might want to list the central idea or theme. This is what you want to say to the audience, and this is tied in with what feelings you want them to experience. The theme should be something important to the audience, something about which they can feel a strong emotion, and something with which they agree. Yet the story has to be more than just a statement of theme, or there's no reason to present it.

Particularly if you are telling a story that has a serious intent, the audience should empathize with the characters and ideas. In a humorous story, this isn't as important since humor is more "intellectual" than emotional. This means that it's easier to laugh at people in humorous stories because we don't identify so strongly with them.

You learned that the theme of a story can be based on well-known sayings and common beliefs. One of the latter ways is to use *humankind's basic needs* around which to build the theme. These include the need for: security, recognition, response, adventure, worship, and self-preservation. Each of these can be broken down further. For instance, there are all sorts of security — protection under the law, financial security, governmental security and so on. You could take any of these and build a story around it. The theme you develop should be in a complete sentence. For example, you might use as one of your themes: Nobody wants to die. You could write many stories around this theme — a person trying to escape a crazed killer, a person stealing to keep from starving, a person refusing induction into the armed forces, and so on.

PLOT AND STORY

Although the terms sometimes are used interchangeably, plot and story are not the same thing. Plot is the action, the forward movement. Story, on the other hand, most often begins earlier than the plot. In "Dead Man's Corner," the man died before the story opened, and something happened to Jeremy.

Story includes all the background information mentioned or alluded to in the story. "Dr. Death" has a whole different culture from ours, and it has existed for the past hundred years.

199

For a long time, there have been mutants in the story "Mutant." The plot occurs only in a short period of time, whereas the story can encompass an entire history. The listener is transported to a world that probably has existed as long as the one in which he or she lives. The characters, situations and events in a story do not exist in a vacuum. Rather, you, as a storyteller, select only those events that have bearing on your plot.

You should try to get your protagonist from Point A (the inciting incident) to Point B (the climax) in as direct a route as possible (except in some tales as shaggy dog stories, where the fun occurs in dragging them out). You have to keep attention on reaching the goal.

In many of the stories in the book, there are either "thinkbacks" or flashbacks. In the former, the character thinks about or remembers prior events, either in general terms or in detail. Cecil remembers what life was like before he became a vampire, and he alludes to this. So does Alicia. On the other hand, some stories actually have the central character remember so thoroughly that the character and the listener are transported back to before the story began. This is a flashback. It can be used in storytelling, but generally it should be used sparingly because it can confuse the listener about when and where he or she is. There are flashbacks in "For Love of Miss Whiffin," where Odelle takes the listener back to when she first met John and spent part of a Sunday afternoon with him.

A storyteller has to be selective in what is included. As you learned, too much detail bogs a story down, too little makes it unclear. You should include only what is necessary to establish the framework and explain the characters' behavior.

FRAME OF REFERENCE

Why are we willing to accept a world in which disease and death have been eliminated and where no children can ever be born?

It has to do with establishing a "logical" frame of reference, one that is consistent throughout. The storyteller has created a world that is different from the one in which we live, but it follows certain "rules" or natural laws that remain in place throughout the story. In "Dr. Death," it would ruin the story to have Penelope or Rollie die of the flu because this is not possible in the world they inhabit.

Thus the audience has, as poet and critic Samuel Taylor Coleridge suggested, a "willing suspension of disbelief." The audience is willing to accept almost anything if the storyteller creates a world in which these things can exist.

If you create a world in which a great flood has destroyed a city, you cannot then go on as if the flood never occurred. The same conditions must continue to exist. If there are unicorns and trolls in the world, they must continue there unless, of course, something that the listener already knows exists in the world destroys them.

It is only when elements of the story contradict the created world or the frame of reference that they become unacceptable or unbelievable. If the idea of magic has not been established at the beginning of the story, you cannot have your protagonist suddenly solve all his problems by waving a magic wand.

Carolyn ("The Olympian") cannot suddenly become well; the narrator ("Night Walk") cannot suddenly soar above the snakes and so escape them.

"Dead Man's Corner" is an excellent example of a story that has no extraneous material and yet includes everything necessary to its understanding. It is based on a place where the author lived in Mexico. Here is the complete piece:

DEAD MAN'S CORNER
by Anne James Valdes

"Did they tell you about the dead man?" Delfina asked as she rinsed the dishes in the *apantle*, the stream flowing through the garden.

"Dead man ... here in the village? In Amatecalpan?"

"*Si, Señora Ellen.* Right here." A plump finger pointed to the stream.

Ellen imagined the current conveying a corpse and

201

depositing it, like a dog with a bone, at her feet. The shriveled face had Jeremy's square jaw, his long nose, his . . . She dropped the plate she was drying. The glazed brown clay broke into four pieces. She picked up a shard, stared for a second at a painted yellow flower, and threw the piece in the water until the flow carried it away. She had to give up. There was no mistake. Jeremy wasn't coming back. Ever. Period. Two men in military uniforms had arrived at her door. "If there is anything we can do . . ." The letter from his commanding officer . . . "Beyond the call of duty . . ." But she refused to accept his death, not until she saw his lifeless body stretched out in a coffin.

Ellen leaned back on her heels. "Where did they find it?"

"Toño found the man in the corner by the aqueduct." The older woman gestured to the wall with no change of expression, as if a corpse turning up in the garden was an everyday occurrence. Neither Delfina nor Toño, her son, were much for conversation but Ellen wondered why no one had mentioned this before.

She considered the age of the place. According to the date carved in the stone, the aqueduct bordering the property was built in the seventeenth century, long before the state of Morelos was overrun by revolutionaries in the war of 1910. This was 1970! In spite of the heat, she shivered, and brushed her arm to erase the sensation of ants crawling up her skin. Uncle Andrew had lived here for twenty years. He recounted stories about the fights for the land annexed by the hacienda. He talked of hangings and executions. The idea of the garden as a mass grave filled her with horror. Hundreds of bodies might be buried here!

She thought of other men interred in far-off places, in unmarked graves, their faces forgotten, their names unknown.

Ellen had come to Mexico three months ago. When he heard about Jeremy, Uncle Andrew invited her to visit. "A change will do you good," he wrote. Andrew

Marsh was her mother's brother. His paintings of the giant amate trees had made him famous. The critics dubbed them "Marsh's trees," and wrote about the recluse living in a remote Mexican village. The amates belong to no one, Uncle Andrew had said, refusing to reveal his whereabouts.

His invitation came as a surprise. His paintings had hung in their living room and haunted her for years. As a child she preferred them to the pictures in her fairy tale books. She climbed them in her imagination, dreaming she discovered what lay in the sky, beyond her reach. The trees possessed a force . . . something she could not grasp, a mood of mystery — relieved only by shafts of sunlight painted with gold dust.

"You are welcome to stay with me," her uncle wrote.

Ellen couldn't turn him down. She and Jeremy had met in Los Angeles at an exhibition of Andrew's paintings. "What do you think?" a voice behind her asked, and she had turned to look into his eyes, glistening like wet green leaves.

As she had with Jeremy, she fell in love with the garden at first sight. But she didn't stay in the house. She preferred to sleep in a tent near the *apantle,* lulled by the trickle of water that washed away her nightmares. It was her private oasis, her haven. She loved the timelessness of this place, the reassuring presence of the amates, the imperious nature of the aqueduct. She inhaled the clear air, observed buds form on branches and birds fly toward the trees with twigs in their beaks. Her bones lost their heaviness, her mouth watered with the aroma of freshly made *tortillas.* The sun removed the pallor from her skin, and Ellen started to write the book she had always wanted.

Delfina came, purportedly to lend her services, but Ellen suspected her real intention was to gather information about "the crazy *Sobrina* of the Señor Marsh, who sleeps in a tent, cooks on a brazier, and washes clothes and dishes in the *apantle.*" Ellen knew the villagers thought all Americans were loony, and Delfina left

203

with plenty of tales to confirm this. The exchange worked both ways. Delfina's penchant for gossip afforded Ellen with plenty of material for her writing, and her comments on the local scene were invaluable.

Ellen focused her attention on the woman beside her. "When did this happen?"

Delfina rinsed out an enamel coffee pot and put it in a big yellow plastic bowl by her side. She dried her hands, freeing them to better illustrate her story. "It was on the Day of Resurrection!" she proclaimed, a sudden oracle of revelation.

"What Day of Resurrection? What are you talking about?"

"*Ay Señora,* last week."

"Last week? But I was here last week. I heard nothing about a dead man."

"It was on Easter Sunday. You went to the city."

It sounded like an accusation, as if she should have stayed to supervise proceedings, instead of going to town to buy provisions and visit a bookstore. Ellen felt herself bristling. "Why was Toño digging up the garden?"

"No, Señora, no one was digging." Delfina seemed anxious to correct the wrong impression. "The man lay on the ground. Men from the village came and took the cadaver — together with the earth which sucked up his life. There was nothing else to do. Don't upset yourself."

So much for the dead revolutionary. This was not a soldier buried in the dust of history. Again she saw Jeremy, his body blown open, gasping for breath, dying . . . alone.

Ellen grabbed Delfina's arm. "Who was he?"

"*Quien sabe, Señora . . .* Who knows . . ." Delfina's eyes widened, surprised by Ellen's concern. She raised her hands to heaven as if she expected God himself to offer an answer. "The *Presidente Municipal* asked around but no one knew him. A drunk. The priest came to bless the body with holy oils. He was buried in the cemetery and covered with the same soil stained with his blood. We all attended the funeral and prayed for his soul."

Ellen fought for control. The midday heat was oppressive. The world turned round and round until east became west, and the past collided with the present. She splashed her face with water from the stream.

"Are you all right?" Delfina asked.

"*Sí*. I want to know what happened. ¿Que pasó?"

"He fell off the wall. *Usted sabe* ... He had a lot to drink celebrating the day our Lord arose from the dead. He must have been at a cantina in San Andrés, but no one knew him there. In San Andrés, the aqueduct is low. Perhaps he wanted to cool himself and decided to wade along the canal. Then he made a wrong turn." Delfina blessed herself, intended no doubt to keep her from making a similar mistake. "Instead of going straight, he crossed onto the wall covered with broken glass. His condition had him confused in the head." She shrugged. Ellen knew this attitude was due to the woman's fatalistic nature, not to a lack of compassion.

"He must have slipped and cut himself," Delfina said. "His thigh was slit, the blood all over ..." Her hand moved up and down, her palm turned outward like a paintbrush against the wall. "The soil soaked it up but still a puddle formed, so big was the wound. When I first saw the man ..." Delfina grimaced. "I thought someone had attacked him with a machete."

Ellen closed her eyes. She heard his drunken pleas mingle with the hum of crickets on a moonless night. She saw the man on the damp ground, blood oozing through the gash in his leg, winding towards the crystal stream. Its coppery smell filled her nostrils, mixed with the sweet, pungent odor of jasmine, *huele de noche* they called it here — night smell. Her wet hands felt sticky and images of Jeremy replaced those of the man.

"How did they find him?" Her voice was softer now.

"Toño was sweeping the leaves. He works so hard,

205

even on Sundays and holidays. Such a good boy . . ." Delfina never missed an opportunity to elaborate on her son's qualifications.

"Yes, yes. I know. So what happened?"

"The man lay here all night, half conscious. When Toño found him at seven in the morning, he was still breathing."

"What did Toño do?"

"He went for a beer."

"A beer? A beer? You mean to say he left the man lying here, bleeding to death, and went for a beer?"

"Si, Señora, but not for himself. For the man."

Ellen shook her head. She was at a loss.

"You see, Señora, he had lost a lot of blood. He was dry . . . thirsty. The beer made him happy. He left this world with a smile on his face. Is there a better way?"

In spite of herself, Ellen smiled. She couldn't think of an answer. It wasn't, after all, an unpleasant picture. "Did he say anything?"

"*No, Señora*. He sipped the beer. I think he was grateful. Toño told the people at the store about the man and the priest came to hear his confession. But he was too late." A frown creased Delfina's forehead. "You're not angry?"

"No, of course not."

"Toño was careful to clean everything. I helped him."

Ellen walked to the corner where the aqueduct and the wall met. Bamboo concealed part of the stone but the top was visible, imbedded with fragments of colored glass to keep intruders out. Ellen discerned a few russet spots on the surface. Blood . . . or something else? The ground showed no sign of disturbance. But after a week, during the dry season, dust covered everything. As far as she could tell, nothing had happened here.

Ellen stared at the spot where she imagined the

man had died. Jeremy lay there, his eyes closed, the corners of his lips turned up the way they did when he listened to Bach, or when she read a passage from Shelley's "The Cloud": "I bring fresh showers for the thirsting flowers, from the seas and the streams . . ." Sometimes she thought he had fallen asleep, until he opened his eyes and looked at her, and she remembered the first time they met and the leaves in her uncle's paintings of the amate trees.

"Where does Toño keep the gardening tools?" She went back and asked Delfina.

"*Allá* . . ." Delfina pointed to an adobe hut with half the roof missing. Under a rat-eaten canvas, Ellen found a shovel. She walked around looking for a sapling. When she found one, she took great care to unearth it.

"Come with me," she directed Delfina.

Delfina followed Ellen across the garden to the corner where the dead man was found. There, Ellen dug a hole and planted the sapling.

"May you and I find peace," she said.

She caught the puzzled expression on the other woman's face. Just a moment of silence, she thought. It was time to let go, time to say good-bye.

The man had died in the right place.

Mostly, we've talked about plotting stories, but, as you know, you can choose to tell a story from your own background, one that does not have a plot. This can be just a reminiscence. You don't have to tell a story with other characters or a made-up plot. Many of the most successful and the most entertaining stories are taken from real life.

This can be a funny happening, or one that affected you strongly in some way. Family stories are of this sort, and often they are just as interesting to an audience. Most often they do build to some sort of climax, but they don't have to.

An example of two types of remembrance follows. They are much different from each other but both could be told to an audience.

SURPRISE PARTY

Mom had a surprise party for me on my birthday. I was seventeen. She sent me to my friend Rick's house to ask if he'd like to go out to dinner and then to a movie to help celebrate. When I was gone, the other kids came to the house. All my friends from school.

Rick and I walked into the living room, and everyone yelled, "Surprise." Then we went to the grove out back to build a fire for a wiener roast, and I started to open my presents. We heard a loud crash and ran to the highway. There was a car in the field up the hill. We ran to see if we could help. The car had crashed through a barbed-wire fence and lay on its roof. A man screamed, "My legs! Oh, my God, my legs!" He was on the driver's side, and someone sat beside him. The roof was crumpled, and we couldn't tell anything about the other person, just that his chest was covered with blood.

Someone said that maybe we should try to get the two men out because the car might explode. Rick said maybe we should wait for an ambulance. Then the driver started to cry. "Please, fellows," he said. "Oh, God, please." So Bob said we should place ourselves around the car, and he called out, "One, two, three, lift."

I was on the passenger side, and oh, God, this guy was lying there with his head against the roof. And his head was cut off, hanging from a little bit of skin in back. I started to puke and choke, but somehow I held onto the car. A couple of my friends pulled the other man out. His legs were smashed and twisted all weird-like. Someone ran to call an ambulance, and we all went back home, except for Bob who said he'd wait till the ambulance came.

We were all sitting around in the living room, not talking or anything. And one of the girls — Sally, I think it was — said that since the fire was going good out back, we might as well have our wiener roast. So we all went out there and tried not to think about the guys up in the field.

We sat around the fire, and it was almost dark, and we tried to pretend that nothing had happened. It's almost a year now, and I can still see this guy's head just hanging there, and the blood — And I'll always remember my seventeenth birthday.

CAMPING

When I was four years old, my parents and I went camping for six weeks one summer on my grandfather's farm. We slept in a tent; my dad built an outside toilet with poles and burlap bags. He built a table and other things as well. This was in what my grandfather called the sugar woods, a wonderful, magical place with tall maple trees and a thick carpet of leaves and no undergrowth.

Once during those six weeks, I was wearing shorts and a maroon short sleeve shirt and suddenly felt something wet on my shoulder. Bird poop! At about the same time I remember wondering that if I swallowed watermelon seeds if a watermelon would grow inside me, much like I was told things could grow in my ears if I left them dirty.

In the sugar woods and on down toward my grandfather's house ran a cold, cold stream. Here we kept things that normally would be refrigerated. Milk, fruit, fresh water. We also bathed in it — brrr — till the skin tingled. I remember looking down stream and seeing Ivory soap scum and bubbles float by.

My dad would leave in the evenings to teach music; at other times my Grandma and Grandpa Spahn would come for a visit and would bring something special to eat, like teaberry ice cream.

Once in the tent where we slept on cots, I became tangled up in the bedding and slipped between the cot and the side of the tent where I became wedged. I was terrified because this was all mixed up with a dream that I was caught and held somewhere.

Another time just my dad and my mother's cousin

and I were sleeping in the tent. I don't know where my mother was. Anyhow the cousin woke up with a kitten sitting on his chest and licking his nose.

It was a wonderful time, eternal, as only a summer or half a summer can be to a kid that age. I knew it would never, never end . . . and yet it did.

ACTIVITIES

1. Choose one of the ideas you began to develop in an earlier chapter and develop the plot using one of the methods discussed at the beginning of the chapter. Plan out the story and present it to the class. It should be about three or four minutes long.

2. Listen to the stories your classmates tell. Then with the rest of the classes, critique what the person has done. Is the story well planned or well plotted? What makes you think so? Is there any extraneous material that could or should be cut? Has the storyteller established and maintained a consistent frame of reference?

3. Think of a setting and from it develop a framework for a story. Don't work out a plotline or complete characters. Now trade papers with someone and using that person's framework, do an outline or summary of a story.

4. Think of a personal experience that you think might make an interesting story to tell to the class. Then develop the story and tell it.

5. What do you think is Ellen's goal in "Dead Man's Corner?" What is her life's goal? Discuss your answer with the rest of the class. Did anyone come up with different goals?

6. Split into groups of three to five people. Now take one of the stories in the book or one that you find elsewhere, and analyze it in terms of:
   a. whether a logical framework was established.
   b. whether there is anything extraneous.
   c. whether the story proceeds logically from start to finish.
   d. whether you think anything could be added to make the story more interesting.

e. whether everything was carefully foreshadowed.

f. in what ways, if any, the world of the story is different from the world in which you live.

7. Figure out a theme, something you believe in strongly, and build a story around it. The story should be three to five minutes. Then have the class try to figure out the theme.

CHAPTER TEN

METHODS OF COMMUNICATING IDEAS

There are different methods of presenting information in a story.

LITERARY VOICE

The one that probably is the most elusive is what is called "literary voice" or simply "voice." This does not refer to the teller's use of tone quality or resonators. Rather it is tied in to point of view, and is the *style* in which a story is presented. For instance, compare these passages:

From **The Music of His Horn**

From somewhere deep inside, Martin pulled forth the courage to risk her anger, to ask Helen, "Can I have a brother?"

"I almost died when I had you," Helen told him. "It could happen again. Do you want me to die? Because if you do . . ."

An ant crawled across the edge of the newspaper.

"Look at me, Martin."

"I don't want a brother," he whispered as the ant crawled down the leg of the table.

From **The Barn**

It came in flashes, bits of memory, incoherent, a disconnected film. He never knew when it would happen — while he was driving home from the office, working in his yard, meeting with a client.

By now, in his fifty-eighth year, he'd be-

come used to it, told himself it didn't matter. A person was what he was; only the present and the future were important. Vern felt proud that he wasn't like some of his friends who prattled on about "the good old days."

From **Beyond the Seventh Day**

In the beginning created I, and stood amidst nothingness and thought infinitesimal fragments of space/time, rending and tearing away a layer of my skin.

Ripped and flayed, fallen around my feet, the skin, whisked by a joyful breeze, became all living things. Wishing to behold this phenomenon, I thought eyes and perceived that I stood on a gentle knoll in tendrils of mist.

Voice refers to the tone, the way in which something is said. We can immediately tell that the narrators in the three excerpts are vastly different from each other. Without being told, we know that the first is a young boy. How can we tell this? He's nervous about asking his mother for a brother. After his mother answers, the boy tries to disassociate himself from what is happening by paying attention to the ant. This and the way he whispers to Helen that he doesn't want a brother tells us he is sad or maybe defeated.

The voice is the personality of the writing, and, is closely tied to point of view and to dialog.

How is the first passage different from the second in voice or tone? What can we tell about the narrator in the second excerpt? Even if the character's age weren't given, we would know that he is much older than the boy in the first excerpt. We can also tell that something is bothering him, though being the sort of person he is, he tries to push it aside. Like Martin, he is trying to disassociate himself from whatever it is. We can tell that he tries to convince himself that he's a no-nonsense sort of person, who won't give in to his problems. He's stubborn and possibly a loner, who tells himself that the past doesn't matter. This isolates him even more from others.

The third excerpt is totally different from the first two. In this story, which is a science fiction tale about time travel, the narrator has lost his mind because he was sent too far back in time — to the very beginning of creation. He becomes confused and thinks he is the one who created the world, rather than God's doing it. Actually, when this scene takes place, he is in the psychiatric ward of a government hospital. You can easily tell that he is mentally disturbed by the way he speaks. He uses English, but his syntax is weird, and although you can figure out the meaning of each sentence, overall he doesn't make much sense.

The *voice* should be consistent with the character. You shouldn't have a boy like Martin sounding old or experienced, nor, on the other hand, should Vern come across sounding like a little boy.

For your own stories, you should have analyzed the character in detail so that you have him or her pretty well in mind. And remember that most often, the narrator has the same sort of voice as one of the characters. Usually, it is the central character, the protagonist, who is telling the story, but this isn't always the case. The narrator in "Pecos Bill and the Rattlesnake" really is a secondary character. Pecos is the more important character because the story is "about" him.

On the other hand, Millie is both the central character and the narrator in "Beneath the Ice Cold Moon." She is uneducated and in ways very naive. This has to come across in the way she tells the story. That's why she sometimes uses very simple sentences and has errors in grammar.

Sometimes the narrator stands entirely outside the realm of the story. This is the case for instance with fables. But usually when a story is told this way, the listener cannot identify with it as much. Compare the following excerpt from Aesop to the three other excerpts:

From **The Travelers and the Bear**

Two friends were walking down the road together when they met up with a bear.

One of the friends, greatly afraid and not

thinking at all of his companion, climbed up into a tree to hide.

The other, seeing what had happened and knowing he alone was no match for the bear, threw himself down on the ground and feigned death for he had heard that a bear will not touch a dead body.

As you can see, there is no close identification with any of the characters because the "voice" used precludes that from happening. It is easy to assume then that the story has an entirely different purpose than to involve the listener. The characters do not matter as such; rather, it is the lesson to be learned from the fable that is important.

POINT OF VIEW

Closely related to "literary voice" is point of view. In the following, it is very easy to see that the story is told from inside Diann Johnson's head. She is the one who wrote the journal entries, so she is the one through whose eyes we view the world created by the story.

From The Experiment

Excerpts from the journal of Diann Johnson:

10 September 1998

I am one of the homeless picked up by the government, and I'm frightened. There are stories about genetic experiments, terrible things.

I hope my husband is okay, and my daughter.

12 September 1998

I was a professor with a Ph.D. in theatre but refused to direct propagandistic plays. I never thought of myself as an activist; I just wanted to be left alone. But I couldn't go against my conscience.

216

The type of story often determines the point of view. Tall tales, as you learned, usually are told from the viewpoint of someone who is observing what the protagonist does. The narrator isn't necessarily standing apart from the story, but rather is to a degree involved. He is part of the world in which the story exists. On the other hand, the narrator for fables and most fairy tales stands completely apart, as if not belonging to the world of the story at all. We can tell nothing about the narrator at all in the fable excerpt.

A story generally is shown and told from only one point of view or perspective. In choosing the point of view character, remember that the character's personality will color the perspective with which he or she views the world. If you were to tell about the confrontation between Martin and his mother from the mother's point of view, it would be a totally different story. It would be the way she viewed the situation, showing why she reacts as she does to the boy's wanting a brother.

You can use an omniscient point of view, which means that the narrator is all-seeing or can get inside everyone's head. But this tends to be confusing for the audience, and also there is no one with whom either the teller or the listener can identify.

You may want to use the omniscient point of view for the sake of humor. "When she climbed the stairs to Mr. Ivanhoe's office, little did poor Sarah know what she was letting herself in for. Mr. Ivanhoe was a knave and liked nothing better than to cheat young women of their savings. He waited above, anticipating the poor girl's appearance."

Of course, this is melodramatic, really a kind of parody. As you can tell, besides seeing into everyone's mind, the omniscient point of view lets the teller step outside the story and make comments about the characters and upcoming events.

As you saw with the fables, another point of view is that of the observer/narrator. An advantage is that this narrator can be more objective about the action and the characters. But, as you can see, this point of view distances the audience from the story.

An audience already is once removed. They stand apart

from the story and only hear it. The narrator/observer takes them even further away. Since the narrator does not "feel" what is happening, neither, of course, does the audience.

Yet this point of view can work when the narrator's purpose is to point out something the central character cannot see himself, such as a personality defect. In the following, the narrator, who stands outside the main character, sees that he has a blind spot in not being able to recognize how people feel about him:

From **Family Man**

I felt sorry for Ned. He never could see that a lot of people loved him. It was as if he completely blanked out any behaviors that showed love. This happened when his business failed. He blamed himself for the trouble he brought on his family because of it and didn't see that to them it didn't really matter. I remember just after it happened. I was visiting Nellie when Ned came home that night.

Nellie immediately knew something was wrong. "Ned?" she said going toward him.

"It's finished, Nell. Everything we've worked for. Gone."

"What do you mean?" She stood and threw her arms around his neck.

"The business. The bank's foreclosing. The creditors . . . God, Nellie, I never wanted this to happen."

"It doesn't matter," she said.

"Doesn't matter! It's what I worked for, spent my whole life doing. And you say it doesn't matter."

"We have each other. We have the children. Don't you see that I love you, Ned?"

It was like he hadn't heard, like he wouldn't recognize that he stood apart from his

business failure, that he was still a man. Still my sister's husband. Still the father of his two kids. I doubt he even heard the words. A few weeks later he was gone. He wrote me a letter later. I don't know why; we weren't that close. But he said he could read the contempt in everyone's eyes.

Nellie wrote to him, even went to see him. Maybe because he was an utter failure in his own eyes, he felt he was in everyone else's as well.

Here the narrator is a part of what is happening, but is able to back away from it and report on it. He sees Ned's continued deterioration, despite the fact that Nellie still loves him and doesn't blame him for the business failure. This is an effective way of showing something a character couldn't see by himself.

You can also tell a story from more than one viewpoint. As you know, this is the case with "Mutant" where alternate sections are shown from alternate points of view. This shows that there are two sides to something; that each views the world differently and each is valid. Milt needs to care for himself and his family, and so does Pierre. For this reason, Pierre needs to escape.

The most common point of view to use is that of the protagonist. He or she sees, hears, feels and reacts to everything. Because of the protagonist's background, he or she views the world in a certain way, different from that of anyone else. Helen, in "The Music of His Horn," certainly would view the world differently than would Martin.

You also need to consider whether to tell the story from first or third person point of view. (You can use second person, but often it's jarring because you're asking the audience to imagine they are engaging in some action: You are sneaking through the living room, afraid you'll awaken the killer. You feel a tightness in your chest . . .) Most often, it doesn't matter a great deal whether a story is told from first or third person. In your own stories do whatever you feel most comfortable doing.

219

The biggest advantage of the first person point of view is that it can sound more intimate. That is, the audience is not quite so distanced. If you empathize with the "first person" from whose perspective the story is told, you feel closer to the character.

There are disadvantages. It can sound unnatural or egotistical for first person characters to describe themselves accurately. Also, you cannot describe how a first person character looks, that is, facial expression and so on. If you are the first person narrator, you can actually show the facial expressions to the audience. You have to weigh one thing against the other.

With third person point of view you can describe more objectively, but then you are talking about someone outside of yourself, and this distances the listener from the character. First person point of view can establish an intimacy with the audience, and have them identify more closely with the teller.

Take some of the stories from the book and see what would happen if you changed from first person to third person point of view and vice versa. How does this, for instance, change "Pecos Bill and the Rattlesnake"?

DIALOG

The dialog you use in a story has to be natural to the character, that is, it has to reflect background, personality and the current situation. But it also has to be "natural" for you the storyteller. You have to feel comfortable with it. This depends somewhat on your personality. One person may be able to do a Scottish dialect very well, while another not only wouldn't be able to do it, but would be very inhibited about trying. So when you develop a story and characters to fit into the story, you need to keep both the characters and yourself in mind.

Go back over the stories in the book and figure out what sorts of things the dialog is implying. For instance, what can you tell about the following dialog from "The Flight of the Niños"?

"You too?" Eduardo said. "You are flying. I

myself have never flown before. I find it a little bit frightening."

First, you should be able to tell that the rhythm of the dialog is suggestive of Spanish. It is a little bit more formal than the English language. You can also tell that Eduardo doesn't want to admit that he really is afraid of flying.

Or from **Beneath the Ice Cold Moon**

"You ain't afraid of me, are you? I don't bite."

This dialog shows that Arnie is uneducated, just like Millie. In the context of the scene where he says this, he also probably has a high opinion of himself and is egotistical enough to know Millie won't turn him down.

For the most part, this sort of thing develops naturally if you actually put yourself into the character's shoes, if you immerse yourself in the persona. Yet you do need to be careful that there are no slips, that the dialog is consistent with the character's personality.

There are, of course, a lot of different things that determine how a person speaks. When you meet someone for the first time, you can often tell a lot by the way the person talks. Hints about schooling, geographic origin, cultural background and personality can be revealed in dialog. You often can tell the type of job a person has by the use of jargon.

Just as important, you can tell how a person is feeling — sad, depressed, happy, and so on. People who are frustrated or angry often speak in choppier sentences than do people in quieter moods.

Dialog in a story also has to get to the point more quickly than does conversation. It can't change direction too quickly or so often as conversation sometimes does, and it has to be more condensed or selective. Each line and word of dialog should have meaning. For instance:

"Am I failing to see some obvious humor?" Alicia asked with a hint of a pout. A pout,

**for God's sake. She was more than eighty
earthly years old. Why would she still want to
swell those cherry lips like a girl's? Well, it was
only a minor thing after all, and in every other
way, she'd always been more mature in outlook
than he.**

**"No, my beautiful one," he said, "it's just
good to be alive."**

**"Alive! Everyone knows your views,
Cecil."**

**"Cecil, is it? Now what would make you
mad enough to call me Cecil?"**

"Ceece, then, is that better?"

We know even without being told that in the first line,
Alicia is resentful (pouty). We can tell also by Ceece's next
line that he is feeling, at the least, contentment and perhaps
even anticipation or happiness.

When Alicia says, "Alive! Everyone knows your views,
Cecil," we understand that she is being argumentative. We
also can pretty much tell that the characters are not young by
their choice of words and the way they put the sentences together. This is particularly apparent in Cecil's line: "Cecil, is
it? Now what would make you mad enough to call me Cecil?"
It's also apparent that he is just a little bit patronizing.

EXPOSITION

Exposition is any information necessary for the listener's
understanding of a story. It's this sort of thing you have to
take into consideration when constructing the world in which
the story exists, the framework.

Background Exposition

As you learned, "story" includes the characters' entire
lives up to the point where the plot begins. These "lives" are
exposition. Often, it is enough to suggest certain things about
a character without going into great detail. When we say something like, "He was the son of a man and woman who had

222

helped colonize Mars," we can know almost immediately that this is a science fiction tale and that it takes place in the future. The storyteller doesn't then have to spell this out.

But the exposition does have to include any prior events and conditions that have a bearing on what happens within the space of the story, on the "given circumstances" (the way things are now in the world of the story), on personality traits and on the relationships among the characters. Going on with the science fiction idea, "He was a moody lad, not fitted to a life of exploration. There were those who argued that he should be gotten rid of immediately. Yet his parents loved him, his peers for the most part tolerated him, and his enemies despised him."

Right away you are introduced to a young male (a lad) who for some reason isn't suited to life on Mars. Some people feel strongly about him, which seems to suggest that there will be a clash between him and them. On the other hand, some of his relationships are not so bad (love; tolerance). Yet there are enemies who apparently are going to cause big problems.

Earlier you learned that in creating the world or framework you shouldn't include anything that isn't important to the story. If being on Mars isn't important, why mention it? If the character is never going to come into conflict with his enemies, they shouldn't be mentioned.

Here is an example of background exposition that was not necessary at the beginning of the story but which was important later on:

> **She walked to him and drew him to an ancient sofa against the far wall. "It's been condemned, don't you understand? We leave them alone; the People all agreed."**
>
> **"And you agree too, do you?"**
>
> **"Oh, Ceece." She closed her eyes and sat unmoving, bringing a stab of regret to his heart. When he saw her like that, it was brought home anew how he and she and the other People truly were separate from those whose pulses throbbed**

inside their breasts. For the most part, he agreed that the People could no longer be tied to what they once were. Yet he couldn't help feeling a tinge of sorrow at the passing of those who'd once been dear to him. At least, he mused, the closest ones had lived long lives.

Gradually, like the rest of the People, Ceece and Alicia, through necessity, had abandoned families and friends. Thank the saints, they'd at least had each other, unlike most People who transmogrified all alone.

Progressive Exposition

There is a second type of exposition. Whereas the first includes anything that the listener needs to know before the opening of the story, the "progressive exposition" refers to the changing situation and involves character revelation. For example, we can see a change taking place in Penelope Eddyns here:

She hadn't been out of the house in months except to buy groceries; there was no need, and she had no place to go. The friends she and Lewis had cultivated during their twenty years of marriage had gradually drifted away. She truly had become a pariah.

It was early spring, a hint of California winter still in the air. She grabbed a cardigan from the hall closet and threw it across her shoulders. Deviating from her usual custom, she wore heels and a dress, pale yellow with a pattern of fall leaves. She wondered at her motives, if the dress was really for Rollie's sake.

Penelope is acting differently now because things are changing; she's going to see Rollie. This is an example of progressive exposition because Penelope is going out for the first time in a long time, and "deviating from her usual custom," she's dressing up. This signifies that her mood and general state are undergoing a change.

It is better to weave exposition throughout the story. If you gave the background all at once, the story would get bogged down. If you told everything about a character right away, the audience probably would not stay interested because they'd already know everything you could tell them. For instance:

The kids were already twelve and thirteen before I finished graduate school and took a job at a little college in New Jersey. So what with paying back student loans and finance companies to whom we'd gone into hock, things were awfully tight those first few years. We had to make every penny count. *(Here there is only one paragraph about "general conditions" of the characters' world.)*

Just before school started, Julie took Bobbie and Andrea shopping and by hitting all the sales outfitted them on a little more than $300. *(This brings us almost up to the present.)*

I'd had a tech assistantship in theatre, so all through grad school I wore grubbies and hadn't a tie or white shirt to my name. I had to hit the sales too. There were weeks of little more than packed peanut butter sandwiches I ate in my office for lunch and Hamburger Helper for dinner. *(This tells more about the current situation.)*

The second day of school Bobbie came home, refusing to wear her "ape shoes." *(This goes right into moving the story forward.)*

Bits and pieces of exposition appear in other places:

Julie sat in the living room watching a PBS program on Zaire. I was at my computer in the alcove by the bay window trying to convert my notes on the acting book into interesting exercises. *(This last sentence, although occurring in the present, gives background on the father's occupation. You can assume that he's a theatre prof*

225

who is in the midst of writing an acting book.)

"What do you mean?" Julie asked. She stood and snapped off the TV set.

Andrea, a year older, came in, tossed her books on the hall table and threw a disgusted look at Bobbie. *(This moves the story forward and also provides progressive exposition, especially about Andrea.)*

"I told you once about how I felt wearing the oufits Mom made me. Different from the other kids' dresses." She turned back. "I can't make her wear those shoes." *(This is important to the plot, but also refers to long-ago conditions, when the mother was a girl.)*

It can help as you're developing a story to write out all the exposition that you think necessary. Then when you do your outline of the story, figure out which pieces of exposition are important that the audience knows at the beginning of the story, before the end of the second scene and so on. But be sure that if it's something that has a bearing on the whole story — like space travel in the science fiction story that takes place on Mars — be sure that you include this near the beginning, or the reader will feel cheated. You can't suddenly have the boy in the science fiction story escape his enemies by leaping through time unless you've established early on that time travel does indeed exist.

A lot of exposition had to be worked into the following story to develop the character, to establish the framework, and to make the ending convincing. This is different from the other two stories by Bill Jarosin because it takes a more serious tone.

UNDER THE HOUSE
by Bill Jarosin

The drains were clogged — no doubt about it. Sinks filled with streaked gray water. Plunger didn't work, neither did Drain-O; ditto the little plumber's snake he'd

bought once at Thrifty Drug Store. Paul'd just have to go under the house and pull the pipes apart himself.

He hated to do it, knew his wife could fix it. Martha enjoyed that kind of thing, but she was at work, and the water was backing up in the bathroom, making little smelly rivulets down the outside of the tub. At least it was no surprise; this had been happening off and on for a month, and Martha had asked him to handle it, since he worked at home. But this wasn't a good time: three articles to write, another very important one for *Gourmet Magazine* waiting, a torn typewriter ribbon, and no place to wash his hands.

He took his arms out of the sink's scummy water, straightened his back, looked at the reflections of his lined face in the bathroom mirror, knew his worry showed — his fear about the kidnappings that had occurred during the past month in the neighborhood. He looked at his watch — one hour until Barb was out of school. He'd meet her, walk her home . . . the Johnson's kid was gone, two others before that, and Jimmy next door was taken last week on his way to a little league game.

Paul scrunched his nose, stuck his finger as far as he could down the narrow pipe, wiggled it around searching for wads of hair or other stuff, felt a suction. There was a loud vibration in the metal, then a strong one, hard. He lost his balance, yanked his hand out. The water slurped down the pipe, then coughed back, blacker, fouler.

He wiped his hands on a coffee-stained shirt, pulled on his shoes, and grabbed the metal flashlight. He stomped heavily through the bedroom, across the living room to the front door, and down the slope beside the house. He stopped momentarily, wiped his hands on his pants, looked at the home's sagging foundation. He was surprised he hadn't noticed it before, wondered if a little paint would hide it. After all, the house is old, he thought as he continued down the hill. Not like the surrounding homes: ticky-tacky concrete slab things built on lots where Victorians once stood. How could those people ever fix a clogged pipe without a crawl space, he wondered.

Paul slid on the unmown grass at the rear of the house. He stepped around the bare spots under the avocado tree, avoiding the mud puddles left from the previous night's rain. Because of the sloping lot, the crawl space here was as tall as a man. Paul stepped to the narrow door, the only opening in the shingled lower wall.

The door's green paint was cracked, black at spots with mold. He had opened the door only once before, when he and Martha had bought the house two years ago. There had been room enough for storage, he remembered, although the earth floor discouraged that. He'd put a clasp and combination lock on the door and then forgotten it.

But now the lock was gone, the missing hasp outlined on splintered wood; the door was pushed open. The late-afternoon clouds cast shadows across the doorway; inside it was black.

He turned the flashlight on, wondering if the old batteries would work. They did. He moved the narrow beam across the timber posts and joists that crisscrossed above a jungle of pipes, which in turn rose over a sharp slope of the earth floor to a ledge two and a half feet below the oak-slat flooring. The pipes ran on into the dark, but the flashlight couldn't penetrate their tangled limbs. Paul played the light over rust and mold, thought he heard a faint scratching somewhere off in the general area of the bathroom, where the pipes would end. Probably just metal expanding after a cold night, he thought.

He stepped further inside, away from the door, and turned the flashlight towards the largest pipe, followed it along the underside of a timber to its hole in the exterior wall. He pushed a finger through. The rotted pine wood crumbled, sap sticking to the back of his hand.

Paul turned around, found the main sewer line and

228

its tar-filled cast iron fittings. Old, he thought, pre-1920 at least. He walked along the pipe to the dirt ledge, judged the metal's diameter to be six inches at this point. The kitchen pipe tied in here; he'd have to crawl to the end of the ledge then scoot in around and work back to the main sewer line. The far corner under the bathroom was twenty feet away in a straight line, maybe fifty on a diagonal. He pulled himself around an iron elbow. The metal groaned, clunked, and shimmied down the line. Just like a cave near the ocean, he thought, all sounds rhythmic, in perfect sync.

He laid on his back and pushed himself twenty feet. An eight-by-twelve-inch timber blocked his progress. He edged his way along, then around, the length of Douglas fir. The door was no longer visible behind him; the flashlight sent a narrow beam ahead along the underside of the floor. He touched the wood, figured he was probably under the bedroom, then noticed long scratches cut deep across the grain, some narrow and almost one-half-inch deep. They were in patches here, and in two other places further up the ledge toward the far corner under the bathroom. He turned the flashlight back towards the door. Couldn't be sure, but the pipe hubs on this side glistened. He reached out, scooted over. Sticky, but not sap, more watery. There was no flow trail down the pipe, and no water was evident, not a leak. Again he saw scratches, small ones on the metal, very bright, not rusted and black like the old pipes. He turned the flashlight ahead, couldn't see any stub-out with the square cap that meant he'd found the sewer cleanout. The far corner was still hidden by several bends of pipe.

He crawled another five feet. It smelled like skunks. He scrunched his nose. No, it was far worse.

Beads of sweat lined his eyes; he wondered if this was worth the trouble. Then he thought of Martha, giggling at him, small hand grabbing a wrench and bounding out the door. He sighed, grasped the pipe and pulled himself forward. The light flickered, glanced off a wet, slick patch of earth, then died. Paul shook the flashlight, but it didn't help. He stuck his hand around the corner, felt the cleanout was open, the plug on the dirt. He pulled his hand back, grabbed the end of the flashlight, stuck it up the hole. It went in, clanked, metal on metal.

He shook the flashlight, rattled it inside the hollow pipe . . . nothing. He leaned back and sighed. No clog. Something stung his back. He jumped, hit the pipe in front of him, turned his head. A large green eye closed. Paul shot past the cleanout. A sharp pain laced his ankle. He hit the wooden foundation at the end of the house, turned himself sideways, and fell in a hole. The flashlight, still tight in his hand, flickered, lit the severed bathroom pipe, it's cut end submerged in a dark pool. Around it were shreds of fabric, bone, a baseball glove with its amputated hand still inside.

The flashlight died again. Paul heard heavy steps above. He opened his mouth to yell. A thick ooze shot from the dark, glazed his mouth, lips, ears. He grabbed his face, tried to scrape the stuff away, pulled off half the skin between his nose and ear. Pain arched down his neck. He clutched the flashlight with the other hand, shook it hard. A beam glanced off a pipe into the dark. A thick, low scream rattled the pipes, penetrated his clogged ears. A black object scuttled backwards. And again the flashlight went out.

He pushed himself further into the hole, kicked backwards, forced himself onto the downwardly inclined tunnel. Something grabbed his shoe, held; a vine slithered around his legs, then let go. He screamed through the glue, kicked the flashlight, pushed himself down the hole. It turned more sharply downward, then opened, turned down more. He slipped, fell, shot forward, and hit a pool of mucus-laced mud.

A minute passed, or two. His feet were entangled in a web-like strand. One hand glued to shreds of skin, he reached with the other to untangle the knots. His arm caught, held fast in the thin, sticky ropes. He needed the flashlight, it had fallen behind him, lay now with a dull yellow glow. It shone on wood shavings and small wrinkled sacs, black and shiny, with numeral-like markings raised in mole-sized welts. The nearest sac was pulsing. Paul pulled his head back, the sac split; a thin wire shot out, laced Paul's nose, which slid to the dirt in a pool of blood. Above, an earthquake of moans; a thick iridescent green limb fell, shattering the flashlight. Legs straddled Paul's body, squeezing him, bending inward, lowering a boulder set with a radiant eye, and a warm long needle entered his stomach. Sap fell over his eyes, his nostrils, trickled down his throat, then a sharper slicing above his heart; phlegm sputtered from the hole in Paul's chest.

Martha looked at the clog — streaks of black and red. She sighed, pulled the plumber's snake out of the closet, and went out to the back of the house. She stepped around the mud, over the trodden grass, found the narrow door. She pushed it open, thankful it wasn't locked.

DESCRIPTION

One type of exposition is description. It can be used for both characters and settings. This too should be woven in because it can bog down a story, particularly a story that is meant to be told rather than read silently.

As you learned, in an oral story, the description should be sharp and concise. In the following, the descriptive words and phrases are italicized:

From **Death by Stages**

Will Shakespeare stared into the mirror at *a face with furrows deep as ditches, pink scalp sticking through wisps of silken hair.* He raised the beaker to his lips and drank. Immediately, the image began to alter into more familiar patterns. No matter how often he went through it, he heaved a sigh of relief with the return of the more familiar self.

Colley Cibber burst through the door.

Will looked over his shoulder. "Why are you always in such a hurry?" he chided.

231

"Dick Burbage of the Duke's Men cannot change back."

Will spun around.

"Tonight Dick played Macbeth and now cannot become himself. His body refuses to alter."

Beads of sweat broke out on Will's forehead. He turned back to the glass. Gone was all trace of King Lear. Before him stood a handsome man in his early thirties. Will closed his eyes and sighed.

"The damned experiments never should have been started in the first place," Cibber said. *Twenty-five years old with a pudgy body and an unctuous voice,* he was an anomaly. All other actors, so far as Will knew, were able to change to the standard roles using formulas that had been determined a hundred years earlier. Cibber's body wouldn't alter. Will had seen him try the potions, but they never worked.

Immediately, with only a line or so, you get a picture of Will Shakespeare in the role of King Lear. With the sweat breaking out, you have a strong image of a man experiencing fear. Later, in just a few words you get an unflattering image of Colley Cibber. There are other descriptive words, but not meant as strong images — the mirror, the beaker, the door and so on. They are stronger as exposition than imagery, though, of course, when you read them, you can't help but get a mental image of the setting. In the following there is much more description — most of the excerpt in fact — but it raises questions that the listener certainly would want answered, and it gives a lot of background exposition while moving the story forward.

From **Mind Swap**

Tomashi Jones stopped singing, *grabbed the neck of his silver-stringed lute and thrust the instrument high above his head. There it trembled and shook, as if fought for by opposing and invisible forces.*

"Aaaagh!" he screamed. "I cannot. I cannot." He *lowered the lute to a small table beside his coat and strapped it into place.* He *punched a tape* and *soothing sounds of a vast organ* filled the *void of his prison sphere.*

Tears oozed from the corners of his eyes, and in the near-zero gravity of the cell became expanding crystals on either side of his nose. He shook his head. The tears, whisked from his cheeks by the movement, broke into tiny droplets, sparkling like diamonds in the diffused lighting. Quickly, the satellite's *recycling system sucked them into the duct-like passageways in the wall* where they would be treated, purified and emptied into Tomashi's drinking supply.

Some stories can better use more description than others.

NARRATION

A good story should be a combination of "showing" and "telling." Showing refers to placing the audience in the midst of the action, such as occurs in the last two examples. Telling or narration is equally as important because there are times the audience should know about what is happening to the characters, but the events are not important enough to know in detail.

The best stories are a blending of the showing and telling. The first part of the following excerpt is narration because it would be tedious and boring to go through what happened to Tomashi during the entire time he was kept imprisoned. It is only when something different or significant happens that the piece goes from telling to showing.

From **Mind Swap**

For days they held him in a damp, musty cell, his only furniture a three-legged stool in one dark corner and on the floor a filthy pallet,

233

filled with straw. At first, Tomashi had been fearful of falling asleep because of the skittering of rats each night. But need had outweighed caution. His only constant was the monotony of having nothing to do and little contact with anyone besides men and women with mind wipes. He pitied these people, and yet selfishly wished he could talk with them. Still, as days went by, he learned never to speak to anyone, or the other person, not he, would be whipped unmercifully.

It was worse than receiving a sentence of death, because he had nothing; he knew nothing. He dreaded a mind wipe, but still he wished something in this dreadful pattern would change. For his needs, a guard daily brought a bucket of fresh water, and another bucket for his waste. Twice a day, a tin plate was shoved through an opening in the bars. The food tasted of nothing more than cardboard, yet seemed to be nourishing for he felt no weakening of strength. *(Here's where the narration ends and the "showing" begins.)*

Thirty-one days after his capture and imprisonment he looked up to see Sarita being led down the hall. "Tomashi," she called. "It's all right. Don't worry; they've allowed us a visit."

He felt his heart pounding as if it were a trapped bird battering against a cage. His first reaction was that she must have been captured and imprisoned. When he realized this wasn't so, he experienced a joy as immense as the despair he'd felt at losing his freedom.

Narration is, in fact, a kind of shorthand that gets the characters and the listener from one important point to another. In effect, the character is "remembering" the narration, rather than being a part of it. It bridges time and events and keeps the story moving.

Narration can also describe — the prison cell and what happened — and it can show how the character is feeling. For example, this implies that Tomashi is both frightened and bored: "It was worse than receiving a sentence of death, because he had nothing; he knew nothing. He dreaded a mind wipe, but still he wished something in this dreadful pattern would change."

THE HOOK

One last thing you might want to include in planning and development of your story is a good hook. That is, the opening should "hook" the audience's attention and interest. It almost always raises or implies a question that the story should answer. Let's look at some of the hooks in stories included in the book:

> **"Did they tell you about the dead man?"**
> **Delfina asked as she rinsed the dishes in the**
> ***apantle,* the stream flowing through the gar-**
> **den. — "Dead Man's Corner"**

Certainly anyone hearing such a beginning would want to know more. Who is the dead man? Why is he mentioned? What is his relationship to the characters in the story?

> **"It happened all of a sudden, near the iron**
> **moons of Cygnus: red, colossal, heavy, sweat-**
> **ing, burlap monsters coming, sneezing, crawl-**
> **ing — I was helpless, helpless!" Mrs. Brundy**
> **wheezed. Strands of long hair caught in her**
> **labored breath and flew like comets across the**
> **table. — "Black Hole Grandma"**

This hook raises all sorts of questions. Who is Mrs. Brundy, and what is she talking about? How did she get out of her predicament?

Here are a few others that certainly would grab a listener's attention for a variety of reasons.

> **Maneul Ortega was twelve years old before**
> **he knew he could fly. — "The Flight of the Niños."**

The moon splashed puddles of silver on the dented lids of garbage cans lining the curb. Although the temperature hovered in the fifties, Millie shivered and grabbed Arnie's arm in both her hands. — "Beneath the Ice Cold Moon."

No one could possibly consider Miss Whiffin pretty. She was short and squat with frizzy grey hair. Her lips were thin and constantly pursed, as if disapproving. But she rarely disapproved; she had, in fact, a great zest for life. — "For Love of Miss Whiffin"

ACTIVITIES

1. What can you tell or infer about the characters in these two excerpts by the literary voice they use? Discuss this with the class and see if anyone came up with anything you didn't see.

Cas hated New York. It was too big, too crowded, too noisy. His friends loved it; they went in often, some of them every weekend.

As he slowed to pay the toll at the Lincoln Tunnel, he felt his eyes fill with tears. His mom had been dead a month, and often it caught him unaware.

Fumes drifting from the tunnel filled his nose, burned his eyes. He remembered his best friend, Ronnie, talking about how he couldn't get along with his folks. How he could hardly wait till he was eighteen to move out and be on his own.

They led her around a corner and into a room similar to the one where she'd spent the last two weeks. In this one there were no windows. "You will be confined here." They shut the door and turned a key in the lock.

The room contained a bed, a small chest of

drawers and a hard-backed chair. An opening led to a bathroom with a sink and shower. In a neat row, toilet articles lay on the counter. She pulled out a drawer — panties, bras, two hospital gowns. In back was a half-used tube of toothpaste. She wondered who had used it and what had become of her.

She sat on the bed. High up in a corner a video camera was mounted.

Diann had never felt so alone. She lay back. It still must be afternoon, she thought. She covered her face with her hands. "Oh, God, George," she said, "what am I going to do?"

No! She wouldn't given them the satisfaction. Kreitzer was right; she was strong.

2. Take one of the stories you've already developed or start a new one. Tell just the first thirty seconds or so to the class using different points of view: first person, second person, or third person.

3. Prepare a one- to two-minute story in which you have at least two scenes, one of narration and the other where the character is immersed in the action. Be sure to develop a good hook for the story.

4. Write three or four sentences of dialog that tell as much about a particular character as possible. Now trade papers with a classmate. See how many things you can surmise about the character developed by your classmate.

5. Using all that you have learned in this chapter and preceding chapters, develop a story of approximately five minutes and tell it to the rest of the class. Have the class critique what you did.

Part III:

Presenting
the Story

CHAPTER ELEVEN

CREATIVE METHODS OF PRESENTATION

Learning a story to tell is easier than learning a recitation or a role for a play because you do not have to learn it word for word. You should have gone over a story at least several times when deciding whether or not to choose it to tell. You've spent more time analyzing the story and working with it.

LEARN THE ESSENCE

The work you've done so far means that by now you are pretty familiar with the story you've chosen. So you already have it well in mind, and the next several steps should be fairly painless.

Step 1: You need to read over the story a few times to capture its essence so that you can think it through or tell it in your own words, so that you are certain you've grasped the way it's structured.

Step 2: Read the story aloud to yourself a few times concentrating only on its style and flavor. If it has a dialect that you feel you can comfortably use, experiment with saying it, not necessarily in the exact way you will in presentation but to become familiar with it.

Step 3: As you go through the story a few more times, learn any phrases or unusual words or expressions that you will want to retain in the telling. If the sentence structure is unusual, you need to consider whether to change it.

Step 4: For the next few readings, concentrate on the imagery. Think about what it means and relate it to your own background. The way you perceive an image will be different from the way anyone else perceives it. But that's okay; your experiences are different from anyone else's. If, in your story, you read about "blowing dust" and it conjures up an image of the dust of a dry country lane roiling and twisting in tiny whirlwinds, take the image as far as you can in your mind. Or if a clanging bell is mentioned, visualize the old courthouse bell that you saw when you visited your grandparents — or whatever the image conjures up in your own mind.

Step 5: Concentrate on learning any lines that you need to say exactly. In the story about the man who fell onto the deck of the ship, it's important for you to keep repeating that he was "rough and tough and used to hardships." "He huffed and he puffed" is exactly what the wolf did in "The Three Little Pigs."

If the story relies on the particular wording of a punch line at the end, memorize that. Memorize any phrases that denote character and are repeated throughout the story. Learn any colorful or unusual words or key phrases that you will want to retain.

To give yourself confidence or as a kind of insurance that you won't forget the story once you are standing in front of an audience, you may want to memorize the first line or two exactly as you will say them. Of course, you don't need to do this unless these lines (or other similar lines throughout the story) are important and need to be related exactly.

Step 6: Next write out the sequence of events and try to get it firmly in mind. Once you can say this to yourself, you should be able to get through the story. An example of a story and how you might write out the sequence follows.

CREOSOTE HOUSE
by Carl Catt

In 1936, Mr. Gravely painted his weathered wooden house with creosote.

"It's black," said Mrs. Gravely. "I don't want to live in a black house."

Mr. Gravely silently counted to nine. Mrs. Gravely puffed up, turned red. He considered counting to ten, thinking she might explode. The thought made him smile, but he decided against it — there were too many dishes in the sink.

"The wooden siding was old and cracked," said Mr. Gravely.

"Creosote was the only way to preserve it." He stared at Mrs. Gravely's face. It too was old and cracked. He contemplated painting it with creosote, but decided against it. He didn't want to preserve it.

"For over forty years," said Mrs. Gravely, "for over forty years, mind you, I've lived in a gray house. Now you've painted it black. Black is the color of the devil."

"The devil is red, Mrs. Gravely, red as hot coals as you will find out soon enough."

"So it is," said Mrs. Gravely, "so it is." She went into the kitchen. The clang of pots and pans echoed through the house. Mr. Gravely moseyed out to the garage, picked up a hoe, dug up weeds. Near the kitchen window he stopped to admire his white roses. They thrived, he thought, because Mrs. Gravely poured dishwater onto them. "How nice you look," he said to his roses. "The black house makes you look a whiter white." He leaned down to smell them, caught his sleeve on a rose thorn. "Damn," he said. Mrs. Gravely looked out of the window, smiled. "Double damn," he said catching his other sleeve on a thorn as he tried to free himself from the first.

Mrs. Gravely poured dishwater out of the window onto the roses. It splashed on Mr. Gravely. "Oh," she said feigning innocence. Mr. Gravely damned and doubled damned until he was free of the roses.

Mrs. Gravely sat on the back porch peeling potatoes. She twisted the knife into a potato eye and into the next and the next, marvelling each time at the similarity of the russet potato skin to the ruddy complexion of Mr. Gravely.

Mr. Gravely fetched a hammer from the garage and pounded dents out of the garbage cans. He stood back, admired his handiwork and said, "There now, Mrs. Gravely, your figure is much improved."

Mr. Gravely mowed the lawn and then plopped exhausted on the back porch with Mrs. Gravely. Myra, Mrs. Gravely's nervous yellow cat, hissed at him. It was *his* rocker which twice attacked her tail and *his* dog,

FDR, who chased her up trees before he went blind. FDR sniffed in Myra's direction. The cat clawed up Mrs. Gravely's leg and onto her shoulder. She damned and doubled damned FDR and Mr. Gravely.

"FDR stinks," said Mrs. Gravely. "He oughta be put away. He ain't no use to nobody."

"Since when," said Mr. Gravely, leaning forward, almost nose to nose with his wife, "is bein' useful a requirement for being alive?"

Mrs. Gravely didn't answer.

"For example," said Mr. Gravely, "that cat."

"Cats catch mice," said Mrs. Gravely.

"What," he asked, "do we want mice for?"

"Not funny," said Mrs. Gravely. She looked down at her potatoes and gouged out a potato's eye with a single stroke.

At supper time, Mr. Gravely set the table. He put the bent fork, the dull knife and the chipped plate at Mrs. Gravely's place and hid a dead roach in her napkin. When she unfolded it, she didn't scream, but smiled at the roach and said, "Mr. Gravely, you're looking a mite bit better today."

Halfway through supper, Mrs. Gravely said, "I hope you liked the meat. It's that big sore-eared dog what got hit on the road the other day."

Mr. Gravely pushed his loose dentures back in place, continued eating.

"I figgered," said Mrs. Gravely, "I oughta practice up my dog cookin' skills. I been thinkin' of FDR for the birthday dinner when Ma and sister Tillie come over."

"I got your ma a special present for her eighty-fifth."

"You," said Mrs. Gravely, "you got *my* mother a present?!"

"Yup," he said, "something she's been a'needin' as long as I knowed her."

Mrs. Gravely, with half-closed eyelids said, "A new son-in-law?"

Mr. Gravely continued eating. He thought of throwing mashed potatoes at his wife, but they were too good. "Well now," he said after several minutes of silence, "I thought of that and, lucky me, I found one, but they wouldn't let him out of the asylum." The dog howled, the cat hissed and Mr. Gravely pounded the table with his fork.

"So then, Mr. Gravely, what did you get Ma?"

"Like I said, somethin' she needs."

"What is it?" snapped Mrs. Gravely.

"Something she really needs."

"Don't try me, old man, or you'll be cookin' your own vittles."

"A moustache cup," he said, "a moustache cup. A big red one to match her nose."

They ate the rest of the meal in silence. Later, sitting on rockers, drinking coffee in the parlor, the Gravelys listened to the radio. Jack Benny said, "Mary, why does Fred Allen talk through his nose?"

"I don't know, Jack, why does Fred Allen talk through his nose?"

"Because," said Jack, "his mouth is worn out."

Mr. and Mrs. Gravely laughed, Myra purred and FDR wagged his tail.

That night as they lay in bed, FDR on the floor next to him and Myra curled up by Mrs. Gravely's side, the old couple dreamed. She dreamed of black widow spiders webbing their way up the bedpost on his side and crawling into his pajama bottoms. He dreamed of a cobra slithering up the bedpost on her side. After swallowing the cat, it curled up on her baggy bosom.

Black clouds, big black billowy clouds raced across the sky. Rain gently tapped on the window and teardropped down the pane. Then, lightning flashed across the sky,

**and a thunder clap shook the house. Mr. Gravely, jolted
awake, grabbed at the snake on Mrs. Gravely's breast.
Mrs. Gravely frantically brushed away the spiders in
his pajama bottoms. They giggled for a moment, and
then she caressed his bald head and he kissed the wrinkles on her face.**

You might write out the sequence something like this:

1. Mr. Gravely painted his house with creosote.

2. Mrs. Gravely complains.

3. Mrs. Gravely goes into the kitchen; Mr. Gravely works on his garden.

4. Mr. Gravely catches his sleeve on a thorn.

5. Mrs. Gravely pours water over him.

6. Mrs. Gravely peels potatoes.

7. Mr. Gravely pounds out dents in the garbage cans.

8. The cat hisses at Mr. Gravely.

Continue this until the end. Of course, your listing may
be more complete or less complete. It may contain different
things altogether. It doesn't matter, just so what you do helps
you to remember the story.

Go over the list until you are sure you know it. You can
do this in odd moments — when you're brushing your teeth,
just before you go to sleep, on your way to class. During the
days when you are concentrating on the list, read through the
story several times to remind yourself how well you're remembering the sequence. If you need to add anything else to it,
now is the time.

Step 7: Put aside the written version now and see how
much you can remember. You may be surprised at how much
it is. If you don't know the story the whole way through, now
is the time to learn it. One way is to learn a certain part of
the story each day. Maybe you want to be sure on the first day
that you know the first page or the first scene. Keep going over
it without worrying about adding on. The next day add a second
scene or page to the first. Go over both of the scenes. The third
day, add a third section and keep going over the story from the

beginning to as far as you've gotten.

Or you may want to try to go over the whole thing at once, rather than adding to it scene by scene. If you get stuck, look at the printed copy. Each time you go over it, you should be able to remember it more completely.

Step 8: As you continue to rehearse the story, visualize your audience and rehearse the story picturing the setting and circumstances.

Step 9: Tape your story and listen to it critically. Are you telling it the way you want? If not, what can you do to improve it? Pay particular attention to *how* you are telling the story, not just what you are saying.

Step 10: Figure out any props you may want and start using them. If you arrange the props in the order in which you will use them, they can be good reminders of what you want to say and when to say it. You might want to change props throughout. An example would be changing hats for different characters or picking up objects that help identify each character. You might want to use drawings or chalk or flannel boards for young children's stories.

Step 11: Now try telling the story to a friend or relative. Don't worry if you falter somewhat here. This is your first live audience, and no matter who it is, this can make you a little nervous. Do remember that this audience, in particular, and almost any audience in general, is rooting for you.

Step 12: You will learn more about this in a later chapter, but you need to pay attention to your gestures and movement and to the way you're speaking in terms of vocal quality and rate.

Remember that whatever works best is what you should do, both in learning and presenting the story.

TWO APPROACHES TO TELLING

There are two ways to present a story. One is performance oriented, the other literary, though there may be elements of both in any presentation. Different stories lend themselves better to one approach or the other.

The *performance approach* involves assuming the role of the characters, even including the narrator. This involves changes in stance, voice, gestures and movement for each character, and is more obviously playing to the audience.

This is similar to acting, but there are several differences. The most obvious is that the teller has more direct contact with an audience than does an actor, at least in a realistic play. The actor usually does not acknowledge the audience, whereas the storyteller always does, talking directly to them, at least in the narrative parts of the story.

Another difference is that representative or realistic theatre *portrays* a location while storytelling *suggests* it. Most often, the actor moves within a setting, while the storyteller, with perhaps a few modifications, uses the setting that already is there — a stage, a library room, a classroom.

With the performance approach, you attempt to step into a characterization, reacting to life as that character.

The *literary approach* is more objective. The teller stands back and says: Here is what the characters say and do, but I am just telling you about them, not attempting to "become" them.

There are advantages and disadvantages to both approaches. The first might be more dynamic, but the second can often allow greater intimacy or communication with the audience. The first is more explicit, the second more suggestive.

Either approach is fine, and you should experiment to see which you like better for each story you tell. "The Hangman's Tree," for instance, seems to lend itself better to the performance approach, while fables or parables lend themselves better to the literary approach.

TWO OTHER METHODS OF PRESENTATION

Throughout the book, you have been learning about telling stories, of adapting them and putting them into your own words. But there are two other ways of presenting a story. One is to memorize a written piece, and the other is to read it. Both of these approaches make up what is called "oral interpretation" as opposed to storytelling.

Certainly, there are many times when people read others' works in public, rather than telling stories. And although one method is not necessarily better than the other, each has pluses and minuses.

Memorizing or reading another person's work is more rigid than telling a story in your own words. Yet you don't have to worry about adapting and changing anything. That part of the work is already finished for you. Otherwise, you go through most of the same steps in analyzing a written story as you do an oral one.

The advantage of memorizing the story is that you can have eye contact and a sense that you are speaking directly to an audience. Reading a story sets up a barrier that includes the book and maybe even a stand on which you place the book. But if you are reading the work, you won't have the problem of forgetting anything — though you could lose your place. This also is a good reminder to the audience that you are not using your own words but someone else's.

Memorization seems more spontaneous, though if you don't know the story as well as you should, you risk forgetting it, and unlike a story you tell in your own words, you'll simply have to stop and try to remember. To counteract that, you can use a note card containing key words or phrases to remind you what comes next. If you are not careful, though, that can be distracting.

There are times when you would want to use a manuscript. Examples are when you are reading a familiar printed story to young children, or even a new story from a new book at a library story hour. This still can come across as spontaneous, *if* you are well prepared. The appearance of spontaneity, in other words, takes a lot of work. Being unprepared is not the same as being spontaneous.

KEEPING TRACK

If you are going to be telling stories to different groups over a period of time, it is important to keep a record. It's simple to get a five-by-eight-inch card file and use a note card for each story.

249

At the top of the card list the story, the author, the type, and the source. Underneath that list a brief description of the characters, the theme, and if you wish, a brief outline or synopsis. List which age group it is for, the time it takes to tell, what types of groups it would fit, and any other comments that help you. Next you might record the first sentence or two to remind you how the story starts, and list the endings and the sequence of events. Keep a numbered list of the places you tell it. This is so that if you are asked to return to a particular group, you will know whether or not you already told a particular story.

You might want to list any properties or costumes you use and anything else that will help you remember the story. As you continue to build your file, look back through your list periodically and go over the stories a few times to keep them fresh in your mind. Of course, you can cut any story you dislike.

ACTIVITIES

1. Take your time in choosing a story five to ten minutes long. Learn it and then tell it to the class.

2. Choose another story of similar length. Experiment in telling it using either the performance or literary approach, or a combination of the two. Now tell the story to the class.

3. As a group, critique each of the stories presented for Activity #2. As part of the critique, discuss in class whether you think the teller used the right approach and if you think the story could be improved using a different approach.

4. Present a ten-minute written story to the class. You can either read it or tell it from memory. Do remember, however, that the preparation is just as involved for this type of story as for one that you tell.

5. Think back over all the stories you've told so far in the class and prepare a card file listing information about each of them.

CHAPTER TWELVE

SETTING THE MOOD

You've done all the preliminary work and know the story and the audience. There are still a few things to do to help assure that the telling will be a success.

SETTING THE RIGHT MOOD

Be sure to dress comfortably. Unless the story is part of a speech you are giving at an after-dinner program or a similar event, you don't need to wear dressy clothing. Of course, you can if wearing them somehow emphasizes the story. What you wear should be comfortable, since you will want to concentrate on the presentation, not on your clothing. Wear something that doesn't call attention to itself unless you want it to, like a witch's costume for Halloween or a Santa Claus or Mrs. Santa Claus outfit for Christmas.

If you like, you can wear a storytelling costume. If you are telling ethnic stories — Irish, Jewish, or whatever — you may want to wear clothing suggestive of the culture. Or you may want to dress in rustic clothing to indicate that storytelling is an old art and comes from an oral tradition.

If the room is empty before the telling and you have access to it, take time to arrange your properties, to dim the lights, and to remove unwanted furniture. Then take a few moments to look around and familiarize yourself with the place.

RELAXING

In addition to checking the room, you need to take some time for yourself. Do some relaxing exercises. If you can do these unobtrusively and shortly before you go in front of an audience, they can help both to relax you and channel your energy constructively.

These can be as simple as doing stretching exercises or neck rolls. You can experiment to see which type helps you, but here are a few you might try.

1. Sit in a chair, lean back and close your eyes. Now take a few seconds to stretch out your arms and legs and to yawn.

2. Stand and stretch. Then stand on tiptoes and reach as high above your head as you can.

3. Let your head hang loose and then roll from left to right around your shoulders. Now roll it the opposite way. Don't do this more than three or four times, or you may start to feel dizzy.

4. Stand and shake your arms and shoulders till they feel loose. Now sit down and lean back shaking each of your legs in turn.

5. Put your left leg in front, your right in back. Now rock gently back and forth, stretching the muscles. Reverse legs and do the same thing.

Next, simply relax. If it helps, go over the story quickly in your mind. If you are worried about forgetting the story, make sure you have the notes you made earlier — the outline or the key words and phrases. Even if you don't use them, they can be a good crutch, a psychological boost.

Always there will be "noise" or interference. But most of the time, unless it's extreme, you can block this out. Don't worry about the test you have to take tomorrow. Don't let your mind dwell on the little aches and pains and itches you feel. Concentrate only on your story and on the telling. Visualize the event from beginning to end, from stepping in front of the audience to the end of the telling.

Nobody will ever make you tell a story in public if you don't want to. Think about this and about how you agreed to the telling because you want to do it, because you have a gift you want to share with an audience. Think positive thoughts about the experience.

It's natural to be nervous, and, though you may not think so, this is a good thing. The nervousness means that you're concerned about doing well. If you let a lot of things worry you — about appearance, about forgetting, about whether you've chosen the right story and whether the audience will like it — then you will experience stage fright. But if you don't think about these things, the nervous energy will be channeled in the right direction, into the kind of energy and the kind of good feelings people have when a performance is going well.

When you are telling a story in front of an audience, you need to be sure that what you communicate nonverbally goes along with the words of the story.

You need to work at giving the signals you want to give and eliminate the other signals in your body language. Nervousness, for instance, can convey a message more strongly than the words of the story, so that the audience will pay more attention to that than to what you want to communicate. Of course, we are all unique, and to a degree we project our own personalities; we simply cannot isolate ourselves from what we are. Yet we cannot let idiosyncracies detract from our telling of a story. Make the kind of person you are work for, not against, you and remember that the more often and the longer you tell stories (or perform at all in public) the easier it becomes.

INTRODUCTIONS

An introduction serves several purposes. First it gives the audience a chance to get used to you and to the new situation of your standing in front of them. If you immediately start in on a story, rather than waiting a few seconds or more, most likely the listeners won't absorb the first few sentences. And since hooks are important, you want to make sure you do everything you can so that the audience hears them.

An introduction allows you to establish a rapport with the listener.

You also will want to create excitement about you and the story. You will want to get the audience interested in what you are going to do, before you ever start the telling. How can you do this? There are any number of ways. But you have to consider that your introduction should fit the audience, the occasion and story, as well as your personality.

Sometimes it's as simple as giving the title and the subject: "I'm going to tell you a story called 'Flight of the Niños,' which is about how it came to pass that certain children in Mexico learned to fly." Then go right into the story.

Or you may want to explain a little more. "I'm sure everyone here today has heard of Pecos Bill? He's similar to Paul Bunyan in that he is much bigger than life, and his accomplishments are highly exaggerated. This story is a tall tale called 'Pecos Bill and the Rattlesnake.'"

This introduction explains the central character, lists the type of story the audience will be hearing and tells a little about this type of story.

The introduction should match the story. You wouldn't give a humorous introduction to "The Ship" or "The Hangman's Tree." On the other hand, you might do so for Carl Catt's "The Creosote House." "It's common nature for people who have lived together a long time to get on each other's nerves and to bicker almost constantly. That's what happens in 'The Creosote House.' But, as in most human relationships, there's more than meets the eye."

If you gave this sort of introduction, you would name the story and its subject matter and also give a hook that would grab the audience's attention and interest and make them wonder what's coming.

The introduction depends on the type of audience. The introduction to the Pecos Bill story probably would fit an audience of older teens or adults or maybe even a mixed audience. For a group of children, you might include the same sort of information in a different way, and at the same time, include some audience participation:

Does anyone here know what a tall tale is? *(You wait for audience members to raise their hands, and then call on them. You may have to call on several before you get a complete answer, or you may even have to explain that a tall tale involves a folk hero, comes from the oral rather than the written tradition, involves a lot of exaggeration, and is bigger than life.)* **All right then, has anyone heard of Pecos Bill?** *(Take what the audience says and let it stand if it's right, add on to, or even correct what has been said. If you do the latter, you need to make sure that you do it without being condescending or hurting feelings. Kids probably will be eager to answer the questions.)* **This is a story called "Pecos Bill and the Rattlesnake." To**

get ready to hear it pretend it's about a hundred years ago. It's wintertime and very cold. Pecos Bill and his friend have been huddled around a campfire on the plains of Wyoming. The wind is whistling, and the air is sharp and clear. Can you picture that? Good. Okay. *(Then you go right into the story.)*

You can adapt the same story to different audiences. If you were going to tell "Who Are You and Why Are You Here?" to a group of fiction writers, you might say something like: "Here's a story you probably all can identify with since I'm sure that all of you have had the sort of experience the central character has in 'Who Are You and Why Are You Here?' "

For a teachers' convention, you might emphasize the dedication of Odelle in "For the Love of Miss Whiffin." But if you were telling the same story to a group of high school dropouts or middle-aged people you might emphasize the idea, like one of the characters in "For the Love of Miss Whiffin," that it is never too late to go back to college, if you really want to do it.

The introduction depends on the type of person you are and what you're comfortable in doing. It should be personal and informal. For example: "One thing I strongly believe is that every person is a human being with human qualities and needs and wants. This is much more important to me than any differences. This is why to me 'The Runaway' makes an important statement. Nobody should be kept from achieving what he or she can. Nobody's abilities and talents should be held down."

This sort of introduction says that the story is important in what it states — important to the teller and to the audience.

You might describe how you discovered a story that has become important to you, whether because of its theme or because it's so funny. You often might tell briefly what the story is about. "Into the Light and the Darkness" (similar to "The Runaway") tells us everyone should be judged individually, rather than in a stereotypical manner because stereotypes dehumanize.

You will want to arouse the audience's curiosity and make them look forward to the story. Maybe by telling why it is important to you, you can accomplish this.

If you are talking to people in a particular locale, you may emphasize that the upcoming story deals with local history or with a local folk hero or with someone well-known in the area. Individualize and personalize each story for each audience.

In some cultures, where storytelling is a common form of entertainment, storytellers sometimes have ritual openings, so that the audience knows that the story is about to begin. These are often thought of as "calling over" symbols because you indeed are calling the audience to come over into a world that is at least somewhat different from the one in which they live. You can develop your own ritual. It can be as simple as sitting down, folding your hands and looking from face to face in the audience. Or it may be a statement: "We are going to travel now to an enchanted land where stories are truth and truth is but stories. Are you ready? All right, here we go."

Many tellers use music or dance to introduce the story. A professional teller in California tells African stories and uses bongo drums to signal that the story is about to start, to emphasize points within the story and as a signal that the story has ended.

If you are going to be telling several stories, then you might think of ways of linking them together. Do they all take place in the same area? Are they all fairy tales? Do they all have the same or similar characters? You can find a way to link most stories.

Throughout the telling you might want to assign different types of audience participation, beyond trying to involve the listeners in the introduction.

In a fairy tale, there might be a repeated chant that shows the evil person is arriving. All you need do is teach the audience the chant, and then point to them and step back a little to indicate that it is now their turn to be a part of the performance.

Depending on the circumstances, you might do things together with the audience — a dance step or even drawing a picture.

CONCLUSIONS

At the end of a story, the audience has to feel some sort of completion. Often this comes about because of the story itself, but this isn't always the case. At any rate, even if the audience knows beyond any doubt that you've reached the end of the telling, you need to maintain the mood for at least a few seconds. This is particularly true when you've told a serious story. The audience doesn't want the mood shattered immediately.

Wait a second or two before saying a simple thank you. Occasionally, an audience will want to raise questions about the story you've told. This is fine; you can lead them in a discussion. But for the most part, let them take the initiative in the discussion. You've already told the story, so you shouldn't need to interpret it further.

On the other hand, if you had told a story like "The Runaway" to a group of middle school students, you might want to lead a discussion about slavery in general.

ACTIVITIES

1. Each of you should come up with a relaxing exercise or two to teach to the rest of the class.

2. Before each session of storytelling, take turns leading the class in relaxation exercises.

3. Present a story in which you use properties and/or costume pieces to denote character. The story should be at least five minutes long.

4. Choose a story to tell and think of three different types of audiences to whom you might tell it. Now develop three different introductions, each geared to one of the groups, and present these before the class.

5. Develop a "calling over" ritual to indicate a story is ready to start. Teach this ritual to the rest of the class.

CHAPTER THIRTEEN

USING YOUR BODY AND VOICE

To be able to present the story to the best of your ability, you should be certain that you are communicating well with both your body and your voice.

USING THE BODY

As you learned in the last chapter, your body plays a big part in any message you send to other people. It is constantly communicating your thoughts and feelings. For this reason, you want to be certain that what your voice says matches what your body says. This is called nonverbal communication because it isn't communicated using words and the meanings of words.

We know that there is explicit body language where meanings are fairly precise. Examples are nodding to show agreement and shrugging to say "I don't know." Most signals are much more subtle.

There are six overall methods your body uses to communicate to an audience: eye contact, stance, facial expression, gestures, movements from place to place, and space. Each of these is important. Let's look at why this is so.

EYE CONTACT

Those who don't look at the people to whom they are talking can appear to be dishonest, nervous and ill at ease, embarrassed or ashamed. None of these are emotions that you want to communicate to an audience.

This means that you should always maintain eye contact, or in the case of large audiences, give the impression of maintaining eye contact with your listeners. This communicates honesty, forthrightness and the idea that you truly are interested in communicating.

But eye contact helps in other ways as well. Communication is a two-way process. Storytelling, of course, is different from having a conversation with friends where there is a verbal give and take. Audiences most often are quiet, but still are sending you messages.

You can usually tell, for example, that someone is interested in what you're saying, or you can tell if the person is bored. If he is the latter, you need to change what you are doing.

One of the reasons for learning a story, rather than memorizing or reading it, is that you can adapt it to your listeners. If an audience is becoming restless, try to figure out the reason. Maybe you are drawing out a part of the story too long, and the audience is bored. Then condense this section or vary the way you are delivering it. The better you learn to read your audience's reactions, the better you can make your story.

There are other reasons for looking into your audience's eyes. If you are using the performance approach and portraying a character, you may very well want to look at the audience as that character. Or you may portray a particular purpose or emotion. Suppose the character is trying to find a murder suspect. You may, as the character, squint, thrust your head forward, narrow your eyes and look from face to face.

At any rate, when people feel you are talking directly to them, they are much more inclined to remain interested and pay attention to the story.

STANCE

The best stance is the one with which you feel most comfortable. Don't be stiff and formal, or the audience may begin to feel uptight. On the other hand, don't slouch or be so sloppy that you will appear apathetic.

It's easy to figure out that a person who stands with arms crossed over the chest is not in an open mood, but rather is perhaps unconsciously saying: I don't want to be here, and I'm not going to be open with you. Furthermore, I'm going to protect myself.

Yet if someone stood before you, hands at their sides or in

their pockets, you would infer that the person does want to communicate, or at least he or she gives the appearance of wanting to.

Just be aware of what certain body language conveys, and strive to stand in a way that communicates positive messages.

FACIAL EXPRESSIONS

Your facial expression should mirror the emotions you are communicating in words. Generally, the broader or more exaggerated the story, the more exaggerated the facial expressions.

Facial expressions often are more subtle than other forms of body language so that if you are speaking to a large group in a big auditorium, they may not register beyond the fourth or fifth row. If the audience is small and everyone can easily see you, then facial expressions are important.

From the time we are small children, we are able to read facial expressions and know that Mom and Dad are happy or angry. In this manner, facial expressions can be more easily discerned than most other body languages. They communicate, sometimes very clearly, a wide range of emotions and feelings from mild dissatisfaction to rage, from enjoyment to sheer delight.

You can use this form of body language very effectively for smaller groups in giving clues as to how the audience should feel, for as you know, sometimes in conversation the words can contradict the true meaning, as when you say something sarcastically.

GESTURES

There are four types of gestures:

A. Directive or indicative.

B. Expressive or emphatic.

C. Descriptive.

D. Private or self-communicative.

Directive or indicative gestures indicate that the person to whom they are directed should do something or change behavior in a certain way. They include pointing, or shaking the head.

City hall is three blocks from here. *(Pointing)* **You should take this street to the traffic signal and turn right.**

And then keep on till I come to it?

No. *(Shaking the head)* **Then you come to a Y and bear to the right.** *(Pointing)*

Gestures such as this are pretty universal and easily understood.

Expressive or emphatic gestures show how we are feeling:

(Forming fists with both hands) **Aaagh, it makes me so angry that he would try to cheat me.**

He seems like a pretty good guy to me. Are you sure it wasn't just a mistake?

(Hands on either side of the head) **You've got to be kidding. This is the third time it's happened in as many days.**

Don't you think it's best to drop the matter?

No! *(Spreading the hands, fingers like claws)* **I need that money.**

Descriptive gestures help define.

This sort of gesture shows such things as size and shape.

The new math teacher is only about this tall. *(Holding hand out and to the side, palm flat and toward the ground)*

Didn't you see him then?

Not at first. I came this close *(Holding index finger and thumb two inches apart, the other fingers curled)* **to bumping into him.**

Private or self-communicative gestures are meant only for ourselves, though they may be the same as we use in wanting to communicate with others. They show our reactions to what is happening around us and are nonspecific, though often readable. For example:

Man, I wish he'd get here. *(Drumming fingers on the table)*

Oh, hi. *(Palms flat together under the chin)* **Sorry I'm late. I got held up in traffic.**

(Rolling eyes and nodding slightly) **Oh, sure, same excuse as last time.**

Gestures, of course, need to fit the emotional content of a story. All four types can be used — even the usually private ones — to show how a character is reacting. They also should grow honestly out of the story you are telling and shouldn't appear planned.

Some people are comfortable using a lot of gestures; they "talk with their hands." Other people use few gestures and feel inhibited in using them.

If you use gestures normally, by all means use them in your storytelling. If not, it's probably better that you don't use them before an audience, at least at first. But you may find that the more often you tell stories to a group of people, the easier it is to use gestures.

Take care that your gestures appear natural. It looks pretty silly for someone to stand in front of a group and suddenly jerk the right arm up and point a finger. If you are going to point, follow through by leaning into the direction you are pointing. Use the whole body, or the gestures will look funny, even if you don't want them to be.

Keep in mind that the bigger the audience, the bigger the gesture should be.

MOVEMENT FROM PLACE TO PLACE

It's very easy to become drowsy or lethargic trying to focus on an unmoving person or object; moving around while telling a story can help keep an audience alert.

But more than that, movement from place to place can

indicate that you have finished one scene in the story and now are going on to another.

When you are portraying different characters, facing slightly to the right for one and then turning and facing to the left can indicate that a different character now is speaking. This is particularly helpful if it's combined with a different posture or stance and different sorts of facial expressions. You may want to devise a characteristic way for each of your characters to stand and move around.

The way you move can indicate moods or feelings. A happy character will have a more lilting way of walking than one weighed down with problems.

You should adapt all body movements to the audience. For a small audience sitting in a circle, you might want to sit in a chair. For a big audience, you would stand and move sometimes, for a bigger audience, you would have a lot of movement.

SPACE

The closer you are to an audience, the more intimate the telling. This can be important in making the listeners know that you care about them and about communicating with them. We naturally feel closer emotionally when we are closer physically. Of course, the most intimate use of space is physical contact, such as touching a person's shoulder or arm.

THE VOICE

You need to relax the voice, to avoid strain and to speak at a proper pitch level.

To relax the throat, let your jaw hang open and draw out a long "ahhhhh." Don't try to focus the sound or make it pleasing; your only concern should be that what you are doing feels comfortable. Carry this relaxed feeling over to your speaking.

Be sure you are speaking at your optimum pitch level. To find what this is, use a piano to match a single note that you sing. Now sing as far down from that note as you can, while playing the notes on the piano. Once you find the lowest pitch which you can comfortably sing, go up the scale to the highest pitch you can reach without straining or using a falsetto voice. Now count the notes; a third of the way from the bottom is your optimum pitch. This note should be the approximate center of your usual speaking/singing zone, the note you hit most often.

Improper breathing is another cause of vocal strain. You should breathe deeply and let the air out in a steady stream. Although most people cannot do this without training or practice, you should be able to hold your breath and exhale slowly over a period of at least thirty to forty-five seconds. Have your teacher time you and see how long you can maintain a tone.

A way to see whether or not you are letting your breath out slowly and evenly is to hold a lighted match in front of your mouth. If the flicker on the flame is steady and even (though "bent" slightly away from you), this means you are breathing properly. If it goes out, you are letting too much air escape at once. If it flickers back and forth, you are letting your breath out unevenly.

Runners and other athletes take shallow breaths, which is good for them. It is not good for speaking (or singing). You need to take in enough air so that it pushes out your abdomen and not just your chest. Then you should push the air out from the abdomen first. If you don't, you are letting your throat do the work, and more than likely you will get a scratchy throat or laryngitis. You may even lose your voice for a day or two.

You are more likely to breathe correctly lying down. If you are having trouble breathing properly, lie on your back and push as hard as you can comfortably against your abdomen. Release the pressure and suck in a big breath of air. Then gently push on your abdomen until the air supply is depleted. Do this several times. Once you know how it feels, stand and do the same thing: push against the abdomen, release, suck in air, and gently push the air out. It may take awhile to get on to doing this, but it is important.

Generally, the more relaxed you are and the more correctly you are breathing, the better you are using the resonators in your body, those cavities which, like the sounding board on a piano or the inside of any non-electric musical instrument, give your voice its distinctive quality and tone. If

265

you are squeezing out the air or speaking at the wrong pitch, you aren't using these resonators, which include the throat, the nose, the mouth, and the bones of the head and chest. Another way to improve vocal production is to have good posture, so that there isn't pressure anywhere on the breathing or vocal mechanics.

Some people have "nicer" sounding voices than others. They have a timbre, a richness and a fullness that most don't. Yet, almost anyone, unless there is a physical reason, can learn to speak in a pleasant sounding voice that is more than adequate for storytelling or any other sort of vocal presentation.

There are some common faults most of us have in speaking. You really just need to be aware of these so you can be careful to avoid them.

The first is speaking too fast. The best way to see if this is the case is to have a friend or your teacher tape one of your stories. Occasionally, people speak too slowly, but this is far less common.

Another fault is speaking too softly. Often this has to do with not breathing properly, not taking in enough air. If you learn to breathe correctly, you should be able to project your voice, without straining, well enough to be heard in almost any storytelling situation.

ARTICULATION

We say, "how ya doin'?" instead of "how are you doing?" Often we don't pronounce "t's" in the middle of words. We say "boddle" for bottle or "rah'n" for rotten. If this is the way a character normally would speak in your story, that's fine. Otherwise, make sure that you are pronouncing all the letters that should be pronounced. On the other hand, don't go overboard and speak so distinctly that the words call attention to themselves.

Tape yourself and listen to the way you speak. If you are not articulating the consonants well enough, practice doing so. Most libraries have speech books that have exercises that will help you with this. If you have a problem and it persists, go to a library and check out a book that gives exercises to help remedy the situation.

VOICE USAGE

There are four facets of voice usage: timing, volume, pitch, and vocal quality. If you are in control of all of them, your voice should be strong enough and flexible enough for any storytelling situation.

Let's look at each of these in turn.

1. *Timing refers to how fast or how slowly we speak.* It can be broken down further into four aspects: rate, duration, pausing, and rhythm.

   A. Rate refers to the number of words you utter per second, the speed at which you deliver the story. Some of us normally talk faster than others. That's fine; don't try to pattern yourself after anyone else.

      When telling a story, you should want to vary the rate according to the emotional content. People speed up when they are excited. In a mellow or relaxed mood, they tend to speak more slowly. You may want to vary your rate of speaking for different characters.

      The mood of the story should also affect the rate. "The Farm in My Mind" would be delivered more slowly than would "Black Hole Grandma." That is, you would deliver a reflective or nostalgic piece more slowly than a funny one.

   B. Duration refers to the length of each sound, and, like rate, depends on the characters and the emotions of the story, and on the importance of particular words or phrases. For example, telling someone, "Go, I don't care" is different from telling the person, "Gooo! I don't caaaare." Drawing out words is a way of emphasizing them.

   C. Pausing is a way to point up a word or phrase. When you deliberately pause, you are saying to the audience that something important is coming up, and they should listen closely to discover what it is. Comedians pause before the punch line because pausing helps to build suspense. "The scholarship is awarded to *(Pause)* Richard Robinson."

      Pauses are a type of verbal punctuation that help

us to understand meaning. Sometimes they match written punctuation, but often are at odds with it. If you paused for each comma in the following, the sentence would sound either funny or tedious: At the grocery store I bought soap, milk, shampoo, celery, and cat food.

But you may want to pause where there is no written punctuation. For example: "What *(Pause)* is the meaning *(Shorter pause)* of this?

Pausing can also point up meaning. For example, compare: "I want some melon, *(Pause)* honeydew, *(Pause)* pass it to me, please" to: "I want some melon, *(Pause)* honey *(Pause)*. Do pass it to me, please." Of course, you can tell the meaning by reading the written words; a listener wouldn't be able to distinguish meaning in this way.

If you were to speak at an even rate as you told a story, the audience would not be able to follow. As an experiment, tell a joke or anecdote to a friend without using any pauses. Chances are, even if the friend understands the words, he or she won't think what you said was funny.

Pauses show how something should be phrased. To a degree, this is up to the individual, for there is no "correct" rule about how to do it. Phrasing depends on the type of story, your own style in delivering it and in the emotional and thought content. For instance, there would be little reason to pause in the following: "I'm leaving for school."

Yet the following sentence would require pauses in several places: "Listen to me and understand there's only one way you are going to get out of here, and that's to do exactly as I say."

To illustrate how someone might say the sentence, we'll use one diagonal mark / to indicate a short pause and a double mark // to illustrate a longer pause. One way of saying this would be: "Listen to me // and understand // there's only one way / to get out of here // and that's to do / exactly as I say."

A variation might be: "Listen to me // and / understand there's only / one way to get out of here // and that's / to do / exactly / as I say."

The idea is to point up the importance of the sentence, to draw attention to what is being said. Pausing also can show emotional state. A character who is very frightened might use a choppy delivery, perhaps even breathing during each pause. "Oh, // God, // I don't // know what / I'm // going to // do."

Here's an excerpt from "Grandaddy and the Lost Violin," marked for pauses. This is the sort of thing you might want to do when learning your story.

> **I'm going to tell you a story / about the time / my grandaddy / was out working the fields in Western Pennsylvania // and this stranger / come a walking down the road // real / slow-like. Grandaddy seen this man, / all dressed / in a black suit / and hat, // though it was the hottest day of summer, // but Grandaddy / finished hoeing a row a taters // and watched / as the man, / careful so as not to ruin the creases in his wool suit, // climbed over the split rail fence / separating the field / from the old dirt road.**

D. Rhythm refers to the flow of the language. A funny story would have a more staccato rhythm, for instance, than would a nostalgic story. You would tell "Pecos Bill and the Rattlesnake" using a different rhythm than you would for "Burdens."

2. *Volume refers to how loudly or softly something is said.* You would use a higher decibel level for words that you wanted to emphasize. In this sentence, the words that would be spoken more loudly are italicized: "I don't *ever* want to *see you* again." If you paused before each of the italicized words, you'd further point them up. You rarely would use one vocal device alone. Rather you use a variety of them in combination.

The size of the room and the size of the audience also help determine the decibel level or volume you would use in telling a story. The larger the room, the more loudly you have to speak. The same holds true for a larger number of people in attendance since more sound is absorbed by clothing and so on.

Here is an excerpt from "Mind Swap." Italicized words indicate a higher volume, and the slashes, of course, indicate pauses.

Two 'Stapo guards / *burst* through the door, / lasers drawn.

"What / *is* this?" / Fillipo demanded. // "What's / going *on* here?"

3. *Pitch refers to the frequency at which a sound is heard.* It also is a means of emphasizing words or phrases. You call attention to a word spoken at a higher pitch level. For example, say the following sentence from "Mind Swap" in a monotone, that is, with no changes in pitch: "Now then," the first man said, "I am Sgt. Miller, and I'm in charge. Is that understood?" You might be able to emphasize certain parts of the sentence by pausing and by changes in volume. But using all three devices is much more effective. Let's take the opening of "Mind Swap" once more and add underlining for changes in pitch:

Two '<u>Stapo</u> guards / <u>*burst*</u> through the door, / lasers drawn.

"What / <u>*is*</u> this?" / Fillipo demanded. // "What's going <u>*on*</u> here?"

Pitch changes from word to word and also within words. The change within words, of course, is called inflection. There are no absolute rules about using inflection. However:

1. A falling inflection can show determination or certainty.

2. A rising inflection can show a question or a sense of doubt, disbelief or shock.

3. Quick and abrupt changes can indicate confusion.

It's best to experiment with each story to see how you

might use changes in pitch and inflection to convey the sense of the piece.

4. *Vocal quality, changes in the overtones in a person's voice, indicates changes in meaning or emotion and shows that a different character is speaking.* Each person has a unique voice with a unique quality.

More than that, however, various qualities indicate certain character traits and certain feelings. A whining voice indicates dependence. A person might use a whining quality when pleading or begging for something. A gruff voice may show depth of feeling. As a character trait, it shows a harshness, perhaps deliberately used to mask something else.

You probably will want to experiment with different vocal qualities for each character or emotion that you portray.

ACTIVITIES

1. How does the rhythm of the following two pieces differ? They both are from "The Music of His Horn." Discuss this with the class.

> **Leaves of a maple tree in the yard brushed gently against the window; a breeze billowed the curtain by Martin's desk as he picked up his trumpet, running his fingers across leaves and stems etched on the gold-plated tubing and the sterling silver bell.**

> **"You have not set the fire," Dan accused, anger pinching his face.**

> **"No." His friends scattered across the grass, disappearing into alley and street.**

> **Dan grabbed his arm, squeezed hard, left his finger marks, pulled him inside and to the upstairs corner that held his bed.**

2. Type or write out the following showing where you might

use pauses:

> **The Brotherhood would call him foolish,
> both for loving his trumpet and pursuing
> magic. They wanted magic for all or for none.
> Since not everyone could have it —**

> **He closed the case. Maybe he wanted only
> to escape through his music; maybe his beloved
> trumpet was only a substitute for love.**

3. What sort of rate would you use in delivering the following
   passage? Why? Discuss this with the class.

> **Helen sat at the kitchen table shelling
> peas. "I'm going to see the Trumpetmaster," he
> told her.**

> **She looked up in surprise. "You've no les-
> son today." She peered at him closely. "Have
> you?"**

> **"No, ma'am."**

> **"Then why —"**

> **"Let the boy go." It was his grandmother,
> standing in the doorway. "He must be allowed
> to pursue the magic," she said. She was a tiny
> woman with dark hair twirled into a bun, a
> faded cotton print dress, black shapeless shoes.
> Martin's mother, even seated, nearly matched
> her height. Grandma turned to Martin as if the
> matter were settled. "I don't have to tell you to
> beware of the Brotherhood."**

> **"No," he said, as she squinted into his eyes.**

4. Type or write out the following passage and indicate the
   different methods you would use for emphasis of words and
   phrases. Then read the passage to the class.

> **Martin pushed open the screen door,
> leaped off the unpainted porch and trotted
> along the boardwalk to the front gate and down
> the unpaved sidewalk of Second Street. Yes, the**

Brotherhood was powerful, he thought. Hadn't they already eliminated most magic . . . except for that of people like Trumpetmaster Carlson? Why was the Trumpetmaster allowed to continue? he wondered. Why was he himself allowed to continue?

Wisps of clouds chased each other across a pale sky. It was near noon, the sun bright. Martin wore thin cotton pants and shirt, but still the air bore him down. None of the Brotherhood was anywhere in sight.

Nearing the final street of the village, he stopped. Maybe the Trumpetmaster wouldn't see him; after all, he had other pupils, though none pursuing the magic. Why were the people taken in by the teachings of the Brotherhood? Couldn't magic cure illness and cast spells of protection? Couldn't it restore lost items and bring comfort in times of sorrow?

As Martin reached the plateau before the final climb, his ears filled with the sweetness of "Carnival of Venice." What powers Trumpetmaster Carlson must have to know the very song Martin had been attempting.

Martin grinned and hurried through the pasture field to the path that led to Trumpetmaster Carlson's cottage. Along the path, the *Arban's* "Carnival of Venice" stopped.

Suddenly, his way was blocked, and he looked up into the eyes of Sean Smithfield.

"Where are you off to, Martin?"

"Nowhere," Martin said. Sean was near Trumpetmaster Carlson's age, though he never seemed to hold a job, his only occupation that of drunkard. Some said he had joined the Brotherhood. Some said he had talked others into starting it.

273

5. Taking all that you've learned in this chapter, choose a story not from the book and tell it to the class. It should be eight to ten minutes long.

6. In the school or public library, find a collection of stories meant for telling. Learn one of them and present it to the class.

APPENDIX

Where to Look for Stories

There are many places you can look for stories to tell. If you are telling stories to children, most fairy tales and folktales are in public domain, which means that they are no longer protected by copyright, and you are free to tell them.

You do have to be careful with copyrighted stories. Reading, writing, or adapting and telling them in class is generally okay, but you couldn't use them if you were going to charge a fee or if it were for a public program. If you do want to tell an authored story at a public gathering, write to the publisher and request permission. Sometimes you will have to pay a fee to use it.

You can find collections of ethnic stories in almost any library. Many of these are from the oral tradition and have been handed down for generations. You might be able to adapt and tell these.

Often, there are collections of stories for telling where the author says that the stories can be adapted and told.

The Bibliography on page 277 lists some books on storytelling. The first is particularly helpful in listing sources for storytellers.

BIBLIOGRAPHY

Bauer, Caroline Feller. *Handbook for Storytellers*. Chicago: American Library Association, 1987.

Breneman, Lucille and Bren. *Once Upon a Time: A Storytelling Handbook*. Chicago: Nelson-Hall, 1983.

Barton, Bob. *Tell Me Another*. Markham, Ontario, Canada: Pembrok Publishers, Limited, 1986.

Chambers, Dewey W. *Storytelling and Creative Drama*. Dubuque, Iowa: William C. Brown Company, Publishers, 1970.

Cook, Elizabeth. *The Ordinary and the Fabulous*. London: Cambridge University Press, 1976.

Cundiff, Ruby Ethel and Barbara Webb. *Storytelling for You*. Yellow Springs, Ohio: The Antioch Press, 1977.

Livo, Norma J. and Sandra A. Rietz. *Storytelling Activities*. Littleton, Colorado: Libraries Unlimited, Inc., 1987.

Livo, Norma J. and Sandra A. Rietz. *Storytelling Process and Practice*. Littleton, Colorado: Libraries Unlimited, Inc., 1986.

Moore, Robin. *Awakening the Hidden Storyteller: How to Build a Storytelling Tradition in Your Family*. Boston: Shambala Publications, Inc., 1991.

Pellowski, Anne. *The Family Storytelling Handbook*. New York: Macmillan, 1987.

Pellowski, Anne. *The World of Storytelling*. New York: Bowker, 1977.

Peterson, Carolyn Sue. *Story Programs: A Sourcebook of Materials*. Metuchen, New Jersey: Scarecrow Press, 1980.

Sawyer, Ruth. *The Way of the Storyteller*. New York: The Viking Press, 1962.

Schimmel, Nancy. *Just Enough to Make a Story: A Sourcebook for Storytelling*, 2nd ed. Berkeley: Sisters' Choice Press, 1982.

Shedlock, Ruth. *Art of the Story-Teller*. New York: The Viking Press, 1962.

Tooze, Ruth. *Storytelling*. Englewood Cliffs, New Jersey: Prentice-Hall, Inc., 1959.

Zuskind, Sylvia. *Telling Stories to Children*. New York: The H. W. Wilson Company, 1976.

ACKNOWLEDGEMENTS

Excerpts from: "Cowboy Parable," "Parable of the Adopted Son," "Grandaddy and the Lost Violin," "The Runaway," "Burdens," "Movie Star," "Mr. and Mrs. Little and Mr. Big," "The Farm in My Mind" (first appearance in *Chiron Rising*), "Paul Bunyan and the Eating Contest," "The Barn" (first appearance in *Triple Fiction*), "Beyond the Seventh Day" (first appearance in *The Cosmic Unicorn*), "The Experiment," "Family Man," *Death by Stages, Mind Swap, Alternate Casts* (Banned Books, 1990), all by Marsh Cassady and reprinted with his permission.

Excerpts from: "Night Walk" by Carl Catt, reprinted with his permission; *Because of Romek* by James D. Kitchen and David Faber, Los Hombres Press, 1990, reprinted by permission of James D. Kitchen.

Complete works: "The Ship" by Pat Cassady, reprinted by permission of Marsh Cassady; "Letters to Whole Wheat Hair Products," "Black Hole Grandma" and "Under the House" by Bill Jarosin, reprinted with his permission; "Creosote House" by Carl Catt, reprinted with his permission; "Dead Man's Corner" by Anne James Valdes, reprinted with her permission.

Complete works: "The Disappearance of Billy Findlay," "Flight of the Niños," "Revival Meeting" and "Surprise Party" (first appearance for both in *By Kids, For Kids,* edited by Catherine Gaffigan, Excalibur Press, 1993), "Into the Light and the Darkness," "Who Are You and Why Are You Here?" "Tradeoffs" (first appearance in *The Voice*), "Pecos Bill and the Rattlesnake," "The Inscription," "For Love of Miss Whiffin" (first appearance in *My Weekly*), "Dr. Death Comes to All," "The Beautiful Dress," "Beneath the Ice Cold Moon" (first appearance in *Bloodreams*), "The Olympian" (first appearance in *Expressions*), "Mutant," (first appearance in *Galaxy*), "Camping," all by Marsh Cassady, reprinted with his permission.

Public Domain: "The Hangman's Tree," "The Travelers and the Bear" and "The Wolf and the Goat."

ABOUT THE AUTHOR

Dr. Marsh Cassady has taught theatre at the high school and college levels for many years. He is currently a director, actor and award-winning free-lance writer. He received both his M.A. and his Ph.D. from Kent State University. He has conducted many workshops on playwriting and has directed and acted in more than 100 plays. Additionally, he as been a columnist, book reviewer, and dramatic writer for radio shows. His list of more than thirty-five books on various theatre arts is widely used in schools throughout the United States and Canada.

ORDER FORM

MERIWETHER PUBLISHING LTD.
P.O. BOX 7710
COLORADO SPRINGS, CO 80933
TELEPHONE: (719) 594-4422

Please send me the following books:

_____ **The Art of Storytelling #TT-B139** by Marsh Cassady *Creative ideas for preparation and performance*	$14.95
_____ **The Theatre and You #TT-B115** by Marsh Cassady *An introductory text on all aspects of theatre*	$15.95
_____ **Acting Games — Improvisations and Exercises #TT-B168** by Marsh Cassady *A textbook of theatre games and improvisations*	$12.95
_____ **Characters in Action #TT-B106** by Marsh Cassady *Playwriting the easy way*	$14.95
_____ **The Art of Storytelling #TT-B139** by Marsh Cassady *Creative ideas for preparation and performance*	$14.95
_____ **Multicultural Theatre #TT-B205** edited by Roger Ellis *Scenes and monologs by multicultural writers*	$14.95
_____ **Great Scenes From Women Playwrights #TT-B119** by Marsh Cassady *Classic and contemporary scenes for actors*	$14.95

These and other fine Meriwether Publishing books are available at your local bookstore or direct from the publisher. Use the handy order form on this page.

NAME: _____

ORGANIZATION NAME: _____

ADDRESS: _____

CITY: _____ STATE: _____

ZIP: _____ PHONE: _____

❑ **Check Enclosed**
❑ **Visa or MasterCard #** _____

Signature: _____   *Expiration Date:* _____
       (required for Visa/MasterCard orders)

COLORADO RESIDENTS: Please add 3% sales tax.
SHIPPING: Include $2.75 for the first book and 50¢ for each additional book ordered.

❑ *Please send me a copy of your complete catalog of books and plays.*